The Great Plains were once characterized by vast expanses of grass, complex interdependence among species, and dynamic annual changes due to weather, waterways, and fire. It is now generally accepted that less than 1 percent of the original tallgrass prairie remains. Habitat fragmentation, the loss of natural predator-prey associations, changes in species composition, and various commercial practices continue to threaten grassland biodiversity.

Recently scholars and conservationists have discussed opportunities for large-scale restoration projects in the Great Plains, but they have provided few details. Daniel Licht offers here a bold new approach to restoring and conserving the grassland ecosystem. In describing hypothetical reserves, he explains how they could help conserve grassland biodiversity, reduce federal expenditures on agriculture, increase recreational opportunities, and sustain rural economies outside the reserves.

Daniel S. Licht is a fish and wildlife biologist at Fort Snelling, Minnesota. His articles have appeared in *Prairie Naturalist* and *Great Basin Naturalist*.

Volume 10 in the Series
Our Sustainable Future

SERIES EDITORS

Lorna M. Butler
Washington State University

Cornelia Flora
Iowa State University

Charles A. Francis
University of Nebraska–Lincoln

William Lockeretz
Tufts University

Paul Olson
University of Nebraska–Lincoln

Marty Strange
Center for Rural Affairs

Daniel S. Licht

Ecology and Economics of the Great Plains

University of Nebraska Press

Lincoln • London

⊗ The paper in this book
meets the minimum requirements of
American National Standard for
Information Sciences—Permanence of Paper for
Printed Library Materials,
ANSI Z39.48-1984.

Library of Congress
Cataloging-in-Publication Data
Licht, Daniel S., 1960–
Ecology and economics of the Great Plains / Daniel S. Licht.
p.   cm.—(Our sustainable future : v. 10)
Includes bibliographical references (p.   ) and index.
ISBN 0-8032-2922-4 (cloth : alk. paper)
1. Grassland ecology—Great Plains.
2. Grassland ecology—Economic aspects—Great Plains.
3. Grassland conservation—Great Plains.
4. Great Plains.   I. Title.   II. Series.
QH104.5.G73L53   1997
333.74'0978—dc20   96-27203
CIP

Contents

Maps

Figures

Tables

Preface

It is here, I repeat, that the voyageur feels most fully that he is gazing upon an unfamiliar land, for the realization of which no previous experiences of travel could have prepared him.

G. D. Brewerton, *Overland with Kit Carson: A Narrative of the Old Spanish Trail in '48*

The forests and lakes of northern Wisconsin were my boyhood home. Since then I have had the pleasure of living along the picturesque coast of Maine and in the alligator-rich bottomlands of South Carolina, the rugged Hill Country of central Texas, and the primeval rain forests of southeast Alaska. I have visited the Rocky Mountains, the Pacific Coast, the desert Southwest, and parts of Canada. I confidently assert that none of these places exceeds the timeless beauty and enduring spirit of the great grasslands in the heart of North America.

True, the great grasslands—also known as the Great Plains and prairies— test a person's fortitude as few other places do. The incessant winds, combined with the searing heat of summer or the bitter cold of winter, can dehydrate a person in hours or cause frostbite in minutes. And the land, already arid, regularly undergoes droughts that last for years. Rainfalls of a few hundredths of an inch are celebrated; dust storms that blot out the sun are routine.

Yet mysteriously, almost imperceptibly, and somewhat like an old adversary, the Great Plains and prairies grow on you. Find a small grassy knoll in the middle of a vast expanse of prairie, and you have traveled both spatially and temporally. You will experience the essence of nature as well as the soul of North America. Walt Whitman came as close as anyone of European descent to capturing the spirit of the grasslands: "While I know the standard claim is that

Yosemite, Niagara falls, the upper Yellowstone and the like, afford the greatest natural shows, I am not so sure but the Prairies and Plains, while less stunning at first sight, last longer, fill the esthetic sense fuller, precede all the rest, and make North America's characteristic landscape'' (Whitman 1982, 864).

Unfortunately most, and by some measures all, of Whitman's prairies and plains are gone. Key species are absent, no longer filling their evolutionary and ecological niches and roles. Critical natural processes have been eliminated, suppressed, or altered. Once clear and limitless horizons are now fragmented, cluttered, and obscured. Lost with these historic elements is much of the spirit and substance of the grassland ecosystem.

This book describes the grassland ecosystem and the consequences of modern settlement (and conversely, how the ecosystem has influenced settlement). It presents and synthesizes new conservation principles and philosophies that can be used by resource managers and private landowners who wish to conserve the biotic integrity of grassland ecosystems. Then it describes and rationalizes additional strategies for grassland conservation that society may wish to consider. These new strategies could benefit residents of the Great Plains and prairies while at the same time saving money for American taxpayers. The arguments are not necessarily new; they have been discussed in the ivory towers of academia and have been casual fodder for scientists, economists, and environmentalists alike. But to my knowledge this is the first time they have been set out in a thorough and detailed analysis, especially from an ecological perspective.

Yet one should view this book not as a prescription but as a possibility. Many other options should also be threshed out. In the end, perhaps a combination of strategies is needed to return vitality to rural grassland economies while conserving grassland biodiversity. I hope that at the very least this book initiates a dialogue on the path we want to take into the twenty-first century. If it is provocative, then it has accomplished a large part of what I set out to do. Even if it is viewed as polemic, the facts do not change.

Most important, I encourage everyone to visit the great grasslands of North America—not just to drive through, as people often do, but to stop and visit. Get to know the flora and fauna, the history, the people, the economies, and most of all the land. Let the warm prairie sun soothe your face. Let your eyes explore unknown horizons. Let your ears discover perfect silence. Let your imagination roll back the clock to the thundering herds of buffalo. If that could happen, then I believe without an ounce of doubt that the restoration and preservation of grassland ecosystems would be as inevitable as a prairie breeze.

Sources and Methods Used in Analyses

Wherever appropriate, I have cited supporting information. In many cases I could have cited more than one study or document, but for brevity I have used only the most recent or comprehensive literature. Information not referenced is either common knowledge, my synthesis of available data, or from my own experience. Unless stated otherwise, all data concerning human demographics, land use, federal expenditures, personal income, and so on came from the U.S. Bureau of Census, specifically the *USA Counties* CD-ROMs published in 1992 and 1994. Unless otherwise stated in the text, all data concerning agriculture came from the previously mentioned CD-ROMs or the U.S. Bureau of Census, Census of Agriculture CD-ROM published in 1995.

Values for tables 7 and 8 are estimates and used for illustration only. They were calculated by multiplying the 1992 Bureau of Census county values by the proportion of the county in the hypothetical reserves. In some cases I substituted data from adjacent and similar counties because some of the counties included in the hypothetical reserves also contained large urban areas or other radically different habitats. The column for set-aside acres was determined by multiplying the 1992 Census of Agriculture values by a correction factor derived from the U.S. Department of Agriculture 1992 yearbook. The correction was necessary because the census tabulates values only for those areas defined as "farms" and therefore excludes many lands where agricultural sales were less than $1,000 for the 1992 calendar year yet government payments were still received.

Acknowledgments

Many people assisted with this effort in one form or another. I thank them all, for this book would not have been possible without their help. However, several people deserve special mention.

Frank Popper graciously read an early draft of the entire manuscript and offered excellent comments. Frank and his wife, Deborah, are leading authorities on land use, demographics, and Great Plains economies and have done as much as anyone to get society to think about the future of the region. Doug Coffman also accepted the exhausting task of reviewing an early draft of the manuscript. I thank Doug for his insightful comments, especially those pertaining to his specialty, anthropology and Great Plains history. Mike Biltonen of the Minnesota Ecosystems Recovery Project (MERP) also diligently reviewed the entire manuscript, as did Bill Simoes of the Canadian Parks and Wilderness Society (CPAWS). Mike and Bill forced me to think in more ambitious and holistic terms than I originally had, for which I am grateful. Paul Waggoner is an expert on global and national agricultural productivity and needs. He generously reviewed large portions of the manuscript and provided valuable information. Willard Cochrane understands as well as anyone the successes and failures of federal farm policies in the United States. His comments on the manuscript helped clarify my thinking in regard to agriculture and farm programs. John Borchert has spent a lifetime studying geography. He also reviewed the entire manuscript and provided helpful advice and, just as important, valuable encouragement. Two anonymous reviewers deserve thanks for their support and thoughtful guidance. Lou Cuicci provided valuable data, encouragement, and friendship.

Most important, I thank Shelley and Brady. Without my wife's tolerance, encouragement, and love I would never have completed this enjoyable but laborious and time-consuming project. Although my son Brady is much too young to have any idea what this book is about (his preference is still for Dr. Seuss), he is one of my greatest sources of inspiration. There can be no more noble pursuit than what is done for the sake of future generations. It is to Brady and all of his generation that this book is dedicated.

Ecology and Economics
of the Great Plains

The Land

We landed, ascended the bank, and entered a small skirting of trees and shrubs, that separated the river from an extensive plain. On gaining a view of it, such a scene opened to us as will fall to the lot of few travellers to witness. This plain was literally covered with buffaloes as far as we could see, and we soon discovered that it consisted in part of females. The males were fighting in every direction, with a fury which I have never seen paralleled, each having singled out his antagonist. We judged that the number must have amounted to some thousands, and that there were many hundreds of these battles going on at the same time, . . . I shall only observe farther, that the noise occasioned by the trampling and bellowing was far beyond description. In the evening, before we encamped, another immense herd made its appearance, running along the bluffs at full speed, and although at least a mile from us, we could distinctly hear the sound of their feet, which resembled distant thunder.

John Bradbury, *Travels in the Interior of America in the Years 1809, 1810, 1811*

Before European settlement, a vast region of grass dominated the heart of North America. In many ways the grasslands were the most striking landscape in a continent that also featured mountains, forests, tundra, swamps, deserts, and lakes. Although magnificent in their own right, the other regions often paled compared with the "sea of grass." The grasslands were the largest in area, contained the greatest concentration of wildlife, and stirred some of the strongest emotions. They appeared to be without limits, a terrain without reference points, a panorama from every perspective, eternal and indomitable, never to be changed. But within one hundred years the pre-Columbian grassland ecosystem was all but gone.

In their geographical distillation the North American grasslands were 1.1 million square miles of grass and savanna in the center of North America, created and evolved in their present form after the last period of glaciation, about twelve thousand years ago. Too dry to be forest and too wet to be desert, the biome stretched from what would become southern Canada to southern Texas and from Indiana to the Rocky Mountains (map 1). The cliché "sea of grass" implies monotony and sterility, but the grasslands were often the opposite. They may have been, before European settlement, one of the richest ecosystems ever to grace the earth.

Of the 1.1 million square miles, 0.3 million were grassland-forest mosaics. Known as savannas, aspen parklands, and foothill prairies, these ecosystems were typically defined as having a patchy tree coverage over 10 to 75 percent of the landscape. Although they are significant ecoregions, composed in large part of grass, I will for the most part concentrate on the 0.8 million square miles of pure prairies, especially those within the United States.

Ecologists typically divide the pure prairies of central North America into three descriptive zones: tallgrass, mixed-grass, and shortgrass prairie. The term Great Plains is commonly associated with the latter two, while the term true prairie is often reserved for the former. For brevity I will refer to the entire region as the Great Plains. Indeed, there are no distinct boundaries between the three zones but rather an east-west gradient that is for the most part a consequence of differing rainfall.

The 120,000 square miles of tallgrass prairie (115,000 square miles in the United States) was the easternmost of the three zones. The characteristic plants of the region before European settlement were big bluestem (*Andropogon gerardi*) and Indiangrass (*Sorghastrum nutars*), grasses that averaged five feet in height, although individual specimens grew to twelve feet. Capable of growing half an inch a day, and with root systems fifteen feet deep, they produced a graminoid biomass that was rarely equaled. While grasses provided the mass, myriad prairie flowers provided diversity. Over three hundred species of plants could be found within 1 square mile of tallgrass prairie, and even more on recently burned areas; 95 percent of the species were perennial, many with life spans of twenty years or more (Risser et al. 1981). The long-lived assemblage made the tallgrass prairie resilient to a wide variety of factors, including drought, saturated soils, fire, frost, and grazing. In addition to the grasses and

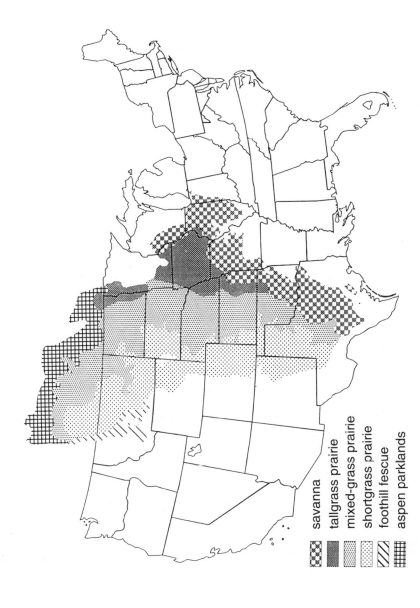

Map 1. Major zones of the contiguous grasslands and savannas. Modified from Omernik (1987) and World Wildlife Fund Canada (n.d.).

savanna
tallgrass prairie
mixed-grass prairie
shortgrass prairie
foothill fescue
aspen parklands

3

wildflowers, scatterings of trees, typically bur oak (*Quercus macrocarpa*), were found on moister soils.

Westward from the tallgrass prairie midsize grasses, one to two feet tall, became dominant (although tall grasses and short grasses could be found on suitable soils). The mixed-grass prairie, a transition zone of 340,000 square miles (265,000 square miles in the United States), may have contained the greatest species diversity of the three grassland ecoregions. Little bluestem (*Andropogon scoparius*) is the plant most frequently identified with the mixed-grass prairie, although junegrass (*Koeleria macarantha*), needlegrass (*Stipa* sp.), and western wheatgrass (*Andropyron smithii*) were also common. The latter grasses grew during the cooler seasons of spring and fall, whereas little bluestem grew best during the heat of summer. The proportion of cool season or warm season grasses in an area often depended on the season when the rains had fallen, or the fires had occurred, in recent years. Trees were found almost solely along rivers, on the edges of larger wetlands, in draws and ravines, or in the infrequent "minimountains" scattered throughout the region (e.g., Wichita Mountains in Oklahoma, Turtle Mountains in North Dakota–Manitoba, Cypress Hills in Saskatchewan-Alberta).

Farther west the midsize grasses disappeared and short grasses became dominant. Unlike the taller and more robust grasses to the east, buffalograss (*Buchloe dactyloides*), blue grama (*Bouteloua gracilis*), and the other shortgrass species were adapted to the climate extremes of the western shortgrass prairie. The grasses grew, flowered, and seeded before the hot dry winds of summer dehydrated the ecosystem. Grasses such as blue grama responded to the harsh environment by producing an abundance of fine, tough seeds (825,000 per pound for blue grama) that lay dormant on the rocklike soil until the next wet cycle (still, most regeneration occurred via vegetative means). Desertlike species such as sagebrush, cactus, and others occurred, and tough, resilient shrubs such as silver buffaloberry (*Shepherdia argentea*), skunkbush sumac (*Rhus aromatica*), and rabbitbush (*Chrysothamnus* sp.) grew where even the grasses could not. Although trees such as green ash (*Fraxinus pennsylvanicus*) and cottonwood (*Populus deltoides*) could still occasionally be found on moist sites, to all intents and purposes the 335,000 square miles (300,000 in the United States) of shortgrass prairie was a treeless ecosystem.

Yet the visible prairie flora was only part of the story. Unknown to most people, the real richness and vitality of the prairie ecosystem was belowground, the third dimension of the prairie ecosystem. Roughly 85 percent of the prairie's vegetative biomass, both living and dead, and 60 percent of net plant productivity occurred beneath the surface (Sims and Singh 1971). Even in the comparatively lush southern tallgrass prairie the belowground live plant biomass exceeded the aboveground biomass for most of the year (Risser et al. 1981). It is commonly noted that one square yard of prairie soil may contain twenty linear miles of roots and root hairs.

Like the prairie vegetation, much of the wildlife biomass lived belowground, at least part of the time. Prairie dogs, badgers, black-footed ferrets, burrowing owls, and swift foxes dwelt in burrows, not only to protect themselves from predators, but also to shelter themselves from the searing summer heat as well as the bitter winter cold. When invertebrates are entered into the equation it is possible that 50 to 70 percent of all prairie faunal species existed belowground at some point in their life cycles. The vitality of the prairie soil was staggering. A yard-square area of tallgrass soil, to a depth of twenty inches, may have contained over 110,000 arthropods and 5.4 million nematodes (Risser et al. 1981). The belowground invertebrate biomass was typically at least ten times greater than the aboveground invertebrate biomass and, even more startling, the soil microbial biomass was generally ten to twenty times greater than the biomass of macroscopic herbivores (e.g., bison, elk, rabbits) (Clark 1975). Although the big creatures got the attention, the little creatures were the engine of the prairie ecosystem.

The big creatures of the Great Plains tended to be more gregarious and visible than the reclusive animals of the forest; hence their numbers were often viewed by the first explorers with incredulity and awe. Indeed, only the great grasslands of Africa rivaled the masses of large animals found in the North American Great Plains.

The most noteworthy creature was the bison (*Bison bison*), commonly known as the buffalo. Powerful beasts weighing up to a ton, bison sometimes traveled in herds that purportedly numbered in the millions. Perhaps thirty to seventy million roamed North America before European settlement, a biomass that would have been over fifty billion pounds (heavier than the current human populations of the United States and Canada combined). The historian Walter Prescott Webb (1931, 44) reported that Plains bison were once "an inexhaustible beef supply, unrivaled by anything elsewhere known to man." Even single herds were mind boggling. Witness this reflection by William Street in 1904:

Many times has the question come to my mind, How many buffaloes were in that herd? And the answer, no one could tell. The herd was not less than twenty miles in width—we never saw the other side—at least sixty miles in length, maybe much longer; two counties of buffaloes! There might have been 100,000, or 1,000,000, or 100,000,000. I don't know. In the cowboy days in western Kansas we saw 7,000 head of cattle in one round-up. After gazing at them a few moments our thoughts turned to that buffalo herd. For a comparison, imagine a large pail of water; take from it or add to it a drop, and there you have it. Seven thousand head of cattle was not a drop in the bucket as compared with that herd of buffalo. (Dary 1974, 26)

Accompanying the bison herds across the vast grasslands were the wolves (*Canis lupus*). Meriwether Lewis recorded in his 1805 journal that "the country in every direction around us was one vast plain in which innumerable herds of Buffalo were seen attended by their shepherds the wolves" (Burroughs 1961, 85). If the 0.8 million square miles of grasslands supported 30 million bison, plus another 10 million antelope, 2 million deer, 1 million elk, and 20,000 bighorn sheep, then there was theoretically enough prey to support 750,000 wolves (Fuller n.d.), an incredible abundance and density by modern standards. However, at high prey densities wolf populations may be limited more by internal social factors than by prey availability; the highest long-term densities recorded are about one wolf per ten square miles (Mech 1970). Based on that, the grassland biome probably conservatively supported 80,000 wolves. Since larger wolf packs tend to be associated with treeless habitats (e.g., the Arctic), large prey (e.g., moose, *Alces alces*), and high prey biomass (Mech 1970), then the bison-hunting wolves of the Great Plains must have formed some of the largest packs found anywhere on the continent. The inference is consistent with the observations of early explorers such as Catlin (1973, 254), who reported in 1844 that wolves could be found in "gangs or families of fifty or sixty in numbers" (this may be an embellishment, but it seems safe to conjecture that grassland wolf packs were very large).

Crossing the paths of the bison and wolves were herds of antelope, deer, elk, and bighorn sheep. Each animal had its own niche, and each was found in abundance by early explorers.

The pronghorn antelope (*Antilocapra americana*)—the only large Great Plains mammal that did not come over the Bering land bridge—was ideally suited to the open grasslands. Fleet of foot, blessed with excellent eyesight, and

6

traveling in small herds, they could be caught by only the most fortunate and skilled predator. Perhaps 10 million antelope inhabited the Great Plains, with the highest densities in the mixed-grass and shortgrass plains.

The characteristic deer of the Great Plains, the mule deer (*Odocoileus hemionus*), was much more sociable than its eastern cousin, especially in the mating season. Whereas the male white-tailed deer (*Odocoileus virginianus*) of the eastern forests, savannas, and riparian woodlands courted only one female at a time, the mule deer buck herded several females. The differing strategies were likely a product of habitat, with the open country of the Plains more conducive to herd formation.

Although now associated with mountainous habitat, elk (*Cervus elaphus*) may have reached their greatest densities in the tallgrass and prairie–oak savanna ecoregions of the eastern Great Plains. The large animals fattened all summer on the lush prairie grasses and wintered on the nearby woody browse. During fall mating some elk herds in the tallgrass region numbered in the thousands (Dinsmore 1994), with the majestic bulls so abundant that they could be heard "whistling in every direction" (Henry 1897, 89).

The last large Great Plains herbivore was the bighorn sheep (*Ovis canadensis*). Numerous small bands of sheep inhabited the rugged buttes and canyons of the mixed-grass and shortgrass regions, blending in perfectly with the clay soils.

Like the large herbivores, many of the smaller animals were sociable. The most notable was the prairie dog (*Cynomys* sp.). The naturalist Ernest Thompson Seton (1929) estimated that there were 5 billion black-tailed prairie dogs (*C. ludovicianus*) about the time of European settlement—a biomass of 10 billion pounds, an impressive one-half to one-fifth that of the bison. Although commonly associated with shortgrass and mixed-grass prairies, prairie dogs were also historically found in some tallgrass areas, where they created conditions like those in shortgrass areas, adding to the region's biodiversity (Osborn and Allen 1949). With the bison and the wolf, the prairie dog was one of the most important vertebrates in the Great Plains.

Other small grassland mammals included the thirteen-lined ground squirrel (*Spermophilus tridecemlineatus*), the northern grasshopper mouse (*Onychomys leucogaster*), and the ubiquitous prairie vole (*Microtus ochrogaster*). Not surprisingly, small mammals in the shortgrass region tended to feed on seeds and insects whereas those in the lusher tallgrass region were more herbivorous (French et al. 1976). Somewhat similarly, seeds were an important part of the

7

diet for songbirds in shortgrass prairies, whereas breeding birds in tallgrass prairies relied almost solely on insects (Wiens 1973).

Compared with forested ecosystems, in grassland ecosystems the number of bird species was relatively poor. It has been suggested that only twelve bird species are endemic to the grassland biome (Mengel 1970) and only nine are not wetland species (Knopf 1988). The harsh climate, especially the periodic droughts, limited the number of species found in the region (Zimmerman 1992). Still, those that did adapt prospered, and the wide-open prairies were once again conducive to grouping behavior and apparent abundance. Greater and lesser prairie chickens (*Tympanuchus cupido* and *T. pallidicinctus*), sharptailed grouse (*T. phasianellus*), and sage grouse (*Centrocercus urophasianus*) all gathered in communal courtship rituals where dozens of birds vied for breeding privileges. Fall flocks of wild turkeys (*Meleagris gallopavo*) numbered in the hundreds (Dodge 1989) to the thousands (Mead 1986), much larger than those found in forested habitats. And flocks of migrating curlews, plovers, cranes, geese, and other birds darkened the spring and fall skies. The ducks alone that migrated through the Great Plains may have numbered in the hundreds of millions.

But not all grassland wildlife was social. The most notable exception, and also the most feared, was the Plains grizzly (*Ursus arctos horribilis*). Now reduced to a mountainous and tundra species, the grizzly historically ranged over most if not all of the grasslands. Based on the records of Lewis and Clark, Botkin (1995) estimated that there were 3.7 to 5.7 grizzlies per hundred square miles in the upper reaches of the pre-Columbian Missouri, densities comparable to those now recorded in mountainous regions. In addition to the grizzly the smaller black bear (*Ursus americanus*) was also found in the grassland biome, especially in the tallgrass and savanna regions (Henry 1897), but also well out into the arid regions along the larger rivers (Audubon 1969).

Although not necessarily the richest habitat in number of species, the grasslands still supported an abundance of wildlife rarely equaled anywhere on earth (early explorers often left the mountains for the vast grasslands because game was more abundant in the grasslands [Thwaites 1905, 16:43]). In addition, the nongrassland habitats within the vast grassland biome were also rich in wildlife and added to the region's diversity.

The meandering Missouri, Platte, Arkansas, Saskatchewan, and other grassland rivers could be at one moment shallow, cottonwood-lined bodies of calmly flowing water and at the next raging, flooding torrents carving new

8

channels through the soft earth. That dynamic would be painfully demonstrated to European settlers when the Missouri River changed its course and swept away pioneer towns such as St. Andrews, St. Anthony, and La Charette in what would become the state of Missouri (Thwaites 1905, 14:149; Bradbury 1986). Yet within this chaotic riverine ecosystem some species not only survived but prospered. The turbid rivers were home to dinosaur-era relics such as the pallid sturgeon (*Scaphirhynchus albus*) and bizarre looking paddlefish (*Polyodon spathula*) . On the countless sandbars that dotted the broad, shallow rivers piping plovers (*Charadrius melodus*) and least terns (*Sterna antillarum*) nested out of reach of most mammalian predators. And the frequently flooded riparian cottonwood groves provided nesting habitat for bald eagles (*Haliaeetus leucocephalus*) and other birds. These linear forests, though composing only 1 percent of the western landscape, provided habitat for more bird species than did the grassland sites (Knopf et al. 1988).

A noteworthy feature of the mixed-grass prairie, and to a lesser extent the tallgrass prairie, was the tens of millions of shallow wetlands dotting the landscape, especially in the region that would become the Dakotas, Minnesota, Alberta, and Saskatchewan. Named the Prairie Pothole Region by scientists, the region encompassed 300,000 square miles and stretched from north-central Iowa to central Alberta. The wetlands, remnants of glaciers that retreated twelve thousand years earlier, were breeding factories for countless waterfowl and other wetland-dependent species. Although constituting only 10 percent of North America's waterfowl breeding grounds, the region produced 50 percent of the ducks. In wet years the landscape seemed more water than land; in dry years it was almost all land.

The southern High Plains of Texas and Oklahoma comprised some of the most arid grasslands in the Great Plains, yet they too contained numerous wetlands. When rain came to the region it was often in the form of a downpour, temporarily filling up twenty to thirty thousand shallow wetlands. These saline pluvial and playa lakes provided wintering habitat for myriad wetland species, including hundreds of thousands of sandhill cranes (*Grus canadensis*).

All these varied habitats formed the grassland biome. Collectively, they made up one of the richest landscapes on earth. Yet the vast grassland biome was more than just a grassland ecosystem in the heart of North America. It was a barrier that separated the flora and fauna of the eastern forests from those of the Rocky Mountains and areas farther west. For example, approximately 130 bird taxa reached the limit of their distribution in the central Great Plains

(Rising 1983). The great grassland effectively created new forest species and subspecies to the east and west though not actually providing habitat for the organisms themselves. It was an ecosystem whose presence defined adjacent ecosystems.

The vast grasslands appeared never changing but were in reality always changing. Indeed, change shaped the grassland ecosystem. Fires frequently swept across great expanses. Severe winters were momentous and inevitable, even ordinary. Periodic droughts eliminated or reduced species not adapted to the region. Incredible herds of bison grazed waist-high grasses down to the earth and then moved on. Rivers reconstructed their course with erratic regularity. The great contiguous grasslands were an odd mixture of timeless stability and regular disruption, a thriving, healthy, and resilient ecosystem that had persisted for thousands of years. That was about to change.

The first Europeans to visit the heart of North America left journals overflowing with extraordinary accounts of abundant wildlife. Major Stephen Long reported on "incalculable multitudes" of large grazing animals (Thwaites 1905, 17:148). Joseph Street wrote of his 1833 trip through what would become Iowa, "I had never rode through a country so full of game" (Dinsmore 1994, 1). Granville Stuart wrote of the northern plains, "The whole country is black with buffalo" (Brown and Felton 1955, 63). George Brewerton traveled the southern High Plains in 1848 and wrote, "Buffalo feed over them by the thousands; the timid deer or graceful antelope meet the eye at every turn" (1993, 222). John Townsend was traveling near the Platte River in 1833 when he reported, "There is not half an hour during the day in which they [antelopes] are not seen" (Thwaites 1905, 21:159). John James Audubon traveled the Missouri River and wrote of the elk, "The number of this fine species of deer that are about us now is almost inconceivable . . . these animals are abundant beyond belief"; in the same region, he noted, "If ever there was a country where wolves are surpassingly abundant, it is the one we now are in" (1969, 2:20, 27, 67). Alexander Henry observed that along the Sheyenne River in North Dakota "grizzly bears are to be seen in droves" (1897, 145). William Clark of the Lewis and Clark expedition was at a loss for words when he wrote, "For me to mention or give an estimate of the different Species of wild animals on this river particularly Buffalow, Elk, Antelopes and Wolves would be incredible. I shall therefore be silent on the subject further" (Burroughs 1961, 85–86).

But impressed as the early explorers were with the wildlife, they were not impressed with the land's potential for settlement, especially the shortgrass and mixed-grass regions. The first Spanish explorers to the arid Great Plains believed the region had value to Spain only because of the bison (Webb 1931). In the early 1800s Zebulon Pike claimed the water-starved region had a barren soil that was dried up eight months of the year and unfit for farming. In Pike's opinion the most positive benefit of the great grasslands was that the biome would keep the citizens of the newly formed United States from "rambling and extending themselves on the frontiers" (as cited by Webb 1931, 156). In the 1820s Major Stephen Long coined the term Great American Desert to describe the region. Long's chronicler, Edwin James, concluded that the region was "almost wholly unfit for cultivation, and of course uninhabitable by a people depending upon agriculture" (Thwaites 1905, 17:147). He went on to say that the land was best "adapted as a range for buffaloes" (148). Likewise George Catlin explored the arid Great Plains from 1832 to 1839 and concluded that the land was best left to the buffalo and that the region was "of no available use to cultivating man" (1973, 262). John Townsend observed that "domestic cattle would certainly starve here [Wyoming], and yet the bison exists, and even becomes fat; a striking instance of the wonderful adaptation of Providence" (Thwaites 1905, 21:188). John Wesley Powell stated that the arid grasses could be "easily destroyed by improvident pasturage, and they are then replaced by noxious weeds" (1970, 63). He concluded that cattle in the region "cannot be inclosed by fences in small fields" and that they should be "fenced only by townships [thirty-six square miles] or tens of townships."

Partly because the land was viewed as poor for agriculture, the newly formed United States was able to purchase essentially the entire grassland biome from France for the astonishing price of less than three cents an acre. Although a bargain by today's standards, the new nation was still cash starved in 1803 and could barely afford the $15 million Louisiana Purchase.

Pioneers soon began apprehensively eyeing the tallgrass prairie. In Europe as in eastern North America, most of the best farmland was associated with cleared forests. Hence the settlers had no experience or knowledge of settling the strange treeless lands, and no appreciation of the region's limitations. The English-speaking pioneers were so unprepared for the new landscape that they did not even have a word for it; hence they adopted the French word *prairie* (Hart 1972).

The first settlers began turning the tough prairie sod in the early 1800s. Once broken, the rich, dark soil of the tallgrass prairie provided some of the best farmland the world had ever seen. In leapfrogging spurts pioneers began swarming over the tallgrass region, quickly dividing up the once vast grassland (Lang, Popper, and Popper 1994). When the easily accessible upland sites were gone the settlers turned to the wet prairies and meadows, draining all but the wettest sites (Hewes and Frandson 1951). By 1890 the tallgrass prairie was essentially gone (Smith 1992), replaced by the plowed field, the shelterbelt, and the rock pile.

Having conquered the tallgrass prairie, the people again looked to the West, the land of treeless horizons and incomprehensible herds of bison. The extermination of the bison deserves special attention in any discussion of Great Plains settlement. In retrospect it appears that the killings were founded at least as much in psychology as in utilitarian need. Granted many bison were killed for profit, and perhaps a few to eliminate the food source of the Native Americans, but the journals of early explorers provide insights into other possible reasons. John James Audubon (1969, 1:509) noted that most of the men were "too lazy . . . to cut out even the tongues," and William Hornaday suggested a moral sickness when he wrote, "It would be an interesting psychological study to determine the exact workings of the mind of a man who is capable of deliberately slaying a noble animal, in the full knowledge that he can make no earthly use of it, but must leave its magnificent skin, its beautiful head, and several hundred pounds of fine flesh to the miserable coyotes and the destroying elements. If such an act is not deliberate murder, in heaven's name, what is it?" (Coffman 1991, 65). Barsh (1990) pointed out that as many as five dead bison were abandoned on the Plains for each one that was shipped back east.

Even before the bison were eliminated, the settling of the mixed-grass and shortgrass regions had begun. Eager for expansion, Washington politicians urged people westward with little thought for the consequences of dense human settlement in an arid landscape. The premise, and promise, was that there was enough human demand in the eastern states, in terms of food and fiber, to warrant the homesteading and exploitation of the entire grassland biome. Expansionists envisioned a Great Plains where every quarter section of land was occupied by a yeoman farmer and his family, with each farmer producing a marketable surplus. How large that surplus would be, and how much was needed, was never scientifically assessed.

Desperate to expedite settlement of the region, the government gave vast tracts of the publicly owned Plains to the railroads in the 1860–80s. (Often the railroads quickly turned around and sold the granted lands to the highest bidder.) The railroads and other land speculators then persuaded President Lincoln to sign the federal Homestead Act of 1862 on 20 May of that year. The act essentially gave 160 acres to any settler who would live on the land for five years. The land giveaway and similar programs were viewed by some as the first direct government agriculture subsidies in the arid Great Plains. Consider the words of the rancher Silas Bent:

> Agriculture has had and is still having more lavish and unpaid-for favors conferred upon it by the government than any other industry among our people . . . ever since Mr. Jefferson began to attract immigration to this country by proclaiming to the world that he would give to the agriculturalist all the land he wanted in fee simple forever upon the payment of the mere cost of its survey, $1.25 per acre, while farmers in Europe are paying an annual ground rent of $20 per acre, agriculture has been and is subsidized to the annual amount of $18.75 an acre. (Webb 1931, 429–30)

The 1862 Homestead Act was soon proved a failure as homesteaders and Congress learned a harsh lesson; land-use practices and philosophies from the eastern United States were often inappropriate for the arid grasslands. Many settlers simply could not survive on such small tracts in such an arid environment. But instead of accepting the limitations of arid-land settlement, politicians continued trying to force eastern-style agriculture on the region. Congress passed a series of successively more liberal land giveaway acts, including the Timber Culture Act of 1873, the Desert Land Act of 1877, the Timber and Stone Act of 1878, the Kinkaid Act of 1904, the Enlarged Homestead Act of 1909, the Three-Year Homestead Act of 1912, and the Grazing Homestead Act of 1916. Other laws and programs were also passed to encourage settlement and exploitation of the region—for example, the Swamp Land Acts of 1849, 1850, and 1860, which promoted and subsidized drainage of prairie wetlands.

Although some had argued for years that the arid climate of the mixed-grass and shortgrass regions was inhospitable to most forms of cultivation, numerous theories were proposed to defy natural conditions. The most common essentially assured the naive settlers that "rain follows the plow," suggesting that the cultivated earth would somehow, perhaps with divine intervention, stimulate bountiful rainfall. Temporary wet periods increased the optimism; witness this report by Cyrus Thomas in 1869 in Colorado Territory: "I therefore give it as my firm conviction that this increase [rainfall] is of a permanent nature, and not periodical, and that it has commenced within eight years past, and that it is some way connected with the settlement of the country, and that as the population increases the moisture will increase" (Powell 1879, 71). Some other rain-making theories were that telegraph wires strung across the Plains would produce rain as a by-product of the electricity generated; that smoke from burning prairies would produce rain; and that planting trees would stimulate precipitation (Webb 1931). Scientists tested myriad other ideas, including numerous experiments involving aerial detonation of dynamite. Needless to say, they all failed to produce rain.

By the middle of the nineteenth century some settlers had had enough. One-third of the population of Kansas fled back to the East during the drought of the 1860s (Burns 1982), leading to the refrain, "In God we trusted, in Kansas we busted." The drought of the 1880s drove reality deeper home as widespread starvation occurred in the Plains. The historian Frederick Jackson Turner observed that "the native American farmer had received his first defeat" in western Kansas in the late 1880s (1901, 813).

While cultivating settlers harvested what they could from the central and eastern plains, cattle ranchers exploited the arid West. The romanticized days of "free" range and cattle drives lasted only a few decades. The increasing numbers of farms quickly fenced off the open range, and in other cases the ranchers themselves illegally fenced and appropriated the public lands to keep homesteaders out (Hurt 1994). By the 1890s the nomadic cattleman and his cattle drives were history.

Confined within small pastures and maintained at unnaturally high numbers, the introduced livestock affected the native vegetation in ways it was not adapted to withstand. Whereas the eradicated bison had grazed an area and then moved on, the fenced cattle did not give the vegetation a rest. Their constant grazing and trampling soon denuded and desertified the arid landscape. In some cases heavy grazing during drought years reduced ground cover by up to 95 percent (Albertson, Tomanek, and Riegel 1957).

By 1885 the western range was overgrazed, and cattle were dying by the tens of thousands (Webb 1931). In the harsh winter of 1886–87 up to 85 percent of some herds were lost in the northern Great Plains, many of the animals freezing to death on their feet (Hurt 1994). By 1895 the western range cattle stock had fallen by two-thirds, creating a vacuum quickly filled by sheep (Barsh 1990). The sheep soon outnumbered the cattle six to one, compounding the pressure on the arid ecosystem.

By the early 1900s poor farming practices, along with widespread overgrazing, had made the Great Plains ripe for a disaster of apocalyptic proportions.

Although efforts were being initiated to correct the problems and to identify the best and most sustainable uses of the region (Guttenberg 1976), the effort came too late.

The drought of the 1930s, and the legendary Dust Bowl that accompanied it, was widely viewed as a great natural catastrophe. In retrospect, however, the drought was not the catastrophe; removing and denuding the natural vegetation that protected the fragile soil was the catastrophe. Great Plains soils were partly the product of windblown loess deposited during the last glaciation. When the settlers started removing and reducing the protective grasses and forbs, the fine material started blowing again. The drought of the 1930s was no different from countless others since the last ice age; the difference was that the shielding vegetation had been ravaged.

At Hays, Kansas, shortgrass vegetative cover of over 85 percent in 1932 was reduced in eight Dust Bowl years to only 21 percent (Albertson, Tomanek, and Riegel 1957). In central Kansas, vibrant mixed-grass prairies were transformed to almost pure short grass (Albertson and Weaver 1946). Meanwhile, tallgrass prairie was replaced by mixed-prairie plants over a swath 100 to 150 miles wide stretching from the eastern Dakotas to central Kansas (Weaver 1943). Blowing dust from cultivated fields and overgrazed range accumulated several inches to several feet deep, practically destroying all native vegetation in some regions. The only sites that weathered the period relatively intact were the ungrazed lands (Albertson and Weaver 1946).

The trees planted by settlers and government agencies were especially hard hit. As early as 1934, at the beginning of the Dust Bowl, 40 percent of all shelterbelt trees in Minnesota prairie were considered dead or dying (Albertson and Weaver 1945). Trees in central Kansas experienced 41 percent mortality or injury by 1936, and those farther west suffered 55 percent. In central Oklahoma, 20–50 percent of trees died, and losses of 35–79 percent were reported in western Oklahoma as early as 1937. Six years later, by the time the drought was broken, almost all the planted trees in the region were dead or dying.

An estimated 2.5 million people abandoned the Great Plains during the Dust Bowl years. Arguably, such an exodus may have been in the best interest of the nation and the region. The mass emigration brought human densities more in line with the carrying capacity of the land. Still, many settlers stayed behind and tried to scratch out an existence, as I shall describe in later chapters.

In retrospect it appears that the gravest misjudgment in settling the grassland biome was that the nation saw the Great Plains not for what they were but as what it imagined, hoped, and prayed they could be (countless small farms, dense populations, thriving communities). *The Oxford History of the American West* (Milner 1994, 151) summarizes the settlement of the Great Plains and the rest of the West: "The full story is not one of great victories and clear successes. It is a story of economic boom and financial bust, of natural resources exploited for distant markets, and of agricultural expansion established with great human cost." The great human cost, as well as the ecological cost, continues to this day.

The Dust Bowl of the 1930s and 1940s did have one positive effect. It forced society to at least tacitly acknowledge that the arid Great Plains had been socially overextended and ecologically abused. In response to the Dust Bowl and farm failures, the federal government's National Resources Planning Board recommended that the federal government acquire 75 million acres of privately owned farmland and rangeland, mostly (about 70 percent) in the Great Plains (Wooten 1965). The U.S. Forest Service went even further, recommending a "conservative initial program" of federal acquisition that would have bought 125 million acres as the first step in a plan culminating in the purchase of more than 200 million acres (Wallach 1985). The goal of these proposals was to offer private landowners a way out of bankruptcy, to conserve natural resources, and to reduce commodity surpluses—that is, to redistribute and restructure land-ownership and land use according to national needs.

The ambitious goals were never achieved. Instead, the government acquired only 11.3 million fragmented acres between 1933 and 1946 (Wooten 1965). Still, twenty-five thousand farm families, many bankrupt and tax delinquent, sold land back to the government. Over eight thousand of these willing sellers received federal help to relocate. All told, removing 11.3 million acres from production cost the federal government a modest $47.5 million for acquisition and another $102.5 million for restoration and development. After indexing to 1992 dollars, the combined cost equates to approximately $1.1 billion.

Approximately 1.3 million of the acquired acres, known as land utilization projects, were given back to Great Plains states, colleges, and local governments. In some cases the tracts were even sold back to private interests. Of the remaining lands, approximately 3.8 million acres of fragmented and degraded tracts were designated national grasslands, ultimately administered by the U.S. Forest Service. Another 1.5 million acres were incorporated into the national forest system and are administered by the same agency. Another 2.5 million acres were transferred to the Bureau of Land Management, 1.9 million of those in Montana. The remaining lands were transferred to other agencies for national parks and wildlife refuges.

The land utilization program was a landmark event in Great Plains history in that it was the first national effort to acknowledge and correct the mistakes of the past. As Wooten (1965, vi) stated, "The land utilization program helped reverse U.S. policies encouraging settlement and development of land whether or not it was suited to cultivation." And Hurt (1986, 104) observed, "The purchase of submarginal land, the restoration of grass, and the wise management of the grasslands enabled the federal government to ensure better use of the land." (A similar sequence of events occurred in Canada, where the government rehabilitated degraded land and converted it to "community pastures".)

Fifty years of hindsight shows that the limited acquisitions of the 1930s and 1940s were inadequate to significantly reduce the nation's surplus agricultural capacity and poorly designed to conserve grassland natural resources. Still, the programs were a noteworthy step in the right direction, and they provide an inspiration and model for future land-use reforms.

In many ways the destruction and degradation of the prairie ecosystem is unparalled in North America. Entire regions have been completely destroyed, especially in the eastern tallgrass ecoregion. Currently, less than 1 percent of the original tallgrass prairie remains unbroken. One study analyzed all the ecosystems of the United States and categorized the tallgrass prairie ecosystem (east of the Missouri River) as "critically endangered" (Noss, LaRoe, and Scott 1995). In Iowa only 0.1 percent of the 30 million acres of tallgrass prairie escaped the plow (Smith 1992); the largest tract in the state preserve system is slightly over 200 acres. In Missouri only 0.5 percent of the tallgrass prairie remains, and almost half of the remaining tracts are 100 acres or smaller (Risser 1988). The Glaciated Plains division of Missouri, which covers the northern third of the state, has been especially hard hit; fewer than twenty prairie remnants are known to exist, all less than 20 acres (Missouri Department of Conservation 1992). An exhaustive survey of the Manitoba tallgrass region found only 370 remnant acres, mostly in railway rights-of-way; it is estimated that only 0.05 percent of the original prairie remains (Joyce and Morgan 1989). In Wisconsin only 0.1 percent of true prairie remains of the original 3.1 million acres, and only 100 acres of the original 1 million acres of mesic prairie. In North Dakota it is estimated that less than 5 percent of the tallgrass prairie survives, mostly in the sandy Sheyenne National Grasslands, and as little as 0.01 percent of the quintessential tallgrass prairie remains in the fertile Red River Valley. In Illinois a 1978 study found that only 0.01 percent (2,352 acres) of high-quality prairie survives (Illinois Department of Energy and Natural Resources and Nature of Illinois Foundation 1994); 80 percent of the remaining sites are less than 10 acres, and a third are smaller than 1 acre. As little as 1 percent of Minnesota's tallgrass prairie may still exist, mostly in small, fragmented tracts along the rugged shoreline of historic Lake Agassiz. Throughout the continent so little tallgrass prairie is left that 100-acre tracts are considered "nature preserves." Ironically, the railroads that first broke open the prairie now in many cases protect the last vestiges of the ecosystem in their rights-of-way. Where large tracts of tallgrass prairie do still exist it is only because the shallow soils deter plowing (e.g., Flint Hills in Kansas and Oklahoma). To all intents and purposes, the virgin tallgrass prairie and associated savannas of the eastern United States have been eliminated.

Farther to the west the mixed-grass prairie has also fallen to the plow, though not to the same degree as the tallgrass prairie. Still, some states have already lost over 70 percent of their mixed-grass prairie (Samson and Knopf 1994). Regionally, the mixed-grass ecosystem may be losing 2 percent of its grasslands annually to cultivation (U.S. Fish and Wildlife Service and Environment Canada 1986). In addition, other problems face the region. Parts of the 174,000 square mile Ogallala aquifer (also known as the High Plains aquifer) of the central and southern plains are predicted to decline over seven hundred feet between 1980 and 2020 (Luckey et al. 1988). Also, the flows of many rivers in the region have been altered, threatening entire aquatic ecosystems.

Other vital elements of the tallgrass and mixed-grass ecosystem have also been decimated. Iowa has lost almost 90 percent of its wetlands owing to drainage (mostly for agriculture), and North Dakota, Minnesota, and South Dakota have lost 49, 42, and 35 percent respectively (Dahl 1990). Even more sobering, these estimates report only on wetlands completely drained. They do not count the hundreds of thousands of wetlands that have lost some of their ecological value because they are cultivated, hayed, or grazed.

The shortgrass prairie has been the least affected by the plow, but the rate of conversion is still dramatic. From 1977 to 1982, 1.8 million acres (shortgrass and mixed-grass) were plowed in Montana, 849,000 in North Dakota, 750,000 in South Dakota, and 572,000 in Colorado (Mooers 1987). Texas has already lost 80 percent of its shortgrass prairie (Samson and Knopf 1994), almost all of it to agriculture. Future conversions of native prairie will likely be most extensive in the shortgrass region, simply because the other two regions have so little left. Even in areas not affected by the plow, the shortgrass ecosystem is radically different than it was before European settlement. The western Great Plains are now dominated by the cow, though bison are more compatible with the ecosystem and by some measures twice as productive (Barsh 1990).

Nowhere in the Great Plains does there exist a vestige of a naturally functioning grassland ecosystem, or even a close simulacrum, because the prairie ecosystem has lost not only grass, but also wildlife. The extermination of Great Plains wildlife was probably the largest human-caused elimination of fauna, in terms of biomass, the world has ever seen. Bison, once numbering 30–70 million animals, were eliminated from the southern plains by 1878 and from the northern plains by 1883 (Barsh 1990). By the turn of the century the world's population was reduced to a mere 1,000 animals, split between a small wild herd in Yellowstone, another small wild herd near Great Slave Lake in northern Canada, and those kept in captivity.

The elk of the grasslands, once found from the tallgrass prairies to the arid shortgrass steppes, was eliminated in the late 1800s. The Audubon bighorn sheep (*Ovis canadensis audaboni*), which inhabited the rugged badlands topography of the Dakotas, Nebraska, Montana, and elsewhere, became extinct about 1925, the consequence of overhunting.

The Great Plains wolf, which may have historically been more common on the Plains than the coyote (*Canis latrans*), was extirpated in the 1920s and 1930s. It is worth noting that the raven (*Corvus corax*)—which was historically common in the Great Plains whereas the common crow (*Cornus brachyrhynchos*) was absent (Thwaites 1905, 16:152)—disappeared from the region about the same time the wolf did. The two species are known to have a close relationship, with ravens often depending on the carrion of wolf-killed prey.

The passenger pigeon (*Ectopistes migratorius*), possibly North America's most abundant bird species (estimated at 3–5 billion individuals [Schorger 1955]), and the Carolina parakeet (*Conuropsis carolinensis*), the continent's second most abundant bird species, were both victims of overhunting, the last birds having died in the early 1900s. The flights of the species used to blacken the skies of the tallgrass prairie as well as the eastern forests and savannas.

Waterfowl populations, decimated by turn of the century market hunting, no longer fill the skies like they once did. Prairie chickens may have occurred in flocks as great as thirty thousand birds in the latter part of the nineteenth century (Dinsmore 1994); by the early twentieth century they were extirpated in many states. Other grassland bird species such as the dickcissel (*Spiza americana*), clay-colored sparrow (*Spizella pallida*), Baird's sparrow (*Ammodramus bairdii*), grasshopper sparrow (*A. savannarum*), and bobolink (*Dolichonyx orizivorus*) have all experienced significant declines. Of the nine upland bird species identified as wholly dependent on the grassland ecosystem, four are candidates for the endangered species list. Overall, populations of grassland birds may have declined by 85–90 percent (Robbins, Bystrak, and Geissler 1986).

Less is known about the status of grassland invertebrates, but where we do have long-term data the trends are just as alarming. For example, in the Loess Hills of western Iowa eight species of prairie butterflies that were present in 1922 were absent in the late 1980s (Orwig 1992).

Canada has suffered an even greater loss of prairie wildlife than the United States, in part because it had less prairie to begin with. Burnett et al. (1989, 74) stated that "relative to its area and population, the Prairie ecozone is the native habitat of a disproportionate number of threatened and endangered species of Canadian wildlife." The greater prairie chicken appears to be extirpated in Canada; the mountain plover (*Charadrius montanus*) consists of only a handful of breeding pairs (if any); Baird's sparrow has declined to less than 5 percent of its former abundance; and the ferruginous hawk (*Buteo regalis*) has declined to only 250–300 breeding pairs from an estimated 5,000 at the time of European settlement (Burnett et al. 1989).

The swiftness and extent of the loss of grassland wildlife are unparalled in human history. Many have accepted the passing without remorse or second thoughts. For others, however, the loss was tragic and sad. L. A. Huffman, a Montana resident, photographer, and bison hunter, both lamented the tragic past and espoused a possible future for the wildlife of the Great Plains. In the early 1880s, with most of the bison exterminated, Huffman, trapped in a Montana prairie blizzard and huddled in a washout with his horse, Crackers, wrote:

> When not busy melting snow in an army cup or toasting hard bread and bits of bacon over my tiny fire I talked to Crackers of my scheme to make a great pasture of the "Flat Iron" [the Montana shortgrass prairie between the Yellowstone and Missouri Rivers], to fence it with a great woven wire to banish forever the skin hunters, maybe enlist them in an army of wardens. How and where the great park gates should be guarded, how tame wild things would get—bison, antelope and elk—and too how splendid twould be when the yellow-green carpet of spring had come, to see it all teeming with life. (Brown and Felton 1955, 49).

Extinctions, the Endangered Species Act, Biodiversity, and Biotic Integrity

We should not knowingly allow any species or race to go extinct. And let us go beyond mere salvage to begin the restoration of natural environments, in order to enlarge wild populations and stanch the hemorrhaging of biological wealth. There can be no purpose more enspiriting than to begin the age of restoration, reweaving the wondrous diversity of life that still surrounds us.

E. O. Wilson, *The Diversity of Life*

It is commonly estimated that about 500 plant and animal species have become extinct in the United States since 1492. Since enactment of the Endangered Species Act of 1973 the rate of extinction in the United States has slowed but not stopped. In the past decade the dusky seaside sparrow (*Ammospiza maritima nigrescens*), Goff's pocket gopher (*Geomys pinetis goffi*), Bachman's warbler (*Vermivora bachmanii*), and ten species of freshwater fish have apparently gone extinct in the contiguous United States. The Center for Plant Conservation estimates that in the United States alone 427 plant species could vanish between 1989 and 1998 (Flather, Joyce, and Bloomgarden 1994). Over 28 percent of the 1,033 freshwater fish species in North America are considered endangered, vulnerable, rare, indeterminate, or extinct (Williams and Miller 1990). All told, 9,000 species in the United States may be at risk of extinction (Nature Conservancy, cited in Blockstein 1994).

The tallgrass prairie ecosystem has been especially hard hit. Dinsmore (1994) listed 29 vertebrate species—6 percent of the original total—that have been extirpated in Iowa and another 57 (13 percent) that are endangered and threatened. In Minnesota, 105 vascular plant and animal species associated with the prairie biome are on the state endangered, threatened, or special concern list (Coffin and Pfannmuller 1988).

In the past most species disappeared because they were shot, clubbed, or harpooned into extinction. Fortunately the world is more conscientious nowadays. Extinction by these means is no longer a major threat to most North American wildlife. Yet the human-caused loss and decline of species continue.

Pesticides once greatly reduced the numbers of bald eagles, peregrine falcons (*Falco peregrinus anatum*), and several other Great Plains raptors. More comprehensive testing, stronger regulations, and a more knowledgeable and concerned society have all helped to reduce the risk of chemical ecocide. Still, pesticides can be an additive factor in the decline of some species. For example, the decline of waterfowl is probably exacerbated by the use of agricultural chemicals, especially aerially applied insecticides. In the grassland biome approximately 21 million acres, 78 million acres, and 2 million acres were treated with insecticides, herbicides, and pathocides, respectively, in 1992 (U.S. Bureau of Census 1995: see preface, "Sources and Methods Used in Analysis"). At an application rate of 2 pounds an acre that equates to over 200 million pounds annually (the estimate is conservative, since many fields are treated more than once).

Humans also release dangerous levels of other pollutants into the environment. Selenium, an element found naturally in the ground, concentrates in irrigation and other water development projects. Selenium has been found at elevated levels in the addled eggs of piping plovers and least terns taken from the Platte River in Nebraska (Fannin and Esmoil 1993) and the Missouri River in South Dakota (Ruelle 1993). Similarly, lead, aluminum, and mercury were also found at higher than background levels at the latter study site, and mercury was near the harmful level at the former site.

Even more alarming, air pollution may disrupt delicate and complex chemical cycles in the prairie ecosystem. For example, increased levels of atmospheric nitrogen associated with air pollution may threaten the stability of tallgrass prairie remnants (Wedin and Tilman 1992). And, the consequences of global climate change may someday have enormous and unforeseen effects on the prairie biome.

A more tangible threat is lead shot (spent ammunition from hunters), which directly poisons waterfowl and indirectly poisons predators that eat them. For example, 9 percent of the eagle pellets found in Missouri contained lead shot (Griffin, Baskett, and Sparrowe 1982).

Outdoor recreation can also indirectly harm some species. Picnickers on

Missouri River sandbars leave food remains that attract predators such as magpies (*Pica pica*) and common crows, reducing the nest success of rare sandbar-nesting birds such as the piping plover. Similarly, off-road vehicles have been associated with lower nesting success of piping plovers on saline wetland beaches in North Dakota (Gaines and Ryan 1988).

Myriad other subtle and little-known threats exacerbate the continuing loss of grassland wildlife. But all these factors together may not equal the loss caused by the most destructive agent of all. The gravest threat to species worldwide is the continuing loss of habitat. The same is true in the United States. A survey of state fish and wildlife agencies found that habitat loss and habitat degradation were the top two management issues out of the thirty identified (U.S. Forest Service 1989c). Flather, Joyce, and Bloomgarden (1994, 9) found that habitat loss or alteration was a factor for approximately 95 percent of the species listed as endangered or threatened in the United States. Cooperrider (1990) listed numerous threats to grassland wildlife and observed that all resulted from habitat destruction and fragmentation.

Although habitat loss is commonly thought of in terms of acres converted to other uses or directly destroyed, that is only a small part of the equation. Owing to many complex ecological factors, small isolated remnants may, for many species, be as effectively destroyed as the habitat converted to other use, a phenomenon I shall examine in much greater detail. But first I need to discuss the limitations of current efforts at conserving grassland species.

Few pieces of legislation have been more maligned, abused, misunderstood, and misinterpreted—or more lauded—than the Endangered Species Act. From that we can conclude only that the act has been both a success and a failure and is definitely worth talking about.

Passed in 1973 and reauthorized several times since, the act explicitly states that one of its primary purposes is to "provide a means whereby the *ecosystems* [emphasis added] upon which endangered species and threatened species depend may be conserved." The keyword is "ecosystems." The creators of the Endangered Species Act apparently recognized that protecting endangered and threatened species ultimately depended on conserving the species' ecosystems. The authors did not use the word habitat, nor did they imply that human-made or human-altered environments would suffice. Demonstrating a profound wisdom, the legislators declared that the species and its ecosystem were inextricably linked and that preservation efforts should include both.

Yet the act has generally been administered as a species-only act, whereby ecosystem conservation is pursued only when it is convenient or noncontroversial. Because of that the act has failed to adequately and efficiently conserve grassland flora and fauna. There are several reasons a species approach is, in the long run, a poor strategy.

A species-oriented act is not preventive. By the time a species is listed as endangered or threatened, it is often too late to efficiently and noncontroversially conserve the species or its ecosystem. It is the old adage, "An ounce of prevention is worth a pound of cure." Because government agencies have tended to use the "pound of cure" mentality in conserving endangered and threatened species, the act becomes extraordinarily expensive. The U.S. Fish and Wildlife Service estimated that $291.5 million was spent by federal and state agencies in fiscal year 1992 to conserve 679 listed species (93 percent of all the listed species in the United States). That is $429,000 per species. The amount spent on endangered and threatened species conservation is expected to increase significantly in the near future. The U.S. Government Accounting Office estimates that $4.6 billion will be needed by the year 2000 to conduct research and recovery work on 2,286 rare species.

This approach is costly not only in dollars but also in terms of public acceptance. The case of the black-footed ferret (*Mustela nigripes*) is a good example. Ever since the last remaining ferret population was discovered near Meeteetse, Wyoming, in the 1980s, antagonism toward prairie dogs, the Endangered Species Act, and government agencies has remained high in the Great Plains. The antagonism was the consequence of having government biologists and other conservationists (along with their regulations) converge on the region to conduct ferret research and recovery. In many cases that antagonism has translated into contempt for ferrets, even though the animal's behavior (they prey on prairie dogs) would normally be considered beneficial by most Great Plains landowners.

Even though the Great Plains has comparatively few endangered species (Flather, Joyce, and Bloomgarden 1994) the potential for conflicts remains high. As of September 1994 twenty-nine federally listed endangered or threatened species were reported by the U.S. Fish and Wildlife Service as being associated with grassland counties (see appendixes A and B). Six of the species are not (or are no longer) strongly associated with the grassland ecosystem but occur in other habitats within counties partly in the grassland biome: grizzly bear, Mexican spotted owl (*Strix occidentalis lucida*), Arctic peregrine falcon (*Falco peregrinus tundrius*), northern aplomado falcon (*Falco femoralis septentrion-*

24

alis), Iowa Pleistocene snail (*Discus macclintocki*), northern monkshood (*Aconitum novaboracense*). Of the twenty-three endangered and threatened species currently associated with the grassland ecosystem, two are migrants only (whooping crane [*Grus americana*], Eskimo curlew [*Numenius borealis*]), and one is an infrequent disperser into the region (gray wolf [*Canis lupus*]). Seven of the twenty-three species are birds, seven are plants, three are mammals, two are fish, two are insects, one is a reptile, and one is a mollusk (appendix B).

Although the grassland biome has few listed species compared with other parts of the United States, the twenty-three species still result in a large perceived social burden. For example, at least one of them is listed by the U.S. Fish and Wildlife Service as occurring, or potentially occurring, in 569 of the 625 grassland counties (91 percent). The sum of county occurrences, or potential occurrences, is 2,241, or 3.6 species per county.

The limited range of some of the listed species does not necessarily lessen the legal ramifications of their status. For example, the black-footed ferret is limited to small reintroduction sites in southeastern Wyoming and north-central Montana, yet it is listed by the U.S. Fish and Wildlife Service as a species of concern in 141 grassland counties. Many actions that affect prairie dogs require precautions to ensure that ferrets are not present. So, although ferrets are unlikely to occur, the legal status of the animal still increases government costs and landowners' antagonism.

Perhaps more significant are the species that may be listed in the near future. The 625 grassland counties contain a minimum of ninety-five candidate species,* of which sixty-four are animals and thirty-one are plants (U.S. Fish and Wildlife Service 1991b, 1993c). In the near future the swift fox (*Vulpes velox*) (75 counties), Dakota skipper (*Hesperia dacotae*) (39 counties), Baird's sparrow (123 counties), and many other grassland species may be placed on the federal endangered and threatened species list. Such actions will have enormous social and political ramifications. Even the prairie dog has been recommended for listing (Miller, Ceballos, and Reading 1994), an action that would surely rate with listing the spotted owl in terms of controversy.

Yet another shortcoming of the act is that it relies too heavily on static definitions of speciation, thereby ignoring evolutionary realities. For example, the

---

*In the summer of 1996 the U.S. Fish and Wildlife Service revised their candidate list. The revised list includes only species for which there are data to warrant listing them as endangered or threatened. Still, the analysis above is useful as an indicator of future trends.

swift fox of the Great Plains may have been diverging into two separate species, yet the act failed to allow for this. Scientists recognized that swift foxes in the northern part of the range were larger and better adapted to harsh winters than animals in the southern part; hence they categorized the northern population as a distinct subspecies. Subsequently the northern population was listed as endangered. But further review by taxonomists determined that the northern animals were not (yet) significantly distinct from those in the south, at least not to a degree that justified subspecies designation; hence the animal was delisted (Stromberg and Boyce 1986). After the delisting the northern population continued to decline to the point where it may now be extinct. The evolving traits and characteristics of the northern swift fox are essentially lost owing to administrative processes.

Like triage, the Endangered Species Act has been somewhat successful in slowing the rate of extinctions. But the time has come to explore more efficient, permanent, and inspiring conservation strategies.

Flather, Joyce, and Bloomgarden (1994, 3) reviewed the history of endangered species protection and concluded that the most significant proposals to improve the effectiveness of the act were proposals for "managing representative ecosystems as complete units for preserving ecological diversity." Rohlf (1991, 278) listed six reasons he believed the act was not working, including that "the Act does not protect habitat reserves sufficiently to sustain 'recovered' populations." Flather, Joyce, and Bloomgarden (1994, 27) also found that "nation-wide, the most frequently cited species recovery management recommendation was land acquisition."

In spite of the controversy surrounding the Endangered Species Act, most Americans still support protection of endangered species (Times Mirror Magazines Conservation Council 1992), even when it conflicts with development (Kellert 1985). Americans are even willing to accept higher commodity prices if necessary to protect endangered species (Kellert 1980, 1985). From that one can conclude that any proposal that both conserves species and saves taxpayers money will be welcomed.

As Noss and Cooperrider (1994, 63) put it, "Species extinction is only the last and most obvious stage of biotic impoverishment." Of much greater concern is the widespread loss of *biodiversity*. Biodiversity, in its simplest distillation, can be defined as the variety of life and its processes (some researchers do not include "processes" within the definition of biodiversity [see Angermeier and

26

Karr 1994]). The protection of biodiversity is now viewed as one of society's most important environmental issues.

Biodiversity occurs at three fundamental levels. The physically smallest and least appreciated is the genetic level. The more diverse a species' genetic pool, the greater the likelihood that some individuals within it can adapt to changing environments, an especially valuable quality in dynamic grassland ecosystems. A second level of biodiversity is species diversity. It is the most commonly understood level in large part because it is the most easily recognizable and classifiable. Species diversity is typically defined as the number of species in an area (species richness) and their relative abundance and distribution. An often overlooked component of species diversity pertains to the vital statistics of a population. For example, most modern game populations (e.g., deer) are healthy in terms of numbers of animals, but few if any have the same age and sex structure as "natural" populations. The long-term effects of such human-induced changes are unknown. The third level of biodiversity is community diversity, a measure of differing plant and animal communities across a landscape. In grassland ecosystems profound changes in community diversity can be attributed to even subtle differences such as those that result from varying grazing histories.

Needless to say, the study of biodiversity is as complex as the study of life itself. Yet it is possible to manage for biodiversity. The wrong way is to try to manage for species preservation per se—the Endangered Species Act approach. The right way is to let natural processes do the work and to deemphasize human interference. According to the U.S. Office of Technology Assessment (1987), most biodiversity can be maintained only in a natural condition. The more the system varies from this "natural condition," the less likely it is to adequately conserve biodiversity.

Angermeier and Karr (1994) argued that "biotic integrity" was a better term than biodiversity. In their opinion biodiversity did not implicitly include natural processes (e.g., fire) but covered only the elements (genetic, taxonomic, and community), was often misconstrued as simply being species diversity, invited inclusions of artificial diversity (e.g., exotic species), and was prone to technological solutions. They argued that "resource policy would be more effective if based on the more comprehensive goal of protecting biological integrity" and that management should "focus on landscapes rather than populations" (690). On the same theme, Knopf (1992) argued that protecting biotic integrity could minimize the need for the costly, crisis-oriented programs used in the past.

27

The conservation of biodiversity and biotic integrity is a natural progression from the first game laws in the 1600s to the Migratory Bird Treaty of 1918 to the Endangered Species Act of 1973 to the present. The U.S. Office of Technology Assessment (1987, 11) stated that a National Biological Diversity Act would be an important step toward designing a comprehensive long-term strategy for conserving biodiversity. As of 1994 there was no such federal legislation that applied a regional approach to biodiversity conservation (Blockstein 1994).

Although Canada does not have a legislative equivalent of the Endangered Species Act, it does have an assortment of national, provincial, and regional laws and policies aimed at protecting biodiversity (e.g., COSEWIC, RENEW). Some of these directives are more visionary and progressive than anything in the United States. Of special relevance is the Wild West Program, conceived in 1985 to conserve the biological diversity found on the Canadian prairies. A Prairie Conservation Action Plan was drafted that elucidated ten goals ranging from identifying remnant prairie sites to protecting rare species to promoting public awareness of the prairie resource (World Wildlife Fund Canada n.d.). Most noteworthy, the plan calls for protecting at least one large, representative area in each of the four major prairie ecoregions (defined as tallgrass prairie, mixed prairie, fescue prairie, and aspen parkland) and at least 10 percent of the landscape protected in each habitat subregion. The emphasis on landscapes is arguably much more progressive than traditional United States measures that concentrate on individual species.

Selected Grassland Species

All things are connected. This we know.
    Chief Seattle

A brief look at of several grassland species can provide insight into the factors leading to the decline of grassland biodiversity. I selected the following species because they represent a wide range of taxa, because they are facing a variety of threats, and because they best represent the concept of biodiversity and the consequences of not conserving naturally functioning ecosystems.

Black-footed Ferret

From a population of perhaps millions of individuals in pre-Columbian times to only eighteen in 1987, the story of the black-footed ferret (*Mustela nigripes*) is one of the best chronicled and most challenging conservation efforts in the grassland biome. The eventual recovery of the ferret will depend in large part on three issues: the stability, distribution, and size of extant prairie dog complexes; the spread of canine distemper; and the degree of predation by coyotes (and to a lesser extent, great horned owls).

Approximately 90 percent of the black-footed ferret's diet consists of prairie dogs. In addition, ferrets use prairie dog burrows for denning and breeding. To briefly sum up the relationship, black-footed ferrets cannot survive in the wild without the right quantity, quality, and distribution of prairie dog colonies.

Before European settlement there may have been 100 million to 250 million acres of prairie dog towns. Assuming that two-thirds of the acreage was within the mixed-grass and shortgrass plains, prairie dog towns may have covered 15–39 percent of the region. Such a distribution and abundance was conducive to ferret survival; as prairie dog towns were extirpated or declined in vigor owing to disease or other factors, ferrets could readily disperse to nearby sites.

Unfortunately for the ferret, the expansive pre-Columbian prairie dog ecosystem no longer exists. Prairie dog populations have declined 98 percent in historical times (Coppock et al. 1983), with hundreds of thousands of acres still being destroyed annually (Miller, Ceballos, and Reading 1994). And just as significant, many of the relict towns are small (in number of individuals) or are isolated from other towns, making them of little value for ferret conservation. Concurrent with the demise of the prairie dog, black-footed ferrets declined from an estimated 5.6 million animals in the late 1800s to only 18 individuals in 1987 (U.S. Fish and Wildlife Service 1988a).

The black-footed ferret recovery plan calls for 1,500 free-ranging breeding ferrets by the year 2010 (U.S. Fish and Wildlife Service 1988a). According to the plan, the conservation of that many ferrets will require 185,000 to 250,000 acres of prairie dog towns. Preferably this acreage will be in the form of several large, stable prairie dog complexes, meaning that each restoration site may have to cover hundreds of square miles.

Current landownership patterns in the Great Plains dictate that private lands will be needed for ferret recovery. Yet private landowners have repeatedly demonstrated antagonism toward prairie dog conservation and hence ferret conservation. Until large tracts of protected land can be established, the future of the ferret will remain tenuous.

A second critical issue concerning ferret recovery is canine distemper, a disease that appears to have been brought to North America by the dogs of European settlers. Because canine distemper is an exotic disease, black-footed ferrets have little immunity to it. The last wild ferret population, in Meeteetse, Wyoming, was reduced approximately 50 percent a month over a three-month period after being exposed to the disease. Black-footed ferrets are so susceptible to canine distemper that scheduled reintroductions may be canceled if it is discovered that the release site is contaminated with the disease.

How to protect wild ferrets from canine distemper is a complex and challenging question. Medical solutions, such as vaccinating ferrets, not only are costly but compromise the spirit of biodiversity conservation. Natural solutions are much preferred. The best of these, albeit not perfect, is to provide a buffer zone between ferret populations and the source of the disease—dogs and human residences. Current landownership patterns in the Great Plains preclude this solution, but should sufficiently large wildlife reserves, with high area-to-perimeter ratio, someday be established in the Great Plains, they would provide some separation between internal ferret populations and external sources of the disease.

The last of the three critical issues influencing ferret recovery is coyote predation. At first glance coyote predation on black-footed ferrets seems natural. Indeed, coyotes and ferrets have always coexisted on the Great Plains. Yet the degree of coyote predation on ferrets in modern times is quite likely very unnatural, and at a level that may threaten ferret recovery. I will discuss this assertion more fully in the section on the gray wolf.

Western Prairie Fringed Orchid

The western prairie fringed orchid (*Platanthera praeclara*), with its spike of a dozen or more large, showy white flowers, is regarded by some as the most stunning plant of the tallgrass prairie. Two feet or more tall, it is also one of the most recognizable. Unfortunately, only seventy-four extant populations of the orchid were known as of 1994, many of fewer than a dozen individuals (U.S. Fish and Wildlife Service 1994). Even more foreboding, only five of the populations occur on federal lands. The lack of public ownership is highly relevant, since the Endangered Species Act affords essentially no protection to plants on private property. However, even public lands are not always managed for the orchid's survival.

One of the largest populations of orchids, approximately 2,500 individuals, occurs on the Sheyenne National Grasslands in southeast North Dakota. Protection there might seem assured. The Forest and Rangeland Renewable Resources Planning Act of 1974 legislated that conservation uses of Forest Service lands be given equal weight with grazing. In addition, the Endangered Species Act mandates that each federal agency "insure that any action authorized, funded, or carried out by such agency is not likely to jeopardize the continued existence of any endangered species or threatened species." Yet even on the national grasslands the orchid is still in danger if not of extinction, then of loss of vitality and vigor.

An unfortunate clause of the Bankhead-Jones Farm Tenant Act of 1937 required grazing on the national grasslands. At the time the provision seemed inconsequential, the main intents of the public-financed acquisition being to relieve settlers of their tax delinquency and emotional suffering while lessening the need for government agricultural subsidies and conserving natural resources. But over time the grazing provision became viewed as paramount by nearby communities. The notion that the areas were established primarily for grazing became ingrained in local cultures and in the minds of local politicians. Lewis (1989, 169) reviewed the history of the national grasslands and concluded that federal laws dictate that "nongrazing uses of the national grasslands are given equal weight with livestock grazing; [yet] in actual practice cattle grazing remains the dominant use."

Heavy cattle grazing on the Sheyenne National Grasslands continues to threaten the orchids' vitality and existence (along with other factors such as invasion by the exotic plant leafy spurge [*Euphorbia esula*]). Heavy grazing can affect orchids in two ways. First, cattle occasionally eat orchids. Second, and perhaps more important, cattle trample them. Although orchids can probably tolerate infrequent injuries, they appear susceptible to repeated harm. Historical grazing patterns by transient bison allowed orchid populations time to recover. Comparatively unremitting grazing by confined cattle does not allow for recovery. Inevitably, the two uses of the grasslands come into direct conflict. As often happens, the battles between ranchers and conservationists are distilled to simplistic and misleading headlines such as "Ranchers Say Flower Threatens Their Way of Life."

Even though the Sheyenne National Grasslands contain one of the largest relict populations of orchids, the heavy grazing pressure on the public land is so threatening that the site was given a conservation rating of only 3 by the draft recovery plan (U.S. Fish and Wildlife Service 1994; a high level of protection rated a 9, while no protection rated a 0). Such a dubious level of protection is not uncommon when rare resources must share public lands with commercial interests.

Eskimo Curlew

Like the legendary flocks of waterfowl, migrating Eskimo curlews (*Numenius borealis*) once blackened the prairie skies every spring (but not in the fall; they take an Atlantic Ocean route to their South American wintering grounds). Terres (1982, 769) reported that the Eskimo curlew was once a "fabulously abundant bird" and that in "migration so resembled tremendous flights of passenger pigeons that they were called prairie pigeons." In the mid- to late 1800s market hunters took incredible numbers of the one-pound, buff-colored shorebirds as they migrated through the prairie states. By the 1990s it was not clear whether the Eskimo curlew still existed.

Although the exact causes for the decline of the Eskimo curlew remain unknown, market hunting was undoubtedly a significant factor. Fortunately it came to an end in the early 1900s, mainly because of dwindling bird populations, but also because of protective legislation such as the Migratory Bird Treaty between the United States, Canada, and Mexico.

Yet something has prevented the Eskimo curlew from recovering. In the past fifty years only about seventy individuals have been reported worldwide, with the last sighting occurring in Nebraska in 1987 (U.S. Fish and Wildlife Service 1990; see Terres 1982 for a summary of sightings). There may be no more than a couple of hundred Eskimo curlews left, if the species exists at all, even though it has been protected from hunting for quite some time and has been covered by the Endangered Species Act since 1974. Therefore factors other than hunting must be preventing the recovery of the curlew. One of those factors may be the conversion, fragmentation, and degradation of the Great Plains ecosystem. At first glance it seems unlikely that habitat destruction in a migration corridor could seriously hinder the recovery of a species, but further examination suggests otherwise.

The Eskimo curlew nests in the tundra region of northern Canada and Alaska, near the Arctic Ocean. Yet even today the Far North remains relatively unspoiled by human activities, so it seems unlikely that events on the breeding grounds have prevented the bird's recovery.

The southern migration of the Eskimo curlew includes one significant stopover. Every fall the birds fatten themselves on berries and snails in the Labrador-Newfoundland area of eastern Canada. Once again the sparsely populated region has changed relatively little since pre-Columbian times.

The third of the four ecosystems significant to the Eskimo curlew is the pampas (grasslands) of southern Argentina and Chile, where the bird is believed to have wintered. Unlike the ecosystems mentioned previously, the pampas has changed since the arrival of Europeans, the most significant change being the presence of cattle. In addition, a relatively small amount of the pampas has been converted to cropland. These factors may have contributed to the Eskimo curlew's failure to recover to its former abundance, but the changes in the pampas pale compared with what has happened along the bird's northward migration path.

The grasslands of central North America have undergone a dramatic transformation from a vast prairie dotted with millions of scattered wetlands to a landscape of cultivated fields, drained wetlands, unnaturally grazed rangeland, and planted shelterbelts. Nowhere from Texas to southern Canada have large tracts of the grassland ecosystem, especially the tallgrass and mixed-grass ecosystems, remained unaffected by European settlement. More than any of the other ecosystems the Eskimo curlew depends on, the vast prairies of North America have changed from historical times.

We may never know for certain why the Eskimo curlew has failed to return to its former abundance. If the conversion of the North American grasslands is partly responsible, however, then that conversion caused the (near) total disappearance of the bird not only from the central United States and Canada but also from the eastern shoreline of North America, from northern Alaska and Canada, and from South America. The curlew is yet another example of how seemingly regional issues in America's grasslands also affect people and ecosystems in other parts of the world. As the case of the Eskimo curlew makes clear, protecting biodiversity is an international issue.

Swift Fox

The secretive swift fox (*Vulpes velox*) is well adapted to the harsh environment of the mixed-grass and shortgrass prairies. A cat-sized canine, it is an opportunistic feeder that makes use of insects, small vertebrates, carrion, and even plants (prairie dogs, grasshoppers, and beetles were the major diet components in South Dakota [Uresk and Sharps 1986]). The swift fox is the true fox of the Great Plains; unfortunately it has been replaced by the larger red fox to such a degree that few people, including Great Plains residents, have even heard of the small grassland fox.

Two lessons can be learned from studying the swift fox. Both apply not only to the swift fox but also to several other Great Plains species. The first lesson is ecological. Like most ecological studies it is fairly complex, highly interwoven with other factors, circumstantial in details, and somewhat speculative. The exact reasons for the swift fox's precipitous decline remain unclear. The easiest theory is that it decreased because of loss of habitat or mortality caused by humans, from being either shot, trapped, poisoned, or hit by automobiles. But further analysis reveals inconsistencies and shortcomings with this theory.

The swift fox originally inhabited most if not all of the mixed-grass and shortgrass prairies from southern Canada to central Texas (map 2). Because of its broad distribution and because of differences in climate between the northern and southern parts of its range, swift fox populations differed not only morphologically but perhaps also behaviorally and ecologically. Soon after the elimination of the bison and the settlement of the Great Plains, the swift fox disappeared from most of the northern part of its range. If it was still present in

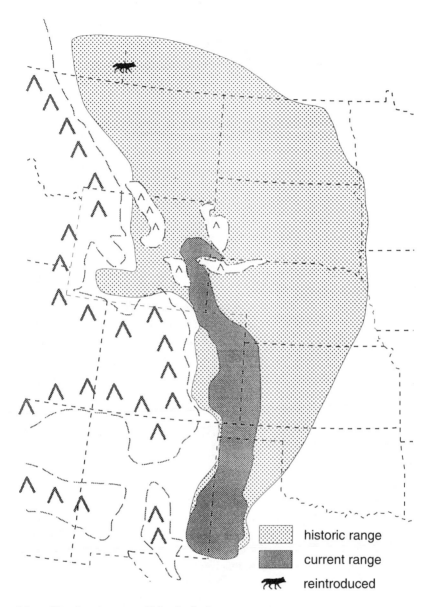

historic range

current range

reintroduced

Map 2. Historic and current swift fox distribution.

western North Dakota at the beginning of the twentieth century it had become very scarce; a turn of the century fur trader in Walhalla, North Dakota, reported that although it was once common, none had been seen since the buffalo disappeared (Bailey 1926, 164). The last specimen in Saskatchewan was collected in 1928 (Carbyn 1989).

But the swift fox still persisted in fair numbers in the southern half of its historic range. Although virtually eliminated from the northern half, the animal persevered southward from approximately Lusk, Wyoming. As late as 1994, apparently viable populations still survived in eastern Colorado, eastern Wyoming, and eastern New Mexico. Yet the obvious reasons for the swift fox's demise in the north (habitat destruction, elimination of prairie dog colonies, hunting, trapping, poisoning, automobiles, displacement by red fox, predation by coyotes) were not noticeably different from those in the south. Therefore some other factor must be responsible for the different rates of persistence between the two populations. One possible explanation has to do with subtle ecological processes.

Winter is a well-documented problem for most species in northern latitudes, in large part because food is scarce at that time of year. Historically, the swift fox in northern latitudes probably depended in large part on carrion to survive the winter months—unlike the southern swift fox that could overwinter on insects, small animals, and even plants. The most significant source of winter carrion in pre-Columbian times was undoubtedly bison—more specifically, wolf-killed bison. It seems reasonable to conjecture that before European settlement wolves indirectly aided the swift fox by providing a relatively abundant source of carrion. But after the elimination of wolves and bison this vital food source was no longer available. The swift fox might have survived mild northern winters without carrion, but harsh winters with prolonged deep snows and cold temperatures may have eliminated entire populations. Over time the northern swift fox population disappeared. This possibility has also been proposed by other researchers. Carbyn (1986) speculated that the loss of wolves from the prairie reduced the amount of winter carrion and that limited food damaged northern foxes more than those farther south.

In addition to the bison killed by wolves, natural mortality of bison and other ungulates was also high in late winter. Concerning the wild bison in Yellowstone National Park, Meagher (1978, 127) stated that "aged and otherwise weakened animals can be expected to die every year" and that such deaths "often [occur] in late winter and early spring." These are the same periods when

36

swift foxes in northern latitudes were probably most in need of food. But because of modern wildlife management practices, few ungulates live to an advanced age where they are vulnerable to winter mortality. Unlike historical times, now there is little if any late-winter carrion available in the northern Great Plains. An integral ecological process is missing.

It is worth noting that as formerly cropped areas revert to grassland the swift fox has begun reoccupying parts of its historic range. For example, it has naturally reestablished itself in western Kansas to the point where there is now a harvestable surplus. Yet no similar reoccupation has been noted in the northern part of the range. Indeed, it appears that the swift fox is still declining in South Dakota, the last remnant of the once vast northern population (some animals have been observed in Montana in recent years, but most if not all appear to have dispersed from a recently reintroduced population in Canada).

The second lesson to be learned from the swift fox is political. Since the delisting (from the endangered species list) of the northern swift fox because of taxonomic questions, several attempts have been made to list the species rangewide or by population. All these efforts have failed. Biologically, it seems that the swift fox warrants listing, especially the northern population. Therefore the reason it is not listed must be administrative or, more specifically, political.

The swift fox is very susceptible to nuisance-animal control, including leghold traps and poisons used for controlling coyotes. Swift foxes are also strongly associated with prairie dog towns, the scourge of many western ranchers. Because of these and other factors, listing the swift fox as an endangered species might result in restrictions on traditional ranching or at least be perceived as having the potential to do so. It seems reasonable to surmise that the federal government's reluctance to list the swift fox as an endangered or threatened species is due in part to the political consequences.

Dakota Skipper Butterfly

The Dakota skipper butterfly (*Hesperia dacotae*) is an unpretentious member of the family Hesperiidae, commonly known as skippers. Skippers are thought to be more primitive than the "true" butterflies (e.g., monarchs, swallowtails, and fritillaries) and are typically not as colorful, as large, or as charismatic. Indeed, they are rarely seen at all, their flight from danger often being described as "suddenly vanishing." That makes their conservation more challenging in the sense that public support is only lukewarm.

A second management challenge concerning the Dakota skipper has to do with its not traveling great distances; indeed, individuals are believed to rarely travel more than a mile from their birthplaces. This characteristic makes the skipper, and many smaller grassland organisms, susceptible to habitat fragmentation.

Before historical times the Dakota skipper was probably distributed throughout most of the northern tallgrass and mixed-grass prairies (map 3). The extent of the range may have been 200,000 square miles, within which the occurrence of skipper populations was likely patchy and not uniform, with high densities in favorable habitat (lightly grazed or ungrazed tallgrass and mixed-grass prairies) and low densities, if any, in unfavorable habitat. As habitat conditions changed through natural succession, fire, or bison grazing, the species' local abundance would change accordingly. Sites that changed to a more suitable habitat would be colonized from nearby skipper populations. Conversely, occupied habitats would be altered by natural events (e.g., fire, heavy bison grazing), and the local skipper population would be extirpated or greatly reduced. Through this ebb and flow the species persisted for thousands of years. But landscape fragmentation disrupts these spatial processes, threatening the skipper's survival.

For example, should an isolated Dakota skipper population on a 160-acre remnant tract of native prairie within an agrarian landscape be extirpated because of pesticides, overgrazing, haying, or some other calamity, there is little chance of the species' naturally recolonizing the site even if the habitat returns to favorable conditions. The problem is common among many invertebrates, making the group especially vulnerable to habitat fragmentation. Indeed, a road as narrow as twenty feet may provide a barrier to some invertebrates (Mader 1984). As the prairie landscape continues to be fragmented by cultivation, shelterbelts, roads, and other human influences, more and more invertebrate populations become isolated. As these isolated populations disappear owing to both natural and human-caused events, the species head inexorably toward extinction, one population at a time. Compounding the problem, even those populations that do persist are often weakened genetically.

Like many less mobile invertebrates, the Dakota skipper probably occurred throughout the vast pre-Columbian grasslands in numerous and dynamic metapopulations comprising numerous local populations that contain unique adaptive traits, often genalogical, and capable of interacting with the other populations via dispersing individuals. Such interchange not only helps local populations rebound from declines but may also be critical for the genetic vitality of the species. Unfortunately, the current fragmentation of the prairie biome prevents remnant skipper populations from exchanging their genetic material.

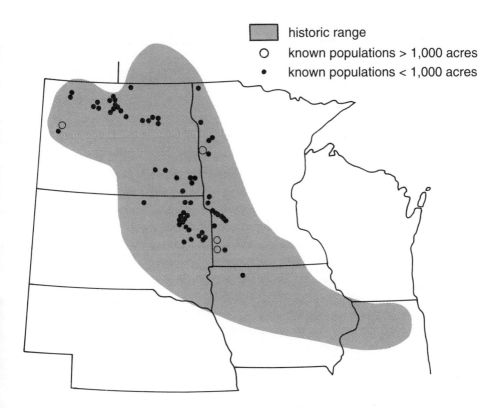

legend:

historic range

○ known populations > 1,000 acres

• known populations < 1,000 acres

Map 3. Historic and current Dakota skipper distribution (includes only populations known to be extant in late 1980s or later). Data from Royer and Marrone (1992), Coffin and Pfanmuller (1988), Schlicht and Saunders (1994), and J. Fleckenstein, Iowa Department of Natural Resources, personal communication.

Without the infusion of outside genetic material, local populations may suffer inbreeding depression, resulting in less adaptability to environmental changes, lower fecundity, and decreased disease resistance, among other factors.

In other cases species in fragmented habitats may suffer hybridization when a species mates with a closely related species, often a consequence of a lack of conspecific mates. For example, if an isolated Dakota skipper population is reduced to only a few individuals, they may mate with more available skipper species (e.g., Ottoe skipper [*Hesperia ottoe*]), resulting in no offspring, sterile offspring, poorly adapted offspring, or successful hybrid offspring that eventually breed. The breeding of the hybrids back to either founder ultimately threatens the genetic integrity of the founder species.

As of 1994 there were only seventy-six known Dakota skipper populations

39

remaining. These populations, many of which occupied habitats of ten acres or less, were distributed among the Dakotas, Minnesota, and Manitoba. (The possible sighting of a single male and two female Dakota skippers in Iowa in 1992 suggests that it may still exist there.)

The aggregate acreage of known Dakota skipper populations appears to be less than 10,000 acres, or 0.008 percent of its probable pre-Columbian distribution. What is especially disconcerting is that few if any of these sites are large enough to ensure the long-term conservation of the species. Because of the myriad threats facing remnant tracts of butterfly habitat (e.g., cultivation, invasion by exotic plants), Orwig (1992) called small butterfly reserves "survivia" in contrast to "refugia." Small remnant populations of skippers may precariously survive there, but they are not necessarily protected from external factors. Although not referring directly to the Dakota skipper, the management concerns expressed by Landres (1992, 302) apply to the skipper: "Management plans that maintain a single population of a species, or several populations with no means for dispersal among them, will likely result in extinction of that species because of natural and human threats to these populations. For the long-term persistence of a species, the metapopulation must be maintained." The most efficient and effective butterfly conservation strategy consists of protecting large, contiguous blocks of habitat. Theoretically, society could establish 128,000 160-acre fragmented tracts of northern prairie butterfly habitat (totaling 32,000 square miles), each separated from the next by a mile, but they would not necessarily ensure the long-term survival of the Dakota skipper. In contrast, a few large reserves, totaling just a fraction of the hypothetical 32,000 square miles, could sustain the species for thousands of years.

Although the Dakota skipper may have little popular appeal, its conservation is no less important. Indeed, it is one of a relatively few northern tallgrass and mixed-grass endemics. But more important, the Dakota skipper, like many other insects, is an important pollinator of prairie plants. Without prairie insects, many prairie forbs would cease to exist or would be greatly reduced in numbers. For example, the decline of many prairie milkweed species may be due in part to the decline of insect species, a consequence of fragmented habitats (Betz and Lamp 1992). Likewise, the western prairie fringed orchid may depend on pollination by species of prairie hawkmoths (*Sphinx* sp.), an obscure group of nocturnal insects that may be vulnerable to habitat fragmentation. The Dakota skipper may be a humble cog in the prairie machinery, but it is an important cog nevertheless.

Prairie Dog

I have already discussed the importance of prairie dog ecosystems from the per-spective of black-footed ferret conservation. Yet prairie dogs (*Cynomys* sp.) benefit so much more than just ferrets. From a biodiversity perspective prairie dog towns may be the most significant microhabitat of the mixed-grass and shortgrass prairies. Small rodents weighing only about 1.5 pounds, they create unique ecosystems within the grassland landscape. Prairie dog burrows provide shelter for swift foxes, burrowing owls (*Athene cunicularia*), rattlesnakes (*Crotalus* sp.), and many other animals. The abundance of invertebrates in prai-rie dog towns attracts large numbers of insectivorous birds (Agnew et al. 1986). Nearly twice as many small mammals, excluding prairie dogs, are found in prairie dog colonies as are found in nearby mixed-grass prairie (Agnew, Uresk, and Hansen 1988). The prairie dogs themselves are prey for black-footed fer-rets, ferruginous hawks, golden eagles (*Aquila chrysaetos*), and numerous other predators. A South Dakota study found that at least 40 percent (134 spe-cies) of all vertebrate species found west of the Missouri River are associated with prairie dog towns (Sharps and Uresk 1990).

It is worth noting that although bison are commonly thought of as the pre-eminent Great Plains grazer, the truth is that the prairie dog probably has the most influence on the ecosystem. In many cases bison (and antelope and other grazers) are mere tagalongs relying on the nutritious forage produced by prairie dogs (although the relation between the two is best described as mutualistic). For example, in Theodore Roosevelt National Park in western North Dakota, bison spent over 24 percent of their time in prairie dog towns even though the towns made up only 1.2 percent of the available land (Norland and Marlow 1984).

Unfortunately, prairie dogs may also be the most persecuted of the re-maining Great Plains fauna. Many ranchers zealously poison them with zinc phosphide, strychnine-treated oats, and other substances in the belief that prai-rie dogs degrade rangelands (Miller, Ceballos, and Reading 1994). Besides the obvious effect of killing prairie dogs and other nontarget species, poisoning also disrupts the size, spatial arrangement, and stability of prairie dog colonies. Small, isolated, and persecuted prairie dog towns, even when they are situated in large blocks of contiguous prairie habitat, are not nearly as species rich or as stable as large ones. Clark et al. (1982) recorded 107 vertebrate species and sub-species in prairie dog towns in Colorado, Utah, and New Mexico, yet they noted that fewer species were associated with small towns than with large towns. In Montana, Reading et al. (1989) found 163 vertebrate species in black-tailed prairie dog towns, and they too noted that vertebrate species richness decreased with colony size and regional colony density.

According to Miller, Caballos, and Reading (1994, 680), the control and persecution of prairie dogs will "undermine all efforts to conserve biological diversity on the western grasslands." It seems likely that prairie dog conservation on private lands will continue to be contentious and difficult. Only on large tracts of unfragmented public lands can the conservation of large, viable complexes be reasonably assured.

Ferruginous Hawk

The ferruginous hawk (*Buteo regalis*) is a bird of vast grasslands, representing the essence of the Great Plains more than any other hawk and perhaps more than any other bird. Its striking rusty red coloration and diagnostic V-shaped belly marking make it easily identifiable as it soars on warm prairie currents. Other names for it include eagle hawk and gopher hawk, in reference to the bird's large size and typical diet.

Before European settlement the ferruginous hawk ranged throughout the shortgrass and mixed-grass prairie. Unusual among birds of prey, it often nested on the ground, typically on a prairie summit (Rolfe 1896). This peculiar strategy was successful because historically there were few midsize nest predators on the treeless sea of grass. Red foxes, which are known to currently be predators of ferruginous hawk nests (Lokemoen and Duebbert 1976), were absent from much if not all of the bird's historic range (Sargeant 1982). Coyotes were probably much less dense than they are today and were apparently common only in parts of the southern plains. The only serious threat to the ferruginous hawk, the gray wolf, was more interested in bison than in hawks or their nests.

After European settlement, and the rapid conversion of prairie to cropland, the ferruginous hawk population was reduced in both distribution and abundance. The bird does not adapt well to areas with large amounts of cropland (Gilmer and Stewart 1983, Schmutz 1984); so not surprisingly the demise of the hawk has been most pronounced in the eastern part of its historic range. In the western part of the Great Plains the ferruginous hawk can still be found, especially where remaining tracts of shortgrass and mixed-grass prairie are large enough to accommodate the bird's vast hunting areas (up to 8.4 square miles [Wakeley 1978]).

Whether these remnant tracts of prairie can provide the habitat diversity necessary to sustain the species remains to be seen. For example, ferruginous hawks avoid nesting on heavily grazed areas (Lokemoen and Duebbert 1976), yet they seem to prefer feeding in those areas, because of the abundance of ground squirrels and other small prey (Kantrud and Kologiski 1982). Before historical times the great herds of bison moved through an area, grazing it heavily and then not returning for long periods. This grazing pattern provided the diversity preferred by ferruginous hawks. Unfortunately modern grazing practices, with cattle confined to fenced pastures, rarely exhibit this landscape diversity.

A more interesting and profound question concerns the bird's nesting strategy. Historically the bird typically nested on the ground, yet in modern times it seems to be shifting toward nontraditional nesting sites such as trees and telephone poles. For example, in north-central South Dakota 48 percent of all nests were reported to be in trees, 44 percent on the ground, and 7 percent on haystacks (Lokemoen and Duebbert 1976). Not surprisingly, all the ground nests were on sites that had a significantly higher proportion of prairie and were farther from human activity than were randomly selected points. A North Dakota study (Gilmer and Stewart 1983) found only 21 percent of ferruginous hawk nests on the ground, and those nests were also in more isolated areas. Habitat deterioration—that is, lack of large tracts of prairie and invasion by trees—is likely responsible for the behavior shift.

At first glance it seems that the invasion of trees (and telephone poles and power lines) into the Great Plains has benefited the ferruginous hawk by providing new nesting sites that apparently can produce higher reproductive success than traditional ground nests. There are two faults with this conclusion.

First, although tree nests may be marginally more productive in the currently altered grassland ecosystem, they may not have been so historically. It is probable that under natural conditions ground nests were more successful than tree nests. For example, the ground nests in the Lokemoen and Duebbert (1976) study contained 0.6 more eggs than the tree nests, and the successful ground nests produced 1.2 more young than the successful tree nests. In other words, when we exclude clutches destroyed by ground-nest predators—most of which are alien to the ecosystem—ground nests produced more young than tree nests. The assumption that trees and telephone poles are good for the ferruginous hawk needs to be placed in the proper context.

Second, even if the ferruginous hawk should persist by nesting on telephone poles, power lines, and hay stacks rather than on grassy prairie knolls, it will be a behaviorally different bird than existed before European settlement. Having ferruginous hawks survive by nesting on telephone poles may aid the species' survival, but is it good biodiversity conservation? Have we conserved the native ferruginous hawk, or have we essentially created a new bird? Is the nest on the power line pole, rimmed by transformers and wires, as aesthetically pleasing as the nest on the prairie knoll, rimmed by stones and bison bones? These questions are more than aesthetic or philosophical; they are fundamental to how wildlife conservation will proceed into the next century. They address whether species' existence per se is the objective or whether conservation of the species and its ecosystem is the ultimate goal.

Gray Wolf

Three vertebrate species constituted the cornerstones of the historic Great Plains ecosystem: the prairie dog, the bison, and the gray wolf. Prairie dogs, the only one of the three that still exists in meaningful numbers, are finally being appreciated for their significance to Great Plains ecology. The historical significance of bison to the grassland ecosystem has always been readily acknowledged by both professionals and laypeople. It is the third species of the Great Plains triad that most people do not acknowledge, appreciate, or understand.

The eradication of the gray wolf from the North American grasslands is well chronicled, although the exact motivation for the extermination may never be fully comprehended or rationalized. It is somewhat ironic that to this day the most effective and conclusive of all federal government programs in the grassland biome may still be the turn of the century program to eliminate the wolf. The last Plains wolves were apparently extirpated in the 1920 and 1930s in the rugged badlands country of the western Dakotas and eastern Montana. Even though there have been recent occurrences of Minnesota and Canadian wolves dispersing into the Dakotas (Licht and Fritts 1994) and Rocky Mountain wolves venturing onto the Montana prairie, the gray wolf is still essentially absent from the Great Plains, with little likelihood of reoccupying its former range anytime in the near future.

So why spend time discussing a species that no longer exists in the Great Plains and has little chance of returning? Because it is more than the wolf itself that is absent—the animal's ecological role is also missing. And that absence may be indirectly responsible for the dire status of many grassland species.

When people think of wolves in the Great Plains they also think of bison. The historical association is well known but poorly understood. The only op-

44

portunity to study the relationship currently occurs in Wood Bison National Park in northern Canada (Carbyn, Oosenbrug, and Anions 1993). But the sedge-meadow ecosystem in the park is radically different from the arid grasslands of central North America and therefore not readily comparable. Still, we can infer from that study and others that grassland wolves commonly preyed on less fit bison (old, young, or weakened). Since there were 30–70 million bison in North America before European settlement, we can also infer that wolves did not limit bison populations.

But I want not so much to describe the wolf-bison relationship as to describe the lesser known wolf-coyote relationship. A study of these two canid species lays a foundation for explaining the decline of several grassland species.

In pre-Columbian times the gray wolf could be found throughout almost all of North America, including the entire grassland ecosystem (wolves are commonly believed to be second only to humans as the most widely distributed mammal on earth). The naturalist Vernon Bailey (1926, 154) reported that the wolf was found in almost every habitat in North America but was "nowhere more numerous than over the Plains in the days of the great buffalo herds." The naturalist also made another interesting observation: "In the buffalo days the large wolves were more abundant than the coyotes" (151).

In contrast to the wolf, the coyote (*Canis latrans*) was rarely seen by the first Europeans in the region, especially in the northern plains. This may be due in part to the more secretive nature of the coyote and in part to its being less note-worthy than the wolf, but a large reason for the scarcity of reports appears to be that the animal was absent from much of the region and scarce where it did exist. Unlike in modern times, the coyote may have ranged no farther east than Indiana, and only rarely farther north than South Dakota and Wyoming (Nowak 1979).

So why were coyotes historically restricted in distribution and abundance? And what natural process has been altered so as to result in a dramatic expansion of the animals' range?

Although not definitive, modern science has collected enough data to strongly suggest an answer. Thanks to modern technology such as radiotele-metry, biologists have found that interspecific aggression between canines such as wolves and coyotes can cause the displacement or "control" of the smaller animal. In other words, the presence of wolves in an area can preclude or limit the presence of coyotes.

Trappers and biologists have long known that wolves kill coyotes caught in traps (Carbyn 1982). That the coyotes are often left uneaten (of twenty-three coyotes killed by wolves in one study, none were consumed [Paquet 1991]) suggests that something other than food motivates the wolves.

This aggression toward a similar species may result from perceived competition. Wolves may view coyotes as rivals for limited prey. Perhaps less significant, wolves may see coyotes as a threat to wolf pups. Whatever the reason, it seems generally correct to say that many wolves try to kill coyotes when the opportunity presents itself. Over time mortality or the threat of mortality from wolves may be enough to reduce coyote numbers in a given area.

This may have been especially true in the historic Great Plains, which apparently had very high wolf densities owing to the high prey biomass (bison) and only sparse escape cover for coyotes. Modern research has documented that coyotes prefer rough topography with cover (Gese, Rongstad, and Mytton 1988) or savanna-type habitats (Litvaitis and Shaw 1980) in contrast to wide open grasslands. This may be due to food preferences, but it may also be a hereditary predisposition. Thousands of years of evolution may have ingrained in coyotes the tendency to avoid open areas where they were vulnerable to wolves.

Biologists have documented several instances in which gray wolves appear to have displaced coyotes or reduced their numbers (Fuller and Keith 1981; Carbyn 1982). Isle Royale National Park in Lake Superior is a striking example. When the current Isle Royale wolf population first colonized the island in the winter of 1948–49, coyotes were already present. Yet within nine years of the wolves' arrival the coyote population had disappeared, probably a result of canid competition (Mech 1970, 284).

Although there are still questions about how far wolves might displace coyotes (in some forested environments wolves do not seem to displace coyotes although they do opportunistically kill them [Paquet 1991]), generally speaking the evidence supports the hypothesis that wolves may have suppressed coyote numbers in the open Great Plains. With that in mind, it is not surprising that it was not until the eradication of the gray wolf in the early 1900s that the coyote began its remarkable range expansion.

If, as the evidence suggests, wolves did displace or limit coyotes in the Great Plains, then certain species would have evolved and prospered under the wolf's protective umbrella. For example, small mammals such as the swift fox and black-footed ferret are known to suffer high mortality from coyotes in today's wolfless Great Plains. But in historical times the two small predators existed in a relatively coyote-free ecosystem. The same is true for the ground-nesting ferruginous hawk. Therefore adaptations to evade coyotes are not well honed in these three species.

Of course an obvious rebuttal is that wolves could have also preyed on swift foxes, black-footed ferrets, and ferruginous hawks, but this is unlikely for three reasons. First, wolves are best adapted to preying on large animals and would not be so adept at catching the smaller species. Even if they did, they would have received relatively little nutritional benefit. Second, wolves, even at high densities, are not nearly as dense as modern coyote populations. Therefore the chance of a wolf's encountering one of the smaller animals was relatively low. Third, the swift fox and black-footed ferret are both nocturnal. This habit appears to be inherent in the species and not human influenced (as it may be in deer and other animals). In contrast, the observations of early explorers indicate that grassland wolves were often active during the day. Further proof of the wolf's diurnal tendencies can be found in the High Arctic, among wolves that seldom encounter humans. Because the plains wolf was diurnal whereas the swift fox and black-footed ferret were nocturnal, the animals probably rarely encountered one another. In contrast to the wolf, the coyote is generally nocturnal, a trait that may have evolved recently as a behavior to avoid humans but may also be a hereditary adaptation to avoiding wolves.

American Burying Beetle

The American burying beetle (*Nicrophorus Americanus*) has a life history every bit as fascinating as that of the gray wolf, the black-footed ferret, and the ferruginous hawk. But because it is a nocturnal, carrion burying, grub rearing "bug," it will never win a popularity contest. Nevertheless this engaging species is as much a part of the grassland ecosystem as are better-known species.

The American burying beetle is the largest carrion beetle in North America, measuring 1–1.8 inches long. The shiny black body has several distinctive orange-red markings, making it easily identifiable. As its name suggests, it buries pieces of carrion as food for its offspring. It prefers larger pieces than do other carrion beetles, weighing 3.5–7 ounces (about the size of a mourning dove [*Zenaida macroura*] or bobwhite quail [*Colinus virginianus*]). Within two days of burying the carrion, the female lays eggs in a tunnel connected to the carrion chamber. The larvae hatch four to six days later and work their way to the stored food, where they feed until they are able to leave the chamber, generally consuming about a third of the carrion (the rest is left to decompose, thereby increasing soil fertility [Wells, Pyle, and Collins 1983]). During the entire twelve to sixteen days of development the eggs and larvae are tended by at least one parent, usually the female. The male may also stay in the vicinity and guard the site from other burying beetles. This fascinating and devoted reproductive strategy in such a "low" life form contradicts many people's perceptions of insects.

Historically the American burying beetle was known to occur in thirty-five states and three Canadian provinces. Although most of these states are in the eastern forest biome, the beetle has been found as far west as Montana (U.S. Fish and Wildlife Service 1991a). However, by 1974 the once widespread beetle was feared extinct in what is considered one of the "most disastrous declines of an insect's range ever to be recorded" (Wells, Pyle, and Collins 1983, 380). Fortunately a few small remnant populations have since been discovered.

As of the early 1990s the American burying beetle was known to be naturally extant only on an island off the Rhode Island coast and in a small part of Arkansas, two counties in Nebraska, and five counties in Oklahoma (a population has also been reintroduced on Penikese Island, Massachusetts). Several of the county occurrences are represented by only a few specimens.

Although the beetle can survive in a wide variety of habitats, one preliminary study found that more individuals were captured in tallgrass areas than in oak-hickory and bottomland forest. According to the American burying beetle recovery plan (U.S. Fish and Wildlife Service 1991a), the availability of carrion is probably far more important to the beetle's survival than any particular vegetation type (although soil type may also be important). In other words habitat, as it is typically perceived by people (vegetation type), is less significant to the beetle than are ecological processes.

Unfortunately the ecological system the beetle evolved in has undergone dramatic changes in the past two hundred years. Some of the changes are reversible, others are not.

One irreversible change is the extinction of the passenger pigeon. The species may have numbered as many as 3–5 billion individuals at the time of European settlement, composing 25–40 percent of the entire United States bird population (Schorger 1955). Every spring and fall their incredible flocks blackened the prairie and forest skies. Every summer hundreds of millions of new and vulnerable chicks were born high in the treetops. No doubt hundreds of millions of passenger pigeons died annually, their carcasses exposed to myriad scavengers including the burying beetle. By 1914 the passenger pigeon was extinct, and so was its role in the ecosystem.

48

We can only speculate on the effect the disappearance of the passenger pigeon (and Carolina parakeet) must have had on the burying beetle. A potential annual food supply of millions of pounds of carrion was eliminated in less than one hundred years. Nothing has come along to replace the missing biomass, and it is unlikely anything will. In addition, songbirds, prairie chickens, and other potential carrion sources have experienced long-term population declines.

Meanwhile, many mammal species have increased their range since pre-Columbian times, much to the detriment of the beetle. Scavengers such as raccoons (*Procyon lotor*), opossums (*Didelphis virginiana*), and skunks (*Mephitis mephitis*) are now found in much higher densities, and in regions where they were historically absent. For example, the opossum is now found as far north and west as southern Minnesota. These scavengers not only compete with burying beetles for carrion but may also prey on beetles when the opportunity presents itself.

Exotic predators also pose direct and indirect threats to the American burying beetle. The domestic dog and cat are now two of the most common predators and scavengers in the eastern and central United States. There may be 15–25 million stray cats in the United States. Their effects on biodiversity are especially pronounced near urban areas. Not surprisingly, the more recent records of American burying beetles typically occur at least one hundred miles from major cities or towns (U.S. Fish and Wildlife Service 1991a).

Hypothetically, society could establish large nature reserves that exclude most dogs and cats and are less hospitable to raccoons, opossums, skunks, and other animals that proliferate in agrarian and urban ecosystems. But politically it is probably impossible to justify such drastic measures simply to protect a small black-and-orange beetle that buries carrion. Hence a significant question concerning burying beetle management, and invertebrate conservation in general, is how we can gain public acceptance for these species. As confirmed in attitude surveys by Kellert (1993, 845), "the general public and farmers were found to view most invertebrates with aversion, anxiety, fear, avoidance, and ignorance." He found little likelihood of people's developing an affinity or affection for the group, let alone investing thousands or millions of dollars for their protection.

With this in mind it seems prudent to focus on preserving ecosystems, with the understanding that many less glamorous species will also be conserved. Based on his finding that there would be little public support for conservation of

49

noncharismatic species, Kellert (1985, 532) concluded that "the most feasible strategy might appear to be an ecosystem approach, focusing attention on preserving large geographic areas essential to the survival of many imperiled species."

Mountain Plover

The mountain plover (*Charadrius montanus*) is a habitat specialist that requires flat or rolling terrain with very short, sparse grasses. This type of habitat is most commonly associated with the shortgrass regions of the Great Plains (Kantrud and Kologiski 1983) but can also be created in mixed-grass regions by fire or by the foraging of prairie dogs and other grazers. (Mountain plovers, like many species, are most strongly associated with larger prairie dog towns [Knowles and Knowles 1984].) Although heavy short-term grazing is often preferred by the mountain plover, long-term overgrazing may be detrimental to the species.

Although mountain plovers originally bred in twelve states and Canada, today they are known to breed in only seven states. More significant, half of the remaining population breeds in only two counties (Phillips County, Montana, and Weld County, Colorado). Rangewide the species has suffered a 93 percent population decline and now consists of only about 7,500 birds (U.S. Fish and Wildlife Service, unpub. rep.).

This precarious status probably has numerous causes, many previously described for other species. Conversion of prairie to cropland, suppression of fires, eradication of prairie dogs, long-term overgrazing, and changes in predator composition have all undoubtedly contributed to the plover's decline. But the mountain plover faces a new and ironic threat that may exacerbate its decline.

Whereas the decline of the mountain plover has been precipitous, the national interest in bird watching has been just the opposite. Observing birds is now one of the most popular and economically important outdoor pastimes in America, with public lands being some of the most popular bird-watching spots (Wiedner and Kerlinger 1990). Bird watching is so popular on the Pawnee National Grasslands, the last stronghold of the plover, that it may threaten the bird's survival.

Although bird watching is generally benign, harm to birds can and does occur, especially during the breeding season. Birders attempting to get close to plovers sometimes unintentionally harass the adults away from the nests or chicks for extended periods, leaving the offspring vulnerable to predators, weather, and other factors. In other cases automobiles and motorbikes can crush flightless chicks that gravitate toward warm prairie trails.

Because of its proximity to Denver and the populated East Front, and because it is the only substantial tract of public prairie in the state, the Pawnee National Grasslands gets relatively high visitor use. As Denver and the other urban areas become more populated, and as more people turn to outdoor pursuits, the pressure on the Grasslands will continue to increase.

Should the mountain plover become listed as an endangered or threatened species (it is currently a candidate), government agencies will need to make a difficult choice. Support for endangered species protection can best be fostered by allowing people to use the species, either consumptively or nonconsumptively. Yet paradoxically, that same support can threaten the species' existence.

To resolve this dilemma the government will have two options: it can decrease the public's access to the birds by prohibiting or limiting bird watching in areas where the plover exists or it can increase the supply of birds to meet the increasing public demand. In the latter scenario birds may still be affected by humans, but the larger population would be better able to withstand the disturbances.

One effective and long-lasting way to increase the supply of mountain plovers is to increase the amount of plover habitat. Such a strategy would be most effective as part of a larger effort to restore and conserve functioning prairie ecosystems.

The Ecology of a Degraded Ecosystem

These are the most beautiful countries and the most handsome lands in the world. The prairies are like seas, and they are full of wild animals, especially bison and deer, in numbers that stagger the imagination.

Veniard de Bourgmont, quoted in Norall, *Bourgmont, Explorer of the Missouri, 1698–1725*

The factors responsible for the destruction of the grassland ecosystem have been so multi-pronged and so interconnected that it is difficult to know where an examination of them should start. Indeed, many of the destructive processes may still be unknown or unappreciated. Nevertheless we need to identify and explore some of the major influences threatening grassland biodiversity.

Fragmentation

The conventional villain in the destruction of the grassland ecosystem is agriculture. The conversion of native prairie to cropland has undeniably played a major role in degrading the prairie ecosystem. Approximately 77 percent of Iowa is now in cropland, as are 62 percent of North Dakota and 59 percent of Kansas. In all, 43 percent of the Great Plains was cultivated land as of 1992 (including unharvested cropland). Agriculture directly and indirectly effects biodiversity in many ways and has been implicated as the leading cause of species endangerment in the United States (Flather, Joyce, and Bloomgarden 1994). But my goal is not to indict the current level of agricultural production in the Great Plains. Great Plains agriculture is important to the region's economy and provides a large portion of the nation's food. No pragmatist would ever deny that, nor would one argue that we should return the entire prairie biome to its pre-Columbian condition for the sake of grassland conservation.

My assertion is that agriculture, even at its present level of production, and the long-term conservation of grassland biodiversity are both compatible and achievable. The problem is not the current amount of harvested cropland but how those cultivated acres are distributed throughout the grassland biome and the human impact associated with that distribution. It is not so much that agriculture has converted 43 percent of the prairie biome to cropland but that it has *fragmented* virtually 100 percent of the entire prairie ecosystem.

Only in recent years have ecologists begun to understand the detrimental effects of fragmenting extensive tracts of habitat. When fragmentation is severe enough, those effects can include the loss of genetic diversity, the loss of species, and the loss of natural communities—in other words, the loss of biodiversity.

The plight of many of North America's native bird species provides an ominous warning about the dangers of habitat fragmentation. For years scientists have been documenting the steady decline of a group of birds known as Neotropical migrants (birds that winter in the New World tropics of Mexico and Central and South America). These birds, typically warblers, sparrows, and other songbirds, have precipitously declined and disappeared throughout North America. The continuing loss of wintering habitat in Central and South America may contribute to the decline, but it does not appear to be the most significant factor (Bohning-Gaese, Taper, and Brown 1993). Although no single research project has conclusively established the reason for the decline, a mounting body of evidence has made a compelling case that landscape fragmentation in the North American breeding grounds is a leading cause.

Breeding Bird Survey data (collected by volunteers throughout North America every May–June) suggest that the decline is occurring in the Great Plains as well as the better-studied eastern forests. For example, one study found that of the thirty-seven species of birds that are strongly associated with the Great Plains ecosystem (Mengel 1970), eleven declined at a statistically significant rate of 1–7 percent annually from 1966 to 1991 (Knopf 1994). Those eleven are the mountain plover, Franklin's gull (*Larus pipixcan*), Cassin's sparrow (*Aimophilus cassinii*), lark bunting (*Calamospiza melanocorys*), eastern meadowlark (*Sturnella magna*), dickcissel, grasshopper sparrow, Henslow's sparrow (*Passerherbulus henslowii*), lark sparrow (*Chondestes grammacus*), Brewer's sparrow (*Spizella breweri*), and clay-colored sparrow. Concerning

53

the decline of grassland birds, Knopf and Samson (1996) reported that the avifauna of the Great Plains showed a steeper, more consistent, and more geographically widespread decline than any other group of North American birds. What is especially alarming is that the decline includes birds from a variety of grassland types and from different bird groups and has likely been going on for decades (fig. 1), well before the widespread initiation of the Breeding Bird Survey in 1966.

Although most studies of the effects of landscape fragmentation on songbird populations have occurred in the eastern forests, the few published grassland studies also suggest that fragmentation is responsible for the decline. For example, in the tallgrass prairie of Missouri only relict prairie tracts larger than 395 acres were able to maintain stable prairie bird communities from year to year (Samson and Knopf 1982). The study also found that the annual number of prairie bird species was more strongly correlated with the size of the habitat fragment than with other factors (habitat heterogeneity, edge, isolation). In Illinois it was found that larger prairies were more likely to contain upland sandpipers (*Bartramia longicauda*), grasshopper sparrows, Henslow's sparrows, sedge wrens (*Cistothorus platensis*), bobolinks, and savannah sparrows (*Passerculus sandwichensis*), all declining grassland species; whereas smaller prairies were more strongly correlated with red-winged blackbirds (*Agelaius phoeniceus*) (Herkert 1994a). In North Dakota it was found that the highly fragmented tallgrass region supported fewer species than the less fragmented mixed-grass region, even though tallgrass prairie is considered better habitat (Kantrud 1981). Samson (1980) felt that 247 acres was the minimum area needed to maintain viable breeding populations of prairie chickens in Missouri; few Missouri prairies are this large, and hence the species is all but absent from the state.

The effects of remnant prairie size on native species richness apply to other taxa as well. For example, in Nebraska there was a significant positive correlation between the number of plant species present and the size of remnant prairie tracts ranging from three to forty-five acres (Boettcher and Bragg 1989). In Kansas it was found that small prairie fragments were unable to support persistent populations of cotton rats (*Sigmodon hispidus*) (Gaines et al. 1992).

Of course, to better understand the consequences of landscape fragmentation we must identify the specific reasons small fragments support fewer native species than large tracts. Some are fairly obvious. Large fragments can be expected to contain more species because they often cross a variety of grassland successional stages and habitat types that are home to a greater number of spe-

54

cies. Likewise, large tracts usually contain more individuals and hence are more resistant to extinctions. Large tracts are also more likely to accommodate species with wide-ranging or specialized habitat needs. The grasshopper *Melanopus spretus* historically migrated over the vast contiguous Great Plains ecosystem in great numbers. It is apparently now extinct, a consequence of habitat fragmentation. Many snakes migrate ten miles or more between summer breeding ranges and winter hibernacula (Scott and Seigel 1992). Breeding prairie falcoms (*Falco mexicanus*) in Wyoming have foraging territories of approximately 43.6 square miles (Squires, Anderson, and Oakleaf 1993). Even small songbirds sometimes require surprisingly large territories during the breeding season. Herkert (1994b) found that the savanna, grasshopper, and Henslow's sparrows, bobolink, and eastern meadowlark required minimum areas ranging from 12 to 136 acres for breeding. Generally speaking, about two-thirds of all grassland bird species appear to be area dependent during the breeding season; in contrast, many alien bird species that are increasing to pestlike proportions in the Great Plains are area independent (e.g., starling [*Sturnus vulgaris*], common grackle [*Quiscalus quiscula*], house sparrow [*Passer domesticus*]). But size alone does not fully explain why small fragments of habitat have fewer species and lower species persistence than large tracts.

Once again bird studies are shedding the most light on why habitat fragmentation eliminates or reduces many native species. Small fragments of habitat have a high ratio of perimeter (edge) to area. Yet scientists have repeatedly found that nests near the edge of habitat types tend to suffer higher rates of failure than nests in the interior (Paton 1994). Since small fragments have proportionately more edge than large tracts, they would be expected to have lower nest success. Such is the case.

A Pennsylvania study of the ground-nesting ovenbird (*Seiurus aurocapillus*) provides a dramatic example. It was found that 1.19 young were produced per male ovenbird in forests larger than 24,700 acres compared with only 0.06 young per male in forest fragments smaller than 453 acres (Porneluzi et al. 1993). At those rates ovenbirds in large tracts of habitat can sustain their population, but those in small tracts cannot. As a forest becomes more and more fragmented, an increasing percentage of the ovenbird population is forced to nest in small fragments where reproductive success is significantly less. Over time the increasing fragmentation becomes responsible for the overall decline in the species.

Once we have shown that small fragments of habitat are associated with

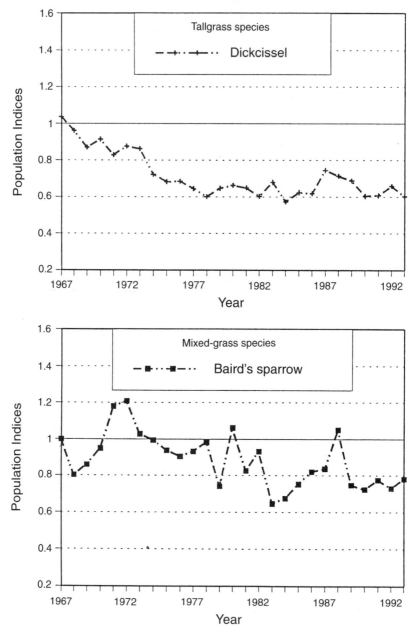

Figure 1. Population trends of representative grassland birds. Data from Breeding Bird Survey and

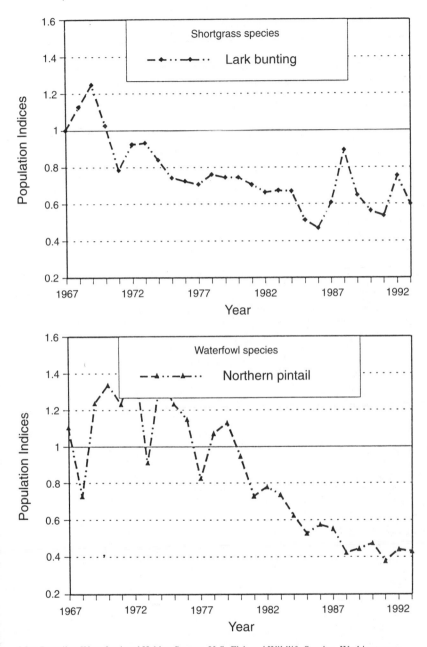

May Breeding Waterfowl and Habitat Survey, U.S. Fish and Wildlife Service, Washington DC.

lower reproductive rates for some avian species, the obvious question is why. The answer seems to be that many predators, especially egg eaters such as raccoons, skunks, opossums, and crows, are most abundant on small fragments, in large part because they have more edge habitat. In the current Great Plains, edge can be found in the form of shelterbelts, farmsteads, cropland, and other human-made features.

Several grassland studies have documented that nest predation is higher on small tracts with a high proportion of edge. In a tallgrass prairie study in Minnesota, Johnson and Temple (1990) found that rates of nest failure owing to predation for five species of prairie birds were higher in small tracts (<321 acres) and higher when nests were within 147 feet of wooded edge. The researchers concluded that "prairie management to maximize nest productivity should provide large, regularly burned prairies with no nearby wooded edges" (106). Another study, this one using artificial nests in Missouri prairies, found that such nests in prairies of less than 37 acres were depredated at a higher rate than those in larger prairies (Burger, Burger, and Faaborg 1994). Yet another study found lower nesting success on small tracts (≤ 40 acres) versus large tracts (79–119 acres), but this time waterfowl were the species in question (Nelson and Duebbert 1974).

Biologists now generally accept that large tracts of grassland have greater potential for nest success of ground-nesting birds than an equivalent area comprising small, disjunct tracts. Samson and Knopf (1982) argued that the best management for native prairie bird species could be accomplished by keeping most land in large, generally undisturbed blocks. When one thoroughly examines the scientific literature, it becomes apparent that almost all grassland songbird species that are declining (e.g., Baird's sparrow, lark bunting, dickcissel, Sprague's pipit [*Anthus spragueii*]) do better on large contiguous blocks of grassland habitat, whereas species that are currently abundant or increasing (e.g., red-winged blackbirds, house sparrows, house finches [*Carpodacus mexicanus*], grackles) survive better in fragmented agrarian habitats.

As important as the issue of fragmentation per se is the question of what is causing it. By that I mean what habitat type is immediately adjacent to the remnant tract. The greater the difference in the two types, the more pronounced the effects are likely to be.

To many people the antithesis of grassland is forest. Because forests are radically different from grasslands, they would intuitively be expected to severely influence grassland ecosystems. Such is the case. Almost as soon as the first pioneers began turning the prairie sod, they began planting trees. The plantings appear to have been partly emotional (a barrier against the frightening expanse of grass) and partly pragmatic. Trees could slow the blowing of topsoil, provide shelter from the scorching summer sun, lessen the wind chill in winter, and bear fruit in the fall. Popper and Popper (1987a, 3) described the tradition of planting trees in the prairie as "a historic Plains occupation."

Arbor Day originated on the Plains in the 1870s, championed by Nebraska congressmen and dryland farmer J. Sterling Morton. The Timber Culture Act of 1873 was an attempt to legislate the growing of woodlots on the Great Plains. The act gave land to anyone who would plant trees on 6–25 percent of the homestead, but as Webb (1931, 500) facetiously pointed out, "the records do not reveal that Congress passed a law increasing the rainfall." In 1924 the Clarke-McNary Act provided additional federal funds for shelterbelts, wind-breaks, and other arid-land tree plantings. By the end of the Dust Bowl many of these early tree plantings were "annihilated" (Albertson and Weaver 1945). But ironically the Dust Bowl, which killed off most prairie tree plantings, stim-ulated a call to plant more trees in the region. A 1935 U.S. Forest Service effort, oxymoronically titled "the Prairie States Forestry Project," was designed to create a forest one hundred miles wide in the Great Plains, stretching from Can-ada to Mexico. Laycock (1991) cites an anonymous source reporting that 223 million trees were planted in the region from 1935 to 1942. Even in recent times another 20.6 million trees were planted annually in the Great Plains (excluding Iowa and Missouri [Griffith 1976]). Government farm programs such as the Conservation Reserve Program (CRP; see below, "The Farm Program") con-tinue to encourage tree planting in the arid region (Mortensen et al. 1989). The state of North Dakota alone has a goal of planting 100 million trees by the end of the century (in a state that was historically 99 percent prairie). The state even publishes a newsletter called *The Prairie Forester*.

Griffith (1976, 6) implied that in the mid-1970s there were 25,000 miles of shelterbelts in the Great Plains. Assuming that the present value is still 25,000 miles and that the average shelterbelt has an effective ground coverage width of fifty feet, then the acreage of shelterbelts on the Great Plains (excluding Iowa and Missouri) is over 150,000 acres, or 0.04 percent of the grassland ecosys-tem. Considering that Iowa and Missouri have some of the highest shelterbelt densities, this is probably a very conservative estimate of the presence of shel-terbelts in the grassland biome. Knopf and Samson (1996) stated that almost 3 percent of the Great Plains is now forested by shelterbelts, probably a more realistic figure. In addition to shelterbelts, most farmsteads and residential areas contain woody plantings that are not typically defined as shelterbelts. There are at least 430,000 farmsteads and a similar number of rural residences in the Great Plains, plus hundreds of thousands, perhaps millions, of abandoned homesites. Almost all of these have some trees present.

In at least two cases the attempt to forest the prairies was successful. The Nebraska National Forest and Samuel R. McKelvie National Forest in the Sandhills of Nebraska—in the middle of the Great Plains—created about 30,000 acres of planted trees (Twedt and Wolfe 1978). The sites probably constitute the world's largest and most bizarrely placed artificial forests.

Last, woody invasion of prairies is inevitable whenever wildfires are suppressed. For example, aerial photographs show that an Illinois prairie decreased from 39.2 acres in 1939 to 17.4 acres in 1988, mainly owing to natural woody succession (Illinois Department of Energy and Natural Resources and Nature of Illinois Foundation 1994). Fire suppression (along with the forestation project mentioned above) is also responsible for the proliferation of ponderosa pines (*Pinus ponderosa*) in the Nebraska Sandhills, where trees were historically very rare or absent (Steinauer and Bragg 1987). Even far to the west in the arid shortgrass plains, the suppression of fire (along with heavy grazing and other factors) has changed once grassy prairies to shrublands in some spots (Fisser et al. 1989).

Whatever the actual figure for artificial woodlands in the Great Plains, it is indisputable that trees are now much more prevalent than they were historically. From the perspective of some native grassland species, planted trees have carved up the prairie biome as effectively as the plow. Knopf and Samson (1996) felt that the fragmentation of the western Great Plains owing to woody invasion has had more severe consequences to the native flora and fauna of the western Great Plains than has had cultivation. Fragmentation in itself negatively affects many species; fragmentation by a dramatically different vegetation type can be disastrous.

So although grassland is still the most extensive vegetative community in the Great Plains (excluding cropland), it is not necessarily dominant. As Saunders, Hobbes, and Margules (1991, 2) pointed out, small, fragmented tracts of habitat are often "predominately driven by factors arising in the surrounding landscape." The remnant tract may look like grassland, but many of its ecological processes may be driven by the adjacent woodland. To put it another way, the landscape no longer comprises distinct grassland ecosystems and woodland ecosystems but is a single grassland-forest ecosystem throughout the entire region.

The obvious rebuttal to this criticism of wooded edge is that trees have always been found in the Great Plains in riparian forests, as isolated copses, and in highly eroded landscapes (e.g., buttes and badlands topography in the Dakotas, Montana, and Nebraska). But wooded edge was never as prevalent as it is now, even in the sites mentioned above. Colonel Richard Dodge (1989, 76) noted that before European settlement "the Platte, the Arkansas, and the Cimarron, filter their waters for hundreds of miles through the sand of their shallow beds without a tree to give life and variety to the scene." These rivers are now forested along a large percentage of their length, mainly owing to disruption of natural processes.

I must digress for a moment and mention that the arborescence of the grassland ecosystem also negatively effects other ecosystems. For example, the fragmentation of the Great Plains, and the associated planting of trees, broke down an important barrier between the eastern deciduous forests and those of the Rocky Mountains. This has led to the hybridization of several forest species that were formerly separated by the great "sea of grass." For example, blue and Steller's jays (*Cyanocitta cristata* and *C. stelleri*), indigo and lazuli buntings (*Passerina cyanea* and *P. amoena*), and rose-breasted and black-headed grosbeaks (*Pheucticus ludovicianus* and *P. melanocephalus*) have all hybridized in the Great Plains in recent years (see Rising 1983). Baltimore and Bullock's orioles (*Icterus galbula galbula* and *I. g. bullockii*) have hybridized to the extent that they are now considered one species. Other eastern forest species such as the tufted titmouse (*Parvus bicolor*) may occur in the western Great Plains in the near future. At least twenty-eight bird taxa (fourteen pairs) have the potential to hybridize in the Great Plains because of fragmentation. So great is the potential for hybridization that the region is now known by ornithologists as the Great Plains Hybrid Zone (Rising 1983).

In conclusion, fragmentation of the grassland landscape and the associated arborescence of the ecosystem have severely affected grassland biodiversity. But that is only part of the story. The rest is how these conditions invite new species, especially predators. Identifying those predators and their impact on the prairie ecosystem is a prerequisite to designing long-term conservation strategies.

Predators

Predators! Farmers, ranchers, hunters, and many biologists are quick to blame predators for almost every imaginable ill caused to grassland wildlife. But predators have always existed in the prairies, so are their arguments valid? The answer appears to be that they are, somewhat.

In the previous section I described how the prairie landscape has changed since pre-Columbian times, and I implied that the predator composition has changed as a result of the altered landscape. But to what degree has the distribution and abundance of predators changed in the Great Plains, and how are these changes manifesting themselves ecologically?

The most despised predator in the prairies, from the hunter's perspective, is the red fox (*Vulpes vulpes*). So strong is the animosity that in 1994 the Minnesota state legislature opened a year-round season on red foxes for the specific purpose of protecting game bird populations. That of course raises the obvious question, How did grassland game birds such as grouse and ducks survive the red fox before the altruistic interference of state politicians?

The answer is that the red fox probably was historically absent from much of the North American prairies, especially the shortgrass and mixed-grass regions, and where the animal did exist it was in very low numbers (Sargeant 1982). Bailey (1926, 163) cited Prince Maximilian zu Wied as reporting in his mid-1800s journals that the red fox was "by no means so numerous as wolves" in the prairie ecosystem. It seems indisputable that the animal was historically much less prevalent in the Great Plains than it is now.

It appears that the red fox began expanding its range in the early 1800s, about the same time the vast prairies were being fragmented and wolves eradicated. By the end of the nineteenth century the red fox's expanding range included most of the eastern and central parts of the Great Plains (Sargeant 1982). The red fox can now be found in virtually all regions of the grassland biome, often in high densities.

Sargeant (1982) listed three general factors that influence the current density and distribution of red foxes in the Great Plains and prairies: human settlement, interspecific competition from coyotes, and harvests by humans, which is directly linked to the price of fur. Each warrants further consideration.

Red foxes find the developed Great Plains much more to their liking than the monotypic grasslands of pre-Columbian times. Modern agriculture, livestock raising, and other land uses provide a variety of food sources for opportunistic red foxes that were not historically available. For example, road-killed carrion provides a dependable year-round food supply. Sargeant (1981) estimated that 4,500 ducks were killed annually on roads in the Prairie Pothole Region of North Dakota during 1969–78, in addition to the countless other road kills. Other new sources of prey for the red fox include domestic fowl and small livestock (e.g., sheep) operations. In winter, historically a limiting period for red fox, the animal readily turns to waste grain such as sunflower seeds. A North Dakota study found sunflower seeds in three-fourths of the red foxes examined in winter, and seeds made up half their stomach contents (Sargeant, Allen, and Fleskes 1986). The myriad food sources in the new Great Plains are ideal for red foxes compared with those in pristine times.

The second factor Sargeant (1982) mentioned—interspecific competition between coyotes and red foxes—is similar to the competition between gray wolves and coyotes described earlier. Numerous studies have documented that coyotes tend to displace red foxes (Sargeant, Allen, and Hastings 1987), sometimes killing them outright (Sargeant and Allen 1989). Sargeant, Allen, and Hastings (1987) speculated that coyote-induced declines in the red fox population occur largely because red foxes do not establish territories already occupied by coyotes. In their study no fox family lived totally within a coyote territory, even though red fox territories (4.6 square miles) were significantly smaller than coyote territories (23.9 square miles). Over time the red fox is gradually and perhaps totally eliminated as coyotes become more established at the site. (A similar situation appears to occur between the red fox and the smaller swift fox, a Great Plains native. Red foxes, through competition and interspecific antagonism, are believed to be one of many detrimental factors depressing swift fox populations.)

The third factor Sargeant (1982) listed as influencing red fox density and distribution is human harvest, mainly for fur. Although the factor was important historically, it seems unlikely that human harvests will significantly affect fox populations in the future owing to changing societal values.

Like red foxes, raccoons (*Procyon lotor*) also appear to be expanding their range throughout the grassland biome (Sargeant et al. 1993). Whereas they probably existed historically only in the larger riparian zones, such as along the Missouri River, they are now abundant throughout the region. This expansion once again appears to be related to European settlement. For example, shelterbelts constitute a vast network of woody travel corridors throughout the grassland biome, and buildings and other structures provide new denning sites. Fritzell (1978) found that 81 percent of all nocturnal raccoon locations and 94 percent of all diurnal locations in his Prairie Pothole Region study area were near buildings, wooded areas, and wetlands, even though these three habitats composed only 10 percent of the study area. Only the latter can be considered natural. The absence of larger predators such as wolves may also aid raccoon expansion (Sargeant et al. 1993).

Modern settlement also means new foods for raccoons. In North Dakota, grain and livestock feed constituted more than half the diet (by volume) of raccoons foraging in upland sites (Greenwood 1982). Greenwood (1981, 759) believed cereal grains such as wheat and barley were a "staple in the diet" of North Dakota raccoons. He surmised that the availability of grains stored on farms may have increased raccoons' survival during emergence from their winter dormancy. In historical times it is likely that late winter was a critical period for raccoons in the drought-prone prairies, with many animals succumbing to starvation. Like red foxes, modern raccoons also benefit from road-killed carrion, domestic fowl, bird feeders, and all the other new food sources associated with settlement.

The striped skunk (*Mephitis mephitis*) also appears to have expanded its range and density in the grassland biome, thanks in part to crops, but also owing to the presence of rock piles and old buildings that it uses for dens. Skunks (which are severe ground-nest predators) may also benefit from the decline in badgers (*Taxidea taxus*) (which are not severe nest predators), another form of interspecific competition (Johnson, Sargeant, and Greenwood 1989). Whereas badgers are intolerant of many human activities and disappear when human presence becomes high, skunks tolerate humans and quickly occupy settled areas.

Franklin's ground squirrel (*Spermophilus franklinii*), another predator of ground nests, has also apparently expanded its geographic range into the grassland biome owing to habitat fragmentation (Robins 1971). Unlike the red fox and raccoon, these seldom-seen predators are only rarely acknowledged for their harmful effects on grassland-nesting birds.

Even the opossum (*Didelphis virginiana*), an animal historically limited to the forests of the southeastern United States, has begun expanding its range into the prairies. Before European settlement the combination of long winters, lack of denning sites, and lack of food probably kept the animal out of the grassland biome. But modern land-use practices create new foods for opossums, much as they do for red foxes, raccoons, and others, and buildings provide relatively warm den sites.

The increase in woody vegetation has also helped many avian predators expand into the grassland biome. For example, crows, magpies, great horned owls (*Bubo virginianus*), and red-tailed hawks (*Buteo jamaicensis*) find abundant perches and nesting sites where historically they were few and far between. Murphy (1993) examined an area in northwestern North Dakota and found that whereas historically the raptor composition had consisted primarily of ferruginous hawks and Swainson hawks (*Buteo swainsoni*), burrowing owls, and northern harriers (*Circus cyaneus*), in the 1990s the dominant species were red-tailed hawks and great horned owls, both tree nesters. Somewhat similarly, Schmutz (1993) felt that the spread of trees into the Canadian prairies has permitted red-tailed hawks to expand into areas formerly occupied by ferruginous hawks. According to the historical records of Judd (1917), red-tailed hawks were only migrants in North Dakota in the latter part of the nineteenth century (at least in most of the state); the species now breeds statewide and throughout the northern plains, thanks in large part to the proliferation of trees.

The dramatic increase in midsize predators in the grassland biome is undoubtedly contributing to the decline of many grassland species, especially birds. But the increase in predators' numbers and distribution is only half the story. Lack of quality habitat is the other part.

As noted above, nest predators such as the raccoon and the red fox can now sustain themselves at unnaturally high numbers through the prairie winter thanks in part to human-created food sources. Come spring and summer, the artificially high predator populations turn to natural foods such as ground nests and ground-nesting birds. Because so little nesting habitat remains, the birds and their nests are concentrated in remnant fragments of habitat, such as road rights-of-way. The predators quickly learn to concentrate their search in these sites and thus have greater success, causing them to spend even more time searching there. Predator foraging in these small, isolated tracts of habitat may be so intensive that the sites can become population sinks for ground-nesting birds such as waterfowl, meaning that reproduction does not compensate for mortality. Over time, the prey population experiences a precipitous decline unless other individuals immigrate into the area.

Waterfowl appear to be especially susceptible to the compounding factors of increased predator density and declining habitat. They also happen to be well studied, so their situation is worth describing in further detail. The nest success of mallards (*Anas platyrhynchos*) in the Prairie Pothole Region of Canada has been estimated at 12 percent (Greenwood et al. 1987). In North Dakota it was

65

estimated to be in the range of 8 percent (Cowardin, Gilmer, and Shaiffer 1985) to 11 percent (Klett, Shaffer, and Johnson 1988), with the lowest nest success occurring in the tallgrass zone where fragmentation, habitat loss, and the influx of nest predators has been highest. Overall, mallard nest success in the Prairie Pothole Region appears to be below 15 percent (Klett, Shaffer, and Johnson 1988), the rate necessary for the species to maintain its population (Cowardin, Gilmer, and Shaiffer 1985).

Red foxes are generally perceived as the most severe predators of waterfowl, because they not only are adept at taking nests but also take adult birds. One Prairie Pothole study found that individual fox families take from 16.1 to 65.9 dabbling ducks annually (Sargeant et al. 1984). These figures, when extrapolated, mean that red foxes may take 900,000 adult ducks annually in the midcontinent area alone (Sargeant, Allen, and Eberhardt 1984), not to mention the eggs and ducklings. Compounding the problem, red foxes often take a disproportionate number of female waterfowl, which are vulnerable to predators while incubating eggs or rearing young. Johnson and Sargeant (1977) found that 79.8 percent of the mallard remains found at fox dens were female. This heavy predation on females further lessens the recruitment potential of the species. Using simulation models, they estimated a current mallard sex ratio in the Prairie Pothole Region of 118 males to every 100 females (the ratio would be even more unbalanced were it not that hunting regulations target males). The same model predicted that in pre-Columbian times, when wolves were the predominant predator on the Great Plains and red foxes were scarce or absent, the sex ratio was probably 110 or fewer males per 100 females.

But red foxes are not alone in affecting waterfowl recruitment. One study found that waterfowl nest success increased from 5 to 15 percent after removal of skunks (Greenwood 1986). A study in Saskatchewan using artificial waterfowl nests concluded that high concentrations of duck nests in small remnant habitats are more likely to be preyed on by crows than nests that are dispersed over wide areas, as was historically the case (Sugden and Beyersbergen 1986). Another study of crow depredation, this time in Manitoba, found that artificial waterfowl nests within 2,289 feet of crow nests—that is, near shelterbelts and other woody vegetation, were more likely to be found by crows (Sullivan and Dinsmore 1990). Last, a study in northwestern North Dakota found that great horned owls and red-tailed hawks, two species that historically were absent from the area, preyed heavily on ducks and many other wetland species; in contrast, the ferruginous hawk, historically a dominant raptor, rarely preyed on wetland species (Murphy 1993). Almost all the midsize predators that prey heavily on waterfowl and waterfowl nests have increased dramatically in the Prairie Pothole Region since pre-Columbian times, whereas those that prey only lightly on waterfowl have been reduced or eliminated (Sargeant et al. 1993). Because of these and other factors, mallard populations may continue to decline as much as 20 percent annually in some areas (Cowardin, Gilmer, and Shaiffer 1985).

Although their statistics may vary, most waterfowl researchers have come to the same conclusion: large tracts of grassland habitat are preferable to small tracts. Greenwood et al. (1987) strengthened that conclusion when they found that mallard nest success in prairie Canada was positively correlated with the amount of grassland habitat. The researchers found that areas with the highest waterfowl nesting success generally "included a large block of land in native pasture, numerous wetlands that contained water and a predator community favorable to duck production" (306). They concluded by stating that "protection of large tracts of native grassland is vital to the production of upland-nesting ducks" (307).

Grazing

A discussion of the increase in midsize predators in the grassland biome, and the concurrent decrease in available nesting habitat, is appropriately followed by a discussion of livestock grazing. Livestock grazing can affect the quality of existing nesting habitat and therefore works in combination with other influences on prairie birds. In addition, livestock grazing can affect many other components of grassland ecosystems.

A convincing argument can be made that grazing is necessary for a healthy grassland ecosystem. Light to moderate grazing stimulates grass growth, disturbs the seedbed, and returns nutrients to the soil through excreta. Even heavy grazing appears necessary for some species and under certain conditions. In fact the variety of life in the great grasslands of North America was shaped in large part by grazing. Next to climate and perhaps fire, it was the grazing effects of ungulates, prairie dogs, insects, and many other species that created and maintained the pre-Columbian grassland ecosystem. Yet modern livestock grazing practices often have negative consequences on that ecosystem.

Once again, the well-studied birds are the best indicators of how current livestock grazing practices affect biodiversity. Light to moderate grazing, especially if it is rotational, does benefit many species of songbirds in the Great Plains. But heavy grazing, especially when incessant, is detrimental to many other species such as Baird's, savannah, grasshopper, and clay-colored sparrows, bobolink, and Sprague's pipit (Kantrud and Kologiski 1982). Likewise, heavy grazing that affects wetland fringes can be detrimental to wetland species such as members of the rail family, plovers (Gaines and Ryan 1988), willets (*Catroptrophus semipalmatus*), marbled godwits (*Limosa fedoa*), and Wilson's phalarope (*Phalaropus tricolor*). Even some upland game species, such as sage and sharp-tailed grouse, show negative responses to high levels of grazing (Kantrud and Kologiski 1982), as do waterfowl (Klett, Shaffer, and Johnson 1988). Yet heavy grazing can benefit some grassland birds such as the mountain plover and burrowing owl (Kantrud and Kologiski 1982). (That is one reason these species are commonly associated with prairie dog towns.)

Although moderate grazing is generally beneficial for grassland birds, in some instances even the slightest amount of grazing is detrimental. For example, one study found that the mere presence of livestock deters nesting by the marbled godwit, willet, Wilson's phalarope, and short-eared owl (*Asio flammeus*), while the upland sandpiper had higher nest success in fields that were not grazed during the nesting season (Kantrud and Higgins 1992). Other studies found that ground-nesting raptors such as the ferruginous hawk and northern harrier tend to establish their nests in prairies that are unused or only very lightly grazed (Lokemoen and Duebbert 1976. Long-term trends in grassland songbird populations provide circumstantial evidence that most Great Plains grasslands are overgrazed in terms of conserving grassland birds. Consider that Breeding Bird Survey data indicate that many species that need or prefer ungrazed or lightly grazed grasslands, such as Baird's and savannah sparrows and Sprague's pipit, are declining in the Great Plains, whereas species that prefer heavily grazed sites, such as the horned lark (*Eremophila alpestris*) and chestnut-collared longspur (*Calcarius ornatus*), are common or increasing (see Kantrud and Kologiski 1982 for grazing preferences). These and other data (a 1982 study found that 61.7 percent of the nonfederal rangeland in the Great Plains states was in poor or fair condition [U.S. Forest Service 1989a]) provide strong evidence that most Great Plains grasslands have traditionally been overgrazed, at least in terms of conserving grassland passerines.

Having said that, it is important to note that heavy grazing may cause an overall increase in bird densities. For example, chestnut-collared longspurs and horned larks may be so abundant on heavily grazed plots that they make up in numbers for the loss of other species from the site (Kantrud and Kologiski 1982). Although apparently desirable, such effects should not be construed as positive for grassland biodiversity.

Last, similar patterns of grazing may influence birds differently in different grassland types. For example, the long-billed curlew (*Numenius americanus*), once wide spread throughout the prairies but now reduced to a few scattered populations, is found in highest densities on lightly grazed aridic ustolls soils (soil type in southeast Wyoming and northwest Nebraska), but it is also found in fairly high densities on heavily grazed typic ustolls (soil type in central South Dakota [Kantrud and Kologiski 1982]). Such extenuating circumstances may help explain why some researchers have reported that waterfowl recruitment was higher on idle lands (Klett, Shaffer, and Johnston 1988) while others felt that grazed lands were more productive (Barker et al. 1990).

Kirsch, Duebbert, and Kruse (1978, 493) reviewed the voluminous literature on livestock grazing and ground-nesting birds and concluded that "higher densities of dabbling duck and upland game bird nests were usually found in undisturbed vegetation than in adjacent habitats that were annually grazed or hayed." Kirby et al. (1992, 620) also reviewed the literature and concluded that "data from appropriately designed studies do not exist to indicate that upland nesting ducks benefit from livestock grazing, and some circumstantial results from poorly designed experiments show the opposite." Generally speaking, it seems reasonable to conclude that the preponderance of studies suggest that most cattle grazing, as now practiced in the Great Plains, is harmful to rare or declining upland nesting birds.

Livestock grazing may also affect mammal species. Goodson (1983) felt that competition from cattle was partly responsible for the declines and die-offs of many native wild sheep populations. Carbyn (1989) suggested that heavy livestock grazing may negatively affect predators such as the swift fox by reducing prey densities. And Risser et al. (1981) found that livestock grazing in a tallgrass prairie decreased both the density and the variety of small mammals. However, in some circumstances heavy grazing and trampling by cattle can create conditions beneficial to grassland mammals. For example, patches of barren ground created by cattle encourage prairie dog colonization (Licht and Sanchez 1993).

As with birds and mammals, livestock grazing affects different plant species in different ways. Generally speaking, light short-term grazing increases plant growth and vigor, but long-term heavy grazing decreases plant productivity (Risser et al. 1981). Heavy long-term grazing can also reduce flora diversity, eventually causing grasses and forbs to be replaced by unpalatable shrubs. For example, in the Jornada Experimental Range in south-central New Mexico, good grass was present on more than 90 percent of the study area in 1858, but by

1963 less than 25 percent of the area had good grass, with most of the rest being replaced by woody shrubs (Buffington and Herbel 1965). The researchers concluded that heavy grazing was partly responsible for the increase in shrubs. Likewise, woody vegetation such as mesquite (*Prosopis glandulosa*), eastern juniper (*Juniperus virginiana*), and Osage orange (*Maclura pomifera*) has invaded large portions of the southern plains in the states of Texas, Oklahoma, and New Mexico, the result of long-term overgrazing and fire suppression. However, some plants, like some birds and mammals, can benefit from heavy grazing. For example, the Nebraska endemic blowout penstemon (*Penstemon haydenii*, an endangered species) is favored by grazing that is so heavy it stimulates erosion in the sandy region (U.S. Fish and Wildlife Service 1992).

Livestock grazing can be especially harmful to riparian areas and woody draws, which some consider one of the most critical and threatened habitat types in the Great Plains. Grazing along streams also threatens water quality and hence fish and other aquatic organisms. Somewhat similarly, grazing in the southern tallgrass ecoregion was found to decrease rainwater infiltration through soil compaction and reduced ground litter (Risser et al. 1981).

In summary, it seems safe to say that livestock grazing is neither inherently good nor bad for biodiversity conservation. It becomes an issue when it is practiced in a manner not analogous to the way grassland species evolved. Based on the available data, it appears that—on a landscape level—most livestock grazing in the Great Plains and prairies has been too heavy for too long. Such a regional pattern contrasts significantly with pre-Columbian grazing patterns.

It is commonly believed that bison grazing is more compatible with survival of prairie birds, prairie mammals, and prairie plants—in other words, grassland biodiversity. Bison are generally perceived as grazing in a more benign and beneficial manner than cattle because they do not naturally concentrate their activities, they graze less selectively (Pedan et al. 1974), and they make more efficient use of Great Plains forage (most domestic cattle descended from wetland species from the humid climates of Southeast Asia). Bison are also generally perceived as less harmful to other habitats within the grassland biome. A study in western North Dakota found that bison grazing had comparatively little impact on woody draws, whereas cattle often degraded the sites (Norland and Marlow 1984).

The ecological differences between cattle and bison go beyond grazing. For example, the tendency of bison to wallow in the earth resulted in unique microhabitats that cattle do not replicate. A study in southwest Oklahoma found that these small depressions served as miniature wetlands by storing rainwater and creating conditions suitable for wetland plant communities (Uno 1987). A Kansas study found that bison wallows over one hundred years old were still providing microhabitats that contained plant species not found in the nearby prairie (Gibson 1989). These small wetlands likely benefit many obscure animal species as well as larger animals like pronghorn antelope. Bison also tend to be better at returning nutrients to grasslands. Whereas cattle prefer to concentrate their resting and defecating in shaded areas (for example, riparian woodlands), bison rest and defecate comparatively uniformly across the prairie.

The nomadic nature of bison also had ecological ramifications that fenced cattle do not fully replicate. For instance, wandering bison herds helped disperse the clingy seeds of the now endangered savanna plant running buffalo clover (*Trifolium stoloniferum*), while the heavy (but brief) local grazing created conditions suitable for germination (U.S. Fish and Wildlife Service 1989). These and many other subtle but important ecological processes are not always replicated by fenced cattle (or fenced bison), even when the best stocking densities are implemented.

Unfortunately, some bison proponents misrepresent the effect bison had on the grassland ecosystem. They envision bison as treading lightly across the prairies, when in reality the local impact of bison could be every bit as pronounced as that of fenced cattle. For example, in the tallgrass prairie area near the present North Dakota–Minnesota border, Alexander Henry (1897, 64) gave this account in August 1800: "The ravages of buffaloes at this place are astonishing to a person unaccustomed to these meadows. The beach, once a soft black mud into which a man would sink knee-deep, is now made hard as pavement by the numerous herds coming to drink. The willows are entirely trampled and torn to pieces . . . and the vast quantity of dung gives this place the appearance of a cattle yard."

When comparing bison grazing with cattle grazing one must keep in mind that the nomadic nature of bison was perhaps the most significant difference between the two herbivores. Bison grazing at any particular site was brief and sporadic, perhaps even random. Bison could and would graze an area hard, but then they would move on, leaving the land to rest. Viewed at the landscape level, bison created a constantly changing mosaic of grassland successional stages. Replicating such a regional grazing pattern on a landscape comprising numerous small private holdings is improbable.

Livestock grazing is not going to be eliminated from the Great Plains anytime in the near future, if ever. Nor should it be. Cattle ranching is too valuable to the region's economy and heritage. And though the current pattern and distribution of livestock grazing is often harmful to grassland biodiversity, it may be optimal for short-term profits, making substantial regional changes unlikely. In contrast, large publicly owned tracts dedicated to grassland conservation can be managed for values not adequately provided by private lands. Few such sites exist at present.

Exotics

It is estimated that at least 4,500 species of foreign origin have established free-living populations in the United States, mainly owing to human activities (U.S. Office of Technology Assessment 1993). These nonindigenous species threaten not only the nation's economy, but also its biodiversity. Exotic species now constitute 2–8 percent of the nation's insect and vertebrate richness. They also threaten the survival of over half the endangered and threatened bird and fish species in the United States (Flather, Joyce, and Bloomgarten 1994). Nationwide, exotic plants rank as the greatest threat to the ecology of our national parks, while exotic animals are the fourth most commonly reported problem (Hester 1991).

The extent of exotics in the Great Plains appears similar to that in the contiguous United States as a whole. For example, of the approximately 410 plant species that occur on the Pawnee National Grasslands in eastern Colorado, it is estimated that 70 are exotics (U.S. Forest Service 1992). Likewise, 16 of the 56 grasses in Badlands National Park in southwest South Dakota have recently been introduced to the continent. Some exotics in the grassland biome are nuisances throughout North America. Examples are the English sparrow (also known as the house sparrow) and the starling, which displace native bird species by occupying their nesting cavities and competing with them for food. Other notable grassland exotics, in terms of ecology and economics, are purple loosestrife (*Lythrum salicaria*), spotted knapweed (*Centourea cyanus*), musk thistle (*Carduus nutans*), leafy spurge, and wormwood (*Artemisia vulgaris*).

Granted, not all exotics are deemed pests by society, for example, the ring-necked pheasant (*Phasianus colchicus*), brown trout (*Salmo trutta*), and alfalfa (*Medicago sativa*). However, even apparently beneficial exotics can sometimes have harmful effects. Ring-necked pheasants negatively affect native prairie chickens by outcompeting them for food, by harassing them at courting grounds, and by parasitizing their nests (Vance and Westemeier 1979). Dinsmore (1994, 113) speculated that the introduction of pheasants may have been the "final straw" in the prairie chicken's disappearance from Iowa. Pheasants are also known to parasitize the nests of waterfowl, quail, grouse, rails, and other species. In time these problems could worsen if pheasants fostered by other species imprint on their hosts (Kimmel 1988).

Exotic grasses such as those used in lawns are also commonly viewed as beneficial, but they too can be detrimental to native ecosystems. For example, Kentucky bluegrass (*Poa pratensis*), along with the exotic leafy spurge, threatens to displace the western prairie fringed orchid in some areas. Brome grass (*Bromus* sp.) is another exotic that is often perceived as beneficial. At least ten different species of brome have been introduced from Eurasia; the aggressive species invade and degrade many remnant prairie sites, including some inhabited by rare prairie butterflies.

Sometimes it takes a while before the detrimental effects of ostensibly good exotics are noticed. For example, the Asian multiflora rose (*Rosa multiflora*) was once promoted and spread by state wildlife agencies as a beneficial "wildlife planting." These same agencies now spend considerable time and energy trying to control the spread of the noxious shrub.

Disturbingly, some exotics with known harmful effects are still promoted and distributed by government agencies. For example, the small tree called Russian olive (*Elaeagnus angustifolia*) is still championed as an ornamental and a windbreak throughout much of the Great Plains. The aggressive shrub outcompetes native trees such as cottonwoods in riparian zones along major Great Plains rivers. It also invades nonriparian sites, where it can turn a native prairie into an artificial woodland. It has been predicted that within fifty years eastern South Dakota will resemble a Russian olive forest (Olson and Knopf 1986). Once established, nuisance trees like Russian olive are extremely difficult to eradicate. Yet in spite of these problems tree plantings of Siberian elm (*Ulmus pumila*), Manchurian apricot (*Prunus armeniaca*), Russian olive, Scots pine (*Pinus sylvestris*), Norway spruce (*Picea abies*), Tatarian honeysuckle (*Lonicera tatarica*), Korean mountain ash (*Sorbus alnifolia*), Japanese lilac (*Syringa reticulata*), and Siberian peashrub (*Caragana arborescens*) continue to be subsidized and promoted by some government agencies.

Some exotic forbs are also promoted by government agencies. In North Dakota the federal government distributes free sweet clover (*Melilotus* sp.) seed to farmers and other landowners. Under certain conditions this native of Eurasia can dominate native prairies. It is also rigid enough to provide nesting structure for red-winged blackbirds—a species that the same federal government invests considerable time and money trying to control for the benefit of farmers. An Illinois study found that most red-winged blackbirds in that state now nest in uplands, whereas historically they nested almost exclusively in wetlands (Herkert 1993); the change is likely due in large part to the proliferation of rigid exotics in the uplands.

In many places the house cat may be the most damaging exotic of all, especially to songbirds. A Wisconsin study found densities of free-ranging cats as high as 114 cats per square mile in rural areas (Coleman and Temple 1993). In contrast, springtime densities of raccoons, striped skunks, and opossums in south-central Wisconsin were respectively only 23, 3, and 10 per square mile. The addition of free-ranging and feral dogs exacerbates the problem.

Other types of exotic species can be much less conspicuous, but even more deadly to Great Plains flora and fauna. Sylvatic plague (known as bubonic plague when it affects people), apparently introduced to North America in the early 1900s, is deadly to prairie dogs and certain other animals, often in epizootic proportions. Wild bighorn sheep are susceptible to exotic diseases transmitted by domestic sheep, an event that has on occasion caused catastrophic die-offs of wild sheep populations (Goodson 1983). Even apparently benign and insignificant exotics can harm ecosystems or at the very least not fully perform functions that native species are capable of. For example, exotic earthworm species were found to be less efficient nutrient processors in tallgrass prairies than were native species (James 1991).

The most prevalent exotics in the Great Plains (excluding crops) are plants used for cattle forage. Planting exotic grasses has been a traditional way of ostensibly improving Great Plains rangeland. Yet these so-called improvements are often detrimental to grassland biodiversity. Numerous studies have found that many bird species indigenous to the grassland biome, especially the rarer species, prefer native grasses to exotics (in certain situations exotic grasses may be on a par with native grasses, typically when structure is more important than composition). For example, species such as the marbled godwit, upland sandpiper, common snipe (*Gallinago gallinago*), Wilson's phalarope, and willet appear to prefer nesting in native prairie rather than areas containing a high percentage of exotic plants (Kantrud and Higgins 1992). Wilson and Belcher (1989) found that in the mixed-grass region of Manitoba the western meadowlark (*Sturnella neglecta*), upland sandpiper, Sprague's pipit, Baird's sparrow, and savannah sparrow were all positively correlated with native plant species and negatively correlated with introduced plants. The ground-nesting ferruginous hawk is known to be strongly associated with areas high in native grass (Gilmer and Stewart 1983). Waterfowl nest initiation (Klett, Duebbert, and Heismeyer 1984) and nest success (Klett, Shaffer, and Johnson 1988) are at least as high in grasslands with a high percentage of native grasses. One reason many birds, especially early spring ground-nesting birds, seem to prefer native grasses is that native species maintain their structure better through the winter and hence provide better cover the following spring.

Even grassland mammals seem to benefit more from native grasses. In North Dakota, Lysne (1991) found that small mammal diversity was low on exotic grasslands compared with nearby native grasslands.

One of the most consequential and well-chronicled species to affect the grassland ecosystem is the brown-headed cowbird (*Molothrus ater*). Although not an exotic in the conventional sense, the cowbird should be considered here because the current status of the species is radically different than before European settlement. The cowbird appears to have occurred in much lower numbers in the pre-Columbian grassland biome, where it accompanied the herds of bison (often riding on their backs) and subsisted on insects flushed by the large beasts. Because of the nomadic nature of bison, cowbirds evolved a reproductive strategy whereby they laid their eggs in the nests of other birds whenever the opportunity presented itself. That way they could continue to move with the bison while their progeny remained behind to be raised by the duped parents (the cowbird chicks would typically outcompete the host chicks for food, resulting in lower reproductive success for the host species). Generally the presence of cowbirds was limited by the movements of bison; their appearance in any locality during the breeding season was a hit-or-miss affair.

But the extermination of bison and the introduction of fenced cattle changed the cowbirds' environment. Cattle and other livestock were distributed uniformly and densely throughout the Great Plains; subsequently, the distribution and behavior of cowbirds changed accordingly. Whereas in historical times the parasitizing effects of cowbirds were localized and brief, in modern times the effects are everywhere and incessant.

Contributing to the cowbird's recent proliferation is the arborescence of the grassland biome. Norman and Robertson (1975) found that (modern-day) female cowbirds often search for host nests by using shelterbelts and other woody vegetation as observation perches, where they remain motionless for hours until a nesting bird reveals its nest location. A study in the tallgrass region of central Illinois found that field sparrow (*Spizella pusilla*) nests parasitized by cowbirds averaged forty-four feet from adjacent woody vegetation, whereas nests more than eighty-five feet from the woody vegetation were rarely parasitized (Best 1978). Another study found evidence that cowbirds in treeless habitats are often unable to gather enough information on potential hosts' nests in time to parasitize them (Freeman, Gori, and Rohwer 1990).

Not surprisingly, cowbird parasitism in the grassland biome seems to occur more frequently in fragmented habitats than in large, contiguous tracts of grassland. For example, in southwestern Manitoba, cowbird parasitism occurred at 69 percent of the nests in a 54-acre study site versus 17 percent and 20 percent on two 158-acre sites (Davis 1993). A study by Johnson and Temple (1990) found higher rates of cowbird parasitism of nests of clay-colored, savannah, and grasshopper sparrows, western meadowlarks, and bobolinks in small (40–79 acres) tracts of tallgrass prairie than in large tracts (321–1,200 acres).

The rate of modern-day cowbird parasitism is staggering. A study in Kansas tallgrass prairie found that 95 percent of the dickcissel nests, 70 percent of the eastern meadowlark nests, and 50 percent of the grasshopper sparrow nests were parasitized (Elliot 1978). Another Kansas study, this one in the mixed-grass region, found that 111 of 520 nests (21 percent) were parasitized by cowbirds, and all but one species of grassland birds were moderately to heavily parasitized (Hill 1976). A Nebraska study also found parasitism for many grassland birds, with dickcissels again one of the most frequently parasitized species (53 percent [Hergenrader 1962]). In summary, the alteration of the prairie landscape has benefited cowbirds to the detriment of other grassland passerines. And though cowbird numbers may have reached a plateau in many parts of the country, they may still be increasing in the northern Great Plains (Peterjohn and Sauer 1993).

Like the cowbird, many other species native to the United States but historically rare or nonexistent in the grassland biome now influence the region's ecology as if they were exotics. For example, the slender madtom (*Noturus exilis*) is a small fish of the east-central United States that has recently invaded (possibly by anthropogenic means) the range of the Neosho madtom (*N. placidus*), a small fish endemic to the muddy rivers of the southern mixed-grass prairies. The invasion of the new species may be to the detriment of the threatened Neosho madtom (U.S. Fish and Wildlife Service 1991c). White-tailed deer, an edge-adapted species of the eastern United States, were not even known in Colorado before 1954; now, thanks to habitat fragmentation, they are a nuisance in many areas and compete with the indigenous mule deer. Bullfrogs (*Rana cat-*

esbeiana) are now commonly found in the tallgrass and mixed-grass plains (probably introduced by fisheries biologists). How these large amphibians interact with smaller indigenous amphibians is unknown, but it has been speculated that the larger frogs are partly responsible for the decline of some native species. Last, well-intentioned humans release hand-reared wood ducks (*Aix sponsa*) and establish wood duck nesting boxes in the grassland biome, even though the ecosystem is more suited to ground-nesting waterfowl. Whether wood ducks are detrimental to other waterfowl species, through competition or by other means, is not yet known. The Breeding Bird Survey indicates that between 1966 and 1993, wood ducks increased 100 percent in the grassland biome; meanwhile the northern pintail (*Anas acuta*), a native grassland species, experienced a 54 percent decline in the region.

As briefly mentioned in previous chapters, many eastern forest birds have also invaded the grassland biome owing to the proliferation of shelterbelts, dwellings, cultivation, roads, and general landscape fragmentation. Consider that the Stephen Long expedition up the Platte River in 1820 did not observe a single robin (*Turdus migratorius*) until the party reached the Rocky Mountains (Thwaites 1905, 15:281); nowadays the species is common throughout the Great Plains, especially around residential areas. Knopf (1986) found that virtually 90 percent of the eighty-two bird species breeding in eastern Colorado were not present in 1900. An Iowa study found that between 1940 and 1989, populations of prairie-nesting birds declined while populations of forest and forest-edge species increased on the same area (Bernstein, Baker, and Wilmot 1990). The researchers concluded that "the most obvious reason for the decline in grassland birds was the reduced area of grassland in the study area because of woody succession" (118). Samson and Knopf (1982) reported that a striking feature in species use of prairie relicts in Missouri was the high frequency of nonprairie birds, including the field sparrow, bobwhite, red-winged blackbird, common grackle, brown thrasher (*Toxostoma rufum*), blue jay, and brown-headed cowbird. Although many of these forest and forest-edge species are not generally perceived as directly harmful to native grassland species, they still outcompete and displace many prairie birds. The introduction of forest birds may also exacerbate the spread of cowbirds by providing more host nests.

Preventing and controlling the spread of exotic species will continue to be extremely difficult, if not impossible. Although society may come up with effective control methods for some harmful exotics, others will simply have to be tolerated. But in some cases the harmful effects of exotics on native biodiversity can be lessened by properly designed conservation areas. Generally, larger reserves, with a high ratio of area to perimeter, are less influenced by exotic invasions than are smaller tracts.

Water

Depletion of groundwater and river water for irrigation, livestock, and domestic use threatens not only the aquatic ecosystems within the grassland biome but also the region's economy. Luckey et al. (1988) predicted that at the current rate of water depletion parts of the High Plains could face extreme water shortages by the year 2020, with dire economic and social consequences. The region is already facing the ecological consequences. Kromm and White (1992, 45, 55) observed that "[groundwater] depletion has destroyed much of the water-supported habitat for fish and mammals in the High Plains, and in many areas the water ecosystem is gone. . . . more than 700 miles of once permanently flowing rivers in Kansas no longer flow." Even major rivers such as the Arkansas, Republican, and Cimarron have been degraded to dried-up riverbeds in places that historically were dynamic riverine ecosystems.

At least twelve species of fish in the southern Great Plains are candidates for the endangered species list (the Neosho madtom is already listed). Almost all are small, little-known, and unremarkable species that have great potential for controversy if they are listed as endangered or threatened. Yet all of them are threatened with extinction, largely owing to depletion of groundwater and river water, mainly for irrigation.

In other cases anthropogenic effects have produced too much water, or water at the wrong time. The hundreds, perhaps thousands, of dams in the Great Plains have directly destroyed habitat for many aquatic species. For example, one-third of the historic river habitat of the Neosho madtom, a mostly nocturnal three-inch fish found in Kansas, Oklahoma, and Missouri, has been inundated and destroyed by dams (U.S. Fish and Wildlife Service 1991c). The Missouri River has been almost completely destroyed as habitat for the prehistoric pallid sturgeon (*Scaphirhynchus albus*). Approximately 36 percent of the river has been inundated by reservoirs, 40 percent has been channelized (all downstream of Sioux City, Iowa), and the remaining 24 percent has been altered and degraded by the patterns of water release from the six dams on the river (U.S. Fish and Wildlife Service 1993b). In addition, the dams prevent the sturgeon from migrating upstream or downstream to reach suitable spawning habitat.

Water diversions and changes to natural river hydrographs have also affected associated upland habitats. For example, the South Platte River in northeastern

78

Colorado was historically bordered by a shoreline of prairie and meadow (Crouch 1984). Only when the region was settled, irrigation returns steadily percolated into the river throughout the summer and fall, and wildfires were suppressed did woody vegetation begin to occur along the South Platte. Forested riparian zones where historically there were only wet meadows or grasslands may be deemed an improvement by some, but they are often detrimental to grassland biodiversity, for reasons I have already given.

Throughout the Great Plains and prairies aquatic systems may be the most threatened communities in the biome. The threats come in the form of water diversions, dams, sedimentation from erosion, pollution, and many other factors. Most of these factors can be ultimately linked to irrigation.

Roads

The existence of roads in the grassland ecosystem is probably more of a threat to wildlife than most people acknowledge. Populations of abundant species like white-tailed deer and ring-necked pheasants are little affected by road kills. But road mortality can exacerbate the decline of some species. For example, automobiles appear to be a significant source of death to swift foxes because of the animals' tendency to forage along roads for road-killed carrion (Hines and Case 1991). Likewise De Smet (1993) believed automobile collisions may be a more significant factor than realized in the decline of loggerhead shrikes (*Lanius ludovicianus*), especially in agrarian regions. Mountain plover chicks are also susceptible to road mortality because they are attracted to roads and prairie trails during the morning by the radiant heat they give off.

Roads can also lead indirectly to mortality and extirpation. For example, in the forested region of northern Minnesota it was found that high road densities correlated with low wolf densities (Mech et al. 1988), probably because roads made wolves vulnerable to shooting. Although no similar trends have been documented for grassland wildlife, it seems reasonable to assume that roads may exacerbate illegal shooting of raptors, ungulates, and other medium to large animals.

Roads also serve as barriers to some species. Studies in forested habitats have found that even lightly traveled roads as narrow as twenty feet can be a deterrent to mice and other small animals (Mader 1984). In a Kansas grassland very few prairie voles and cotton rats crossed a dirt track only ten feet wide (Swihart and Slade 1984). The effects of roads are probably especially significant in the tallgrass states, where roads are most prevalent.

Disturbance associated with roads may threaten the survival of some sensitive grassland species in ways we do not yet appreciate. For example, the proliferation of roads in the badlands of western North Dakota, a result of oil development, has long been suspected of limiting bighorn sheep populations. Such cause and effect is difficult to prove, but it appears that the roads effectively fragment sheep populations into small bands with little interaction. Studies in the desert Southwest have found that isolated bighorn sheep populations of fewer than fifty individuals have a high likelihood of extinction (Berger 1990).

Biologists now recognize that roads can limit populations of certain species, some of which are critical to ecosystem functions. Yet in the Great Plains there may be no more than seven roadless areas over 100,000 acres (Wild Earth 1992), and even some of those are laced with prairie trails. Until large roadless (or mostly roadless) areas are established, restoring and conserving functioning prairie ecosystems will be difficult.

Fire

Last, but certainly not least, the wildfires that once rejuvenated, maintained, and shaped the prairies have been suppressed. The effects of this loss cannot be overstated. Wildfires were less a disruption to the great grasslands than the norm. In fact the lack of fire constitutes the disturbance.

In the comparatively humid tallgrass region, fires may have historically occurred every three to ten years. In mixed-grass prairies they were probably more regular, sometimes striking the same site in both spring and fall (Bragg 1982). In the shortgrass regions fires were less frequent (owing to a lighter fuel load), perhaps only every fifteen to thirty years (Wendtland and Dodd 1992). Whatever the frequency, fires were critical to the grassland ecosystem.

Grassland fires historically burned in a patchy pattern, in part because of the wallows, trails, and grazing of bison, in part because of soil types and other natural features, but perhaps also because they were set that way by Native Americans. Colonel Richard Dodge (1989, 77) who traveled the Plains from the 1860s to the 1880s, noted that in the region of present-day Kansas, "the Indians burn portions of the prairie every fall, setting the fires so as to burn as vast an extent of country as possible, and yet preserve unburned a good section in the vicinity where they propose to make their fall hunt." In addition to those set by Native Americans, many other fires, especially during the summer months, were ignited by lighting (Howe 1994). Whatever the source, the burns created a mosaic of grassland successional stages throughout the prairie. After the burns many grasses grew more vigorously and were more nutritious, and flowering increased in many prairie forbs (Risser et al. 1981).

Once grassland fires were suppressed, the grassland biome began to change. Trees invaded the prairie, especially in the eastern regions, which were always a battle zone between forests and grasslands. In other areas species that benefited from fires, such as the blowout penstemon, rapidly declined to the point where they were thought to be extinct (U.S. Fish and Wildlife Service 1992).

Many of the detrimental effects of fire suppression have been documented but are still poorly understood. Johnson and Temple (1990) found that nest success of prairie passerines was lower in grasslands that had not been burned within the past three years, and Kirsch and Higgins (1976) found lower nest success for upland sandpipers on unburned grasslands. Numerous factors may be at work in these situations; burned grasslands may provide better nesting cover because the growth is ranker, or the greater seed and insect production in recently burned grassland may afford incubating birds more time to attend their nests, or the greater food availability may increase prey abundance that helps to buffer predation on nesting passerines.

Scientists now recognize the importance fire plays in a prairie ecosystem. Unfortunately, attempts to conduct burns on small remnant prairies, especially those in populated regions, are often thwarted by expense, liability issues, or neighbors concerned about smoke and wildfires. Even when prescribed fires are conducted on small remnant prairies, however, they can have unforeseen harmful effects if not managed properly. The smaller the remnant, the less margin for error. For example, a small prairie preserve in western Minnesota was "managed" with an intensive burn regime intended to promote floral diversity and vigor, but over time it became apparent that the regime was too intensive for the Dakota skipper butterfly. Hence skipper numbers declined dramatically at the site. Similarly, Howe (1994) noted that many remnant tallgrass preserves are managed with hot spring or fall dormant season burns whereas under historical conditions (vast tracts of contiguous prairie) cooler midsummer lightning burns may have played a more significant role. One advantage of larger prairie tracts is that they are more forgiving of these mistakes and allow for a greater variety of burns in which to test hypotheses. They are also less likely to be frustrated by social or political concerns.

Public Lands

It was that glorious, exhilarating season of the year known as Indian summer. . . . There were buffalo on all sides of us and mingled with them were groups of antelope grazing or playing over the hills. It was the most beautiful scene I ever beheld: an abundance of game on every side, quietly feeding or reposing in the sunshine, and at home as the Great Creator placed them.

J. R. Mead, *Hunting and Trading on the Great Plains, 1859–1875*

Generally speaking, the protection and conservation of our grassland heritage rests with numerous federal and state agencies. These agencies, either through land they administer or by legal authority, are charged with conserving grassland biodiversity for the benefit of present and future generations. Unfortunately, these agencies and their staffs have not always been given the proper tools and laws to tackle this difficult but vital task.

The Metamorphosis of Wildlife Conservation

Wildlife management has changed dramatically since the 1930s when biologists were still wrestling with restoring game populations. A modern wildlife manager is now expected to know about everything from deer to grouse to butterflies to plants to computer models to minimum viable populations. Such a drastic transition has not come easily for some.

Over the past decade the transformation of the wildlife profession has been so spectacular that a new science called conservation biology has arisen. Perhaps the simplest distinction between the new science and conventional wildlife management is that the latter tended to concentrate on maximizing production of game animals for harvest whereas the former emphasizes conserving bio-diversity. The previous discussion of edge habitat illustrates the difference between the two philosophies. In the past, wildlife managers were often unconditional proponents of creating edge habitat because of the benefits to deer and other game species (Robinson 1988). Yet for reasons I have outlined at length, conservation biologists tend to discourage anthropogenic edge habitats. Such an extraordinary reversal in a long-held orthodoxy does not come easily.

Songbird management in the grassland biome is another case in point. Grassland ecosystems are characterized by having relatively few bird species. For example, Wiens and Dyer (1975) found that local prairie bird communities (25-acre plots) averaged 4.1 species in tallgrass prairies, 4.7 species in mixed-grass prairies, and 4.3 species in shortgrass prairies. Yet wildlife management has traditionally striven for lengthy bird lists. In the past many area managers tried to convert "unproductive" grasslands into Garden of Eden habitats by planting trees and shrubs. But conserving grassland biodiversity requires exactly the opposite mentality. It seems a paradox, but as Samson and Knopf (1982, 429) noted, conservation of native biological diversity often demands that resource managers "minimize practices promoting site-specific diversity" in favor of those that promote only endemic species. Similarly, Robinson (1988, 153) recommended that managers "develop management plans centered around native habitat specialists" (e.g., Baird's sparrow, black-footed ferret) in contrast to those centered on habitat generalists (e.g., white-tailed deer, pheasants).

Another significant difference between traditional wildlife management and the new science of conservation biology is their time frames. As Landres (1992) pointed out, most wildlife management plans by state and federal agencies operate on three- to ten-year horizons at best. In contrast, conservation biology is interested in decades or centuries. Such long time frames are more in tune with ecological processes and may provide valuable political spinoffs. As Frankel (1974, 63) wrote, "An evolutionary perspective may help to give conservation a permanence which a utilitarian, and even an ecological grounding, fails to provide in men's minds."

To successfully conserve grassland biodiversity the wildlife manager must consider five topical factors:

Knowledge of pre-columbian conditions. Most wildlife professionals receive exhaustive training in wildlife management techniques but relatively little in pre-Columbian natural history. Without this knowledge they are not equipped to manage for biodiversity.

Understanding regional conditions. Site managers need to manage for conditions and processes that are not provided on nearby private lands. For example, managers in the grassland biome should generally manage for lightly grazed or ungrazed conditions, since most private lands are moderately to heavily grazed.

Managing for native flora and fauna. Invasions by exotic and alien species pose one of the most significant threats to native species. Managers should strive to eliminate alien and exotic species, including those perceived as "good."

Restoring ecological processes. The elimination or disruption of natural processes between species (e.g., wolf/coyote/red fox/swift fox) has led to the loss of biological diversity. Likewise the loss, suppression, and moderation of natural processes (e.g., fire, drought) has negatively affected the grassland ecosystem. These processes should be restored wherever possible. At the same time, management practices and strategies that are artificial should be deemphasized.

Designing and implementing long-term conservation strategies. Long-term planning, on the order of twenty-five to one hundred years or more, better considers ecological and evolutionary processes. Long-term planning also inculcates an intergenerational ethic and obligation.

Since I have been somewhat critical of past management practices, I need to point out that traditional wildlife management was often simply responding to the values and desires of society at the time. As Kellert (1985, 528) noted, the "technological emphasis (of past management efforts) probably reflects an expedient response to the political pressures of a Congress and public that demand immediate remedial action rather than fundamental and long-term social and perceptual solutions." The wildlife profession, Congress, and society all need to shift their thinking from myopic tactics to long-term and permanent solutions. These solutions, in terms of biodiversity conservation, will often center on our public lands.

Several government agencies, all with different missions and policies, administer the public lands and wildlife resources in the Great Plains (table 1). Unfortunately, the differing and often conflicting missions seriously compromise meaningful efforts at coordinating long-term conservation strategies (U.S. Office of Technology Assessment 1987). Yet even if these agencies did mount a coordinated effort to conserve grassland biodiversity, they would likely still come up short in many efforts, for reasons I shall explain in further detail.

Table 1. Federal Ownership in the Great Plains (Acres)

Agency	Tallgrass	Mixed-Grass	Shortgrass	Total
Fish and Wildlife Service	166,599	1,070,698	409,891	1,647,188
	(0.2%)	(0.6%)	(0.2%)	(0.4%)
Forest Service	28,205	758,925	6,494,034	7,281,164
	(0.0%)	(0.5%)	(3.4%)	(1.7%)
Bureau of Land Management	65	880,978	7,922,762	8,803,805
	(0.0%)	(0.5%)	(4.2%)	(2.0%)
National Park Service	0	38,377	295,826	334,203
	(0.0%)	(0.0%)	(0.2%)	(0.1%)
Total	194,869	2,748,978	15,122,513	18,066,360
	(0.2%)	(1.6%)	(7.9%)	(4.2%)

Source: Fish and Wildlife Service and Bureau of Land Management values from unpublished data provided by the agencies. Forest Service values from U.S. Forest Service (1994). National Park Service values from National Park Service (1991).

In addition to the agencies soon to be discussed, the federal government has many other land-administering agencies in the Great Plains. The Farmers Home Administration holds lands that are in default by farmers and ranchers. FHA acreage will likely remain high in the future; as many as 40 percent of the farmers with FHA loans are delinquent in some grassland states. Significant amounts of federal land are also held by the Department of Defense. Some of these lands will be disposed of in the near future as the nation continues to close military bases. Department of Defense lands provide habitat for a surprisingly large number of endangered and threatened species (Flather, Joyce, and Bloomgarden 1994). Similarly, the Army Corps of Engineers administers considerable land along the Missouri and other major rivers in the region. The Bureau of Indian Affairs also administers large amounts of land in the grassland biome in conjunction with local tribes. Because these lands are typically some of the poorest for farming, many are still covered by native vegetation and would be valuable for restoring grassland biodiversity. However, owing to space limitations I will restrict the discussion to the most prominent natural resource agencies in the Great Plains.

U.S. Fish and Wildlife Service

Originally known as the Biological Survey and then as the Bureau of Sport Fisheries and Wildlife, the U.S. Fish and Wildlife Service (called the Service) has changed remarkably since the days when its primary purpose in the Great Plains was to eradicate the gray wolf. As evidence of that, the Service is now the agency charged with protecting and restoring endangered species, including the wolf. In addition to overseeing endangered species, the Service is also responsible for conserving waterfowl populations, an especially important mission in the grassland biome. Indeed, waterfowl garner the bulk of the Service's attention in the region, especially in terms of land acquisition. As a result of that emphasis, most acquisition by the Service has centered on marshes and sloughs. Only in the past few years has it begun acquiring large refuges dedicated primarily to conserving grassland flora and fauna.

This is meant to be not a condemnation of efforts to conserve waterfowl but rather a critical commentary on the lack of grassland conservation. Indeed, waterfowl warrant and deserve special attention because hunters' dollars, in the form of duck stamps, were used to acquire many Service tracts. But it is unsettling that current waterfowl management tactics may not be the most effective and may in some cases hinder the long-term recovery of waterfowl and many other species.

Whereas other federal agencies were granted large acreage as part of massive government programs or acquisitions, the Service has had to purchase most of the lands it now administers from private parties. Because the Service is limited to paying only market value (which has no relation to the ecologic value), and because of the difficulty of coordinating purchases among several adjacent landowners, many of the Service acquisitions were only a few hundred acres. Many of these parcels were subsequently designated Waterfowl Production Areas (WPAS). The Service now administers over 235,000 acres of scattered WPAS in North Dakota alone. Intended for waterfowl, these sites usually consist of a wetland or small wetland complex isolated in an agrarian landscape.

A second waterfowl management technique the Service relies on is purchasing easements to protect habitat on private lands. Easements are legal restrictions placed on landowners to prevent wetland drainage, conversion of grassland, or other activities. As of 30 September 1993 the Service had accumulated 1,543,717 acres of easements in the Dakotas, Montana, and Minnesota. Similar private lands programs include extension agreements and piggyback leases (on farm program set-aside lands), which occur on another 250,000 acres in the region.

Like WPAS, easements often consist of a large wetland isolated within an agrarian landscape. Unlike WPAS and other lands acquired in fee title, however, easements often provide only short-term habitat protection, making their value questionable on a cost-benefit basis. For example, it was found that twenty-year easements in North and South Dakota merely delayed wetland drainage (Higgins and Woodward 1986). The same researchers concluded that there was little price difference between short-term easements and fee title purchases, that resource agencies should offer only perpetual easements or fee title purchases, and that "protection of wetland resources should be viewed in terms of many decades and generations and not in the short term" (232).

The distribution of countless easements, WPAS, and national wildlife refuges throughout the Prairie Pothole Region often fuels a perception by rural residents and local governments that the federal government is taking over. Such concerns are somewhat understandable. The Service now owns or leases 1.4 million scattered acres in North Dakota alone, mostly in the Prairie Pothole Region in the center of the state. Excluding the shortgrass counties in western North Dakota and the heavily cultivated and drained counties along the eastern border, the Service controls 5.1 percent (1.3 million acres) of the remaining thirty-two counties. In some counties, such as Kidder and Burke, the Service either owns or has easements on more than 8 percent of the land. And in some townships (an area of thirty-six square miles), such as Lowenthal and Strassburg, easements cover 75 percent. The short-term benefits gained by easements must be weighed against not only the monetary costs, but also the political and social perceptions.

Unfortunately these scattered WPAS, small refuges, and easements often are only marginally effective for the species they are intended to protect—waterfowl. For example, it has been found that WPAS have lower nest success (8.2 percent) than Farm Program set-aside tracts (23.1 percent [Kantrud 1993]). In retrospect this is not surprising, nor should it be interpreted as a glowing recommendation for farm set-asides. That farm set-asides produce higher waterfowl nest success than WPAS is likely due to two factors: farm set-asides have more upland nesting cover (grassland) than WPAS, and farm set-asides are farther from brood-rearing wetlands and therefore less likely to be searched by predators. Another study found that the number of ducks taken by red fox families is often highest on areas managed by the Service for waterfowl (Sargeant, Allen, and Eberhardt 1984). As Greenwood (1981, 759) elucidated, predators have a high chance of encountering nesting waterfowl on WPAS "because in many parts of the Prairie Pothole Region isolated federal and state-managed areas provide virtually the only remaining waterfowl nesting habitat." Hence both waterfowl and predators home in on these sites, so that they act as population sinks for ducks.

Loss of wetlands, the common lament during the middle of the century, has undoubtedly played a role in the decline of waterfowl, but it does not single-handedly explain it. In fact the loss of wetlands may not even be the major reason for our dwindling waterfowl populations (Johnson and Shaffer 1987). The disappearance and fragmentation of large tracts of grassland nesting habitat appear to be the greatest cause for the decline. Further proof is that the species most dependent on large, contiguous grasslands, the northern pintail, has declined the most (75 percent since the mid-1950s). Pintails' nesting strategy is to select grassy sites great distances from water, typically 0.6 to 1.2 miles (Duncan 1987).

Compounding the problem of small size and inadequate nesting cover, the grass that does occur on Service lands is often compromised for political reasons. For example, livestock grazing can be used as a management tool to improve grassland conditions, but in too many cases it appears that grazing levels are set more to appease local ranchers or politicians than to benefit wildlife. A 1989–91 review of grazing on Service lands found that 38 percent of the Service's 478 refuge system units had grazing (Coleman et al. 1990). The same study found that 42 percent of the refuge managers acknowledged that current grazing leases were harmful, with degraded nesting cover the major concern. Kirby et al. (1992) perceptively observed that cattle grazing on refuge lands also had negative aesthetic effects. They found the naturalness of many refuges compromised by the presence of cattle and, one can assume, cattle trails, watering tanks, supplemental feeders, a network of fences, and so on. They suggested that "one unexplored avenue for modifying the plant community to achieve specific objectives may be the judicious use of native grazing herbivores" (622). One way to make the use of native grazing herbivores—bison—more logistically feasible is for the Service to expand and consolidate its properties.

These arguments are not meant to discredit past efforts by Service employees. Without their hard work and dedication, the present waterfowl situation would likely be even worse. And with only limited funding, authority, and vision from Washington DC there was only so much they could do. But the strategy of minutely integrating waterfowl habitat into intensively farmed areas has proved dubious. Wall maps with hundreds or thousands of widely distributed pushpins denoting waterfowl production lands are an impressive sight, stimulating idyllic visions of waterfowl flourishing side by side with cropland, but we now know that for waterfowl and many other species such a relationship is marginal at best. Society will need to acknowledge that the highest (natural) waterfowl recruitment will occur not across the street from a farmstead but over the horizon. Metaphorically speaking, waterfowl managers and conservationists need to reconsider the fine-pellet shotgun approach toward land acquisition in favor of a coarse-pellet pattern.

In the past the argument used for the small tract approach to habitat acquisition is that it was the only means politically possible. But at the same time the strategy was politically damaging. Every new acquisition, no matter what size, stirred resentment among county commissioners, residents, and farmers who felt threatened by the government's mushrooming and apparently insatiable presence (compounding the antagonism, many residents were already distressed because of the region's economic and demographic woes). They saw no end to the piecemeal approach and hence felt their way of life was being insidiously destroyed. Their arguments have some merit. By acquiring countless small tracts throughout the Prairie Pothole Region, the Service was exacerbating the sparseness of rural farming communities, which inevitably led to the decline of rural towns (while paradoxically other federal agencies such as the Economic Development Administration infused massive amounts of money into rural development). Hence the relationship between the Service and some local grassland governments borders on hostile. For example, the Service's Devils Lake Wetland Management District in northeastern North Dakota has been called the "Vietnam of the wetland wars." The analogy is more accurate than it first appears. Like the military when involved in Vietnam, the Service apparently has no clear long-term strategies except to keep pouring in more money and more manpower.

Meanwhile rare grassland species have been comparatively ignored in the Service's acquisition efforts. According to the U.S. General Accounting Office (1994), the only Great Plains refuge that provides a significant portion of the habitat of an endangered or threatened species is the Charles M. Russel refuge in Montana, where black-footed ferrets were recently reintroduced. The only refuge established in the Great Plains specifically for a listed species is the 1,063-acre Karl E. Mundt refuge in the forested Missouri River floodplain along the Nebraska–South Dakota border, which provides roosting habitat for bald eagles.

But there are reasons to feel encouraged. A tallgrass refuge (albeit small) has been established just southeast of Des Moines, Iowa. Restoring the ecosystem will necessitate (re)creating prairie on abandoned farmland, yet the Service has admirably taken on the challenge. And a Northern Tallgrass Prairie Refuge is being considered for western Minnesota. Such formidable tasks are made more difficult by the prevailing perception that valuable and much needed farmland is being taken out of production, a misconception I shall examine later.

Large contiguous blocks of grassland, with a full (or mostly full) complement of grassland species, represent the best opportunity to conserve grassland biodiversity. Research by the Service's own biologists has demonstrated that large contiguous complexes of grassland and wetlands, with the presence of upper-level predators, have the highest waterfowl productivity (Greenwood et al. 1987). Large wetland complexes also benefit many other birds. A study in Iowa found that they supported more bird species than large isolated wetlands (Brown and Dinsmore 1986). And researchers in North Dakota concluded that the best conservation strategy for marbled godwits was to use an ecosystem approach that conserved "wetland complexes, as opposed to the acquisition of single, large, more permanent ponds" (Ryan, Renken, and Dinsmore 1984, 1216). In a study of Waterfowl Production Areas in the Prairie Pothole Region, Niesar (1994, ii) concluded that biodiversity would benefit most if the government would purchase as large an area as possible for waterfowl production.

U.S. Forest Service

Herbert Hoover's secretary of agriculture, Arthur Hyde, was all in favor of what he called "a new epic" of land retirement. After the hard lessons of the 1930s Dust Bowl, it was proposed that the United States government acquire a minimum of 125 million acres of submarginal farmland, mostly in the Great Plains, and permanently retire it from cultivation (Matthews 1992). Of the proposed 125 million acres, only 11.3 million were actually acquired. And of those only 3.8 million were transferred to the U.S. Forest Service to be managed as national grasslands. Although apparently a vast acreage, those lands are generally inadequate to ensure the protection of the black-footed ferret, the mountain plover, and the western prairie fringed orchid, among other species. The reasons are manifold, but two are prominent: the lands are too fragmented and the Forest Service is forced to operate under conflicting policies and regulations directing a "multiple-use" approach for the national forests and grasslands. Unfortunately, multiple use, as currently defined and practiced, is impossible.

The current Forest Service interpretation of multiple use is to try to accommodate every activity on every piece of land. Yet the Forest Service, and more specifically the United States Congress, needs to realize that many demands on the national grasslands are simply incompatible. For example, high levels of oil exploration are generally perceived as incompatible with bighorn sheep populations; wilderness experiences and barbed wire fences are inharmonious and contradictory; and cattle grazing compromises quality hunting experiences in otherwise pristine grasslands.

Of the various groups that are allowed to exploit the national grasslands, the most ubiquitous and controversial is the grazing industry. Virtually every acre of the 3.64 million acres of national grasslands in the grassland biome is grazed to some degree, yet I have already described the effects of grazing in detail and need not repeat them here. What do warrant further discussion, however, are the indirect effects of grazing on public lands. To maximize profits, many public land graziers directly or indirectly eradicate or diminish prairie dog communities, kill raptors and other native species perceived as pests, introduce exotic species, and prevent or devalue many environmental and conservation initiatives. Collectively these effects may be more harmful to grassland ecosystems than all but the most severe overgrazing.

For example, at the urging of grazing associations the Forest Service actively controls prairie dogs, or subsidizes others to control them, even though prairie dogs may benefit cattle (Knowles 1986) and cost-benefit analyses have shown that government agencies do not profit from the practice (Collins, Workman, and Uresk 1984). Yet to accommodate the demands of the industry the internal Forest Service guidelines recommend that prairie dogs be controlled when they threaten primary range (range of superior forage quality) or when there is a potential for them to spread to private lands. The latter is virtually unavoidable whenever public lands are intermingled with private lands, as are the national grasslands. This relegation of prairie dogs to only poor range, and only the largest grassland fragments, severely lessens the value of the public lands for biodiversity conservation.

Even the range "improvements" conducted by public lands graziers are often detrimental to grassland biodiversity. For example, many grass plantings consist of exotic species such as crested wheatgrass (*Agropyron cristatum*) and brome that outcompete and displace native flora. And unlike native grasses, the

exotics do not cure well in situ, a serious shortcoming for native ungulates trying to survive harsh winters. As another example, artificial watering structures
built for cattle attract and support nonindigenous species in an arid environment
(though populations of native species do not really need the water, they may
make use of it), facilitate disease transmission, and directly cause mortality of
grassland birds (Chilgren 1979). Cooperrider (1990) noted that the primary purpose of most rangeland rehabilitation projects has been restoration of livestock
forage and that such projects typically reduce diversity of plant and animal species.

Yet of all the factors that limit the Forest Service's ability to conserve grassland biodiversity, none is as significant as the problem of intermingled public
and private land. Fragmentation of the national grasslands is a by-product of the
way the lands were acquired back in the 1930s and 1940s. Although large blocks
of land were marked for federal acquisition, some landholders did not need or
wish to sell. Understandably, they were not forced to. But in some cases it appears that though all landholders were willing to sell, Congress did not release
the funds necessary to complete the transaction. Hurt (1986, 99) quotes an ad-
ministrator of one of the acquisition projects who stated that "the federal government could purchase 'practically every privately owned acre' within one or
two years, if funds were available."

The 3.64 million national grassland acres in the grassland biome are found in
1,398 noncontiguous blocks (table 2). More telling, the area-to-perimeter ratio
of these blocks is only 2.33:1. Another way of looking at this is that the effective
administrative area of the typical fragment of disjunct national grassland is only
2.96 square miles.

A map of the central United States delineating the location and perimeter
(acquisition boundary) of the national grasslands (map 4) reveals what a golden
opportunity was missed in the 1930s and 1940s. The proposed acquisition
boundaries of the various national grasslands are comparable in size to Yellowstone National Park and in some cases larger.

The deleterious effects of ecological fragmentation have already been discussed in detail, but the administrative problems associated with numerous
small fragmented tracts of land warrant additional attention. Fragmentation of
public lands precludes or frustrates many conservation initiatives such as species reintroductions. For example, the reintroduction of black-footed ferrets
has been hindered by private landowners at Great Plains reintroduction sites.
Likewise, fragmentation makes it difficult to implement controlled burns and

Table 2. National Grasslands in the Great Plains

Grasslands[a]	Acres in National Grasslands System[b]	Perimeter (miles)[c]	Area (square miles) /Perimeter (miles) Ratio	Number of Fragments[c]	Median Size of Fragments (acres)[c]
Little Missouri	1,028,061	3,312.50	1:2.06	283	320
Buffalo Gap	595,673	1,720.75	1:1.85	112	320
Fort Pierre	115,997	380.75	1:2.10	19	320
Sheyenne	70,268	193.00	1:1.76	10	1,760
Cedar River	6,717	58.50	1:5.57	18	320
Cimarron	108,175	336.50	1:1.99	43	160
Black Kettle	31,286	265.50	1:5.43	69	160
Rita Blanca	92,989	408.00	1:2.80	74	480
Kiowa	136,417	602.25	1:2.83	54	320
Pawnee	193,060	870.75	1:2.89	131	320
Comanche	435,319	1,548.00	1:2.28	118	360
Thunder Basin	572,211	2,594.75	1:2.90	410	80
Oglala	94,480	298.50	1:2.02	18	860
Grand River	155,075	651.50	1:2.69	38	280
McClelland Creek	1,449	7.50	1:3.31	1	1,449
Total	3,637,177	13,248.75	1:2.33[d]	1,398	320[d]

[a]Excluded are Lyndon B. Johnson and Caddo National Grasslands in Texas, Crooked River National Grassland in Oregon, and Curlew National Grassland in Idaho.

[b]Acreage includes only National Grassland acreage (not National Forest or other designations) within the National Forest system in the Great Plains and Prairies (U.S. Forest Service 1994).

[c]Perimeter, number of fragments, and size of fragments were calculated from National Grassland maps produced and distributed by the U.S. Forest Service. Fragments that met only at the corners were considered separate fragments.

[d]Weighted total.

other management practices. Public land fragmentation compromises the recreational potential of the land by not providing the backcountry experiences that many recreationist desire. Last, fragmentation of public lands increases the cost of management. Currently, a large portion of a Forest Service employee's time is spent simply driving from one disjunct tract to another. Many sites rarely get visited at all. The large amount of boundary also demands much administrative and enforcement time, and increases the potential for disputes. Like the U.S. Fish and Wildlife Service, Bureau of Land Management, and many other federal agencies, the Forest Service will be forced to make dramatic reductions in

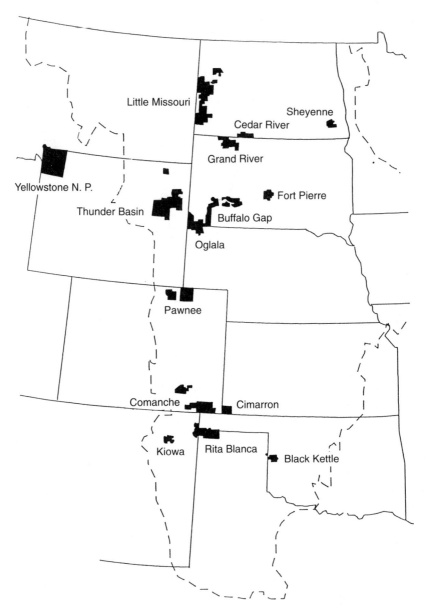

Little Missouri

Sheyenne

Cedar River

Grand River

Yellowstone N. P.

Thunder Basin

Fort Pierre

Buffalo Gap

Oglala

Pawnee

Comanche

Cimarron

Kiowa

Rita Blanca

Black Kettle

Map 4. National grasslands (and Yellowstone National Park for size comparison). Modified from U.S. Forest Service (1994).

personnel over the next several years. Executive orders signed by President Clinton in February and September 1993 call for a reduction of 100,000 federal positions by fiscal year 1995 and a total reduction of 252,000 positions by the end of 1999. These reductions will decrease Forest Service personnel by 12 percent, approximately 4,200 employees. Experiences suggests that a great many of these cuts will occur in the wildlife program.

There is one strategy that addresses the problem of declining government funds and declining biodiversity on national grasslands. That strategy is for the Forest Service to begin consolidating its landholdings, in which case management would benefit from economies of scale. The Forest Service already has the authority to consolidate its landownership by conducting land exchanges with private parties under the General Exchange Act of 1922, the Weeks Law of 1911, and several other pieces of legislation. In addition, numerous other authorities grant the Forest Service the ability to acquire private properties under its Land Acquisition Program.

To date the Forest Service has shown little inclination to ambitiously consolidate the national grasslands. From an ecological perspective, consolidation would greatly enhance the long-term conservation of grassland biodiversity, even if the consolidation resulted in a net decrease in federal ownership. From an administrative perspective, consolidation would decrease the travel time of Forest Service employees and lessen boundary disputes with private landowners. From a recreational perspective, the consolidation of public lands would be a first step in restoring wilderness values to the prairie ecosystem.

Bureau of Land Management

The Bureau of Land Management (BLM) is the largest land administering agency in the federal government, overseeing more than 272 million acres, or approximately 48 percent of all federal lands in the United States. Most of these lands are west of the Great Plains; still, there are significant amounts in the grassland biome, especially in Montana and Wyoming.

Many of the issues concerning the previously mentioned federal agencies (e.g., fragmentation, multiple-use approach) also apply to the BLM, but a few additional points can be made about BLM ownership in the grassland biome.

In spite of the Bureau's administering almost 9 million acres in the grassland biome, BLM lands produce comparatively few recreational experiences. This is in part because of the multiple-use approach where cattle, mining, and other industrial uses are allowed, and in part because of the fragmented nature of the lands. In addition, BLM lands get relatively little recreational use because few people know where they are. This great resource of public land is underused largely because the land is too hard to find. Also, some BLM lands are not used by the public because access is blocked by private lands. In these cases the public lands essentially become the exclusive domain of adjacent landowners.

BLM lands are for the most part leftovers from the public domain (many BLM lands in Montana are an exception—they were purchased during the resettlement programs of the 1930s and 1940s). They are lands that nobody wanted because they had little commercial value, are often arid and inhospitable, and are difficult to reach. For the most part they are poorly surveyed and rarely marked with proper signage.

Should the federal government choose to dispose of many of the isolated and inaccessible tracts in exchange for consolidating its ownership at more accessible sites, such a restructuring would benefit recreational users, the agency, and grassland biodiversity. And since the currently scattered BLM tracts have little commercial value other than for grazing—a use that is already being exploited—they could readily be transferred to private ownership with little loss of biodiversity values.

Last, it is interesting to note that the BLM is part of the Department of the Interior, along with the U.S. Fish and Wildlife Service and the National Park Service. The Department has chosen as its symbol the bison, perhaps the most characteristic of all of North America's fauna and definitely the symbol of the Great Plains. Yet the Department, although it administers almost 10.8 million acres of "wildlife habitat" within the grassland biome, manages only about two thousand bison—about one animal for every 8.4 square miles.

National Park Service

Nationwide, the National Park Service administers over 80 million acres, or about 3.5 percent of the United States land base. About 267 million recreational visits are made annually to the national parks. And a 1988 survey found over 120 endangered or threatened species occurring, or suspected to occur, in more than 140 units of the park system (U.S. National Park Service n.d.). The national park system is truly a national treasure and a legacy of the vision of the great conservationists such as Theodore Roosevelt, John Muir, and others.

However, the National Park Service's role in the Great Plains is more noteworthy for its absence than for its presence. Only two national parks exist within the grassland biome, and both are in the northern shortgrass region. But even those two Great Plains parks do not truly represent the grassland ecosystem. They comprise more rugged and hilly badlands country than Great Plains rolling prairie. The two parks, Theodore Roosevelt National Park in North Dakota and Badlands National Park in South Dakota, are also inadequate because they are not large enough to truly preserve a grassland ecosystem (70,447 acres in two units and 242,756 acres in two units, respectively). For example, the establishment of bighorn sheep in Theodore Roosevelt National Park has failed, possibly because of disease transmission from domestic animals outside the park. Meanwhile, Badlands National Park provides ideal habitat for restoration and conservation of the black-footed ferret and swift fox, but not enough to support viable populations.

At present it appears that the only way the National Park Service lands within the Great Plains can play a significant role in protecting biodiversity is by using the lands as seed from which to create larger protective areas. Because the two shortgrass prairie parks are adjacent to substantial tracts of other public lands, the potential exists to do just that.

State Agencies

Missouri is arguably the most progressive of the grassland states in terms of biodiversity conservation. The state's efforts are guided by a document titled *The Biodiversity of Missouri* (Missouri Department of Conservation 1992). In addition to recognizing the threat to the biodiversity of the state, the document is bold enough to acknowledge that a piecemeal and technological approach to conserving biodiversity is inadequate. The document states that "long-term maintenance of biodiversity can best be achieved by a network of biological reserves. . . . large areas are necessary because conservation of habitats for individual species, or even for single, isolated communities, may overlook processes necessary to the conservation of biological diversity. Large areas . . . allow natural processes, disturbance regimes, and management activities to affect landscapes as they did in pre-settlement times . . . minimize edge effects [and] meet the needs of wide-ranging animals" (45, 46). This acknowledgment by a government entity of the needs and complexity of biodiversity protection is encouraging. The Missouri plan also recognizes that "it is more cost-effective to manage a single large, complex area than many small, widespread areas" (46).

Perhaps the greatest obstacle to state biodiversity conservation efforts is that most states simply have insufficient and poorly distributed land to work with. For example, the North Dakota Game and Fish Department administers 80,180

97

fee title acres as Wildlife Management Areas. Yet this acreage, equal to 125 square miles, is distributed among 134 sites, meaning the average area per site is only 598 acres. The Nebraska Game and Parks Commission administers 116,039 acres of Wildlife Management Areas, but these are distributed among 140 sites averaging 829 acres. As I have noted, such small tracts are often inadequate for long-term conservation. Even the best-intentioned management efforts can be thwarted by the small size of the tracts (Herkert 1994a). And it is important to remember that many of these sites were acquired with funds from hunters, who would likely resist attempts to remove tree plantings (habitat for deer and pheasants) for the benefit of grassland biodiversity.

As the values and philosophies of society change, so do the missions and operations of state agencies. Nielsen and McMullin (1992) predicted that in the year 2020 state agencies will differ markedly from today's agencies. They felt that in the future many state agencies will be emphasizing nonconsumptive uses of wildlife, that general tax revenues will be used to fund the agencies' operations, and that agencies will use a more holistic approach to natural resource issues. These predictions seem realistic; indeed, they are already starting to take place in some prairie states. But the unsettling truth is that even with these philosophical and administrative changes, the conservation of the grassland ecosystem cannot be ensured until sufficiently large tracts of land have been set aside for such a purpose.

Conservation and Private Lands

When we conclude that we must bait the farmer with subsidies to induce
him to raise a forest, or with gate receipts to induce him to raise game, we
are merely admitting that the pleasures of husbandry-in-the-wild are as
yet unknown both to the farmer and to ourselves.

Aldo Leopold, *A Sand County Almanac*

Aldo Leopold is commonly regarded as the father of modern wildlife management, in large part because of his seminal work *Game Management* (Leopold
1933). *Game Management* is a cookbook of techniques and principles that can
be used to produce more deer, rabbits, pheasants, and other game species on
private lands. At the time Leopold wrote many of these species were in short
supply, so the book was much needed. Unfortunately, many people have misunderstood his views on private lands. Leopold recognized that private lands
were critical to the production of many game species and also some nongame
species, but he never implied that true biodiversity conservation could take
place on private lands. In fact he advocated just the opposite.

Leopold's more lasting legacy is the 1949 classic *A Sand County Almanac*
(Leopold 1966). *A Sand County Almanac* is for all intents and purposes an ecosystem book, a biodiversity book, and a wilderness book rolled into one. It is
also his most eloquent and philosophical treatise, working into the equation of
wildlife management such concepts as ethics, aesthetics, and naturalness.
Throughout his career, and especially in his later years, Leopold was a passion-
ate advocate of preserving large tracts of public lands for wildlife. Leopold recognized that there were limits to what could be produced on private lands and
limits to what professional wildlife management could do.

99

It is highly unlikely that the long-term conservation of grassland biodiversity can occur solely on private lands, or even on public lands that are significantly intermingled with those in private ownership or compromised by commercial interests. There are simply too many human-caused effects, too few natural ones, and too much ignorance.

In spite of fifty years of modern scientific research, we still know very little about biodiversity, ecological functions, evolutionary processes, population dynamics, environmental influences, and so on. For example, in the Great Plains nematodes, not bison or prairie dogs, may actually be the predominant grazers in terms of vegetative biomass consumed. Yet we know next to nothing about these soil species. And even apparently insignificant species such as mycorrhizal fungi may turn out to be keystone species on rangeland ecosystems, essential to big bluestem and other grasses and vital to rare plants such as the western prairie fringed orchid (U.S. Fish and Wildlife Service 1994). In human-altered landscapes we are often forced to replace natural processes with artificial ones in order to maintain species, yet to suggest that we can identify and manage for these processes, and the creatures they sustain, denies the complexity of natural systems.

Even exhaustively studied management issues such as grazing continue to confound wildlife professionals. This is partly because they typically distill management to a few simple rules, yet natural systems vary greatly in both space and time. A bird species that responds negatively to heavy grazing at one site may respond positively at another. Plant species such as the western prairie fringed orchid are negatively affected by heavy grazing, whereas others such as blowout penstemon may benefit. Attempting to present all this information to ranchers, politicians, and others is a losing proposition. Any wildlife agency that tries to coordinate grazing regimes across a vast landscape is perceived as arbitrary and capricious.

Another commercial use of private lands in the Great Plains is haying. To many people haying seems superficially similar to grazing, but in practice it is often much more deleterious. For example, waterfowl frequently nest in hayfields but inevitably sustain high nest failures because of haying operations (Klett, Shaffer, and Johnson 1988). One study in an intensively farmed area of North Dakota found that farm work destroyed 49 percent of northern pintail nests (Higgins 1977). The conventional solution to this problem is for government agencies to pay farmers to delay haying until after July 15. That may be fine for waterfowl and some other ground-nesting birds, but it can be catastrophic for some prairie butterfly species. It can also be counterproductive on native grasslands that are being invaded by exotic grasses. For example, a Nebraska study found that repeated late-season haying favored exotic species such as brome grass whereas less frequent early summer haying favored warm-season native grasses such as big bluestem (Boettcher and Bragg 1989). In other words, the haying regime that favors ground-nesting birds may be deleterious to native vegetation. Compounding the problem, new varieties of alfalfa and other hay crops are being developed that mature earlier in the growing season. So whereas haying traditionally did not start until August in the northern United States, now the first cuttings occur in June or even May. The incentive payments to counter the impact of haying will have to get proportionately larger as varieties of hay become more and more productive.

Another wildlife management strategy on private lands is to subsidize no-till farming. In no-till (or minimum-till) farmers do not plow after harvest or before planting, leaving stubble and other debris on the fields. Birds do tend to nest at higher rates in these areas than in conventionally plowed fields, but they are not necessarily more productive. A study in Iowa (Basore, Best, and Wooley 1986) found that nest predation in no-till fields was very high and that productivity was probably below that necessary to maintain viable bird populations; thus conservation tillage practices may produce "ecological traps." Although no-till and minimum-till may be good soil conservation practices, they cannot be relied on to conserve bird populations.

As noted earlier, artificial woody plantings can inflict great damage on native grassland biodiversity. However, trees and shrubs provide important psychological and environmental benefits to arid-land residents. They also attract many wildlife species valued by humans, such as white-tailed deer and pheasants. From the human perspective, a convincing argument can be made that shelterbelts and other woody plantings are not only desirable but necessary. Yet they are often deleterious to grassland biodiversity.

And there are of course numerous other factors present in agrarian landscapes that are impossible to avoid or mitigate. Roads are always going to be necessary, dogs and cats are always going to be present, human disturbance will be frequent, and development is always going to be threatening. Pesticides will likely always be used, and people will always be introducing exotic species.

But let us suppose for a second that conservation of grassland biodiversity depended solely on private lands. How would we approach it? It seems obvious and inevitable that it would be a piecemeal affair. Any attempt at conserving biodiversity on private lands (e.g., eliminating shelterbelts) would soon find that some landowners would cooperate, but many others would not. Other government agencies with conflicting missions (e.g., Natural Resources Conservation Service) may also oppose the initiative. So right away we are forced to eliminate many tracts from the initiative. The ecosystem approach has already become fragmented. From there we move on to the next issue, perhaps grazing and haying. The practices should include the constraints mentioned above, among others. Once again many landowners will drop out of the program, which now contains a large number of nonparticipating landowners within the designated project area.

We can safely assume that we will not reintroduce large predators into our private lands. This greatly compromises the ecosystem for reasons given earlier. Without large predators, many midsize predators will increase in abundance. Therefore, in lieu of natural predator control we are forced to implement artificial control to sustain populations of ground-nesting birds and other species. But for predator control to be effective it must extend at least two miles from the nesting habitat (Lokemoen 1984), and in most agrarian landscapes a distance of two miles will encompass several landowners, some of whom will not want to cooperate and may be actively hostile to the program.

Then there are complaints of damage from wildlife. Many landowners within the project area will care more about their property, especially crops and livestock, than about wildlife. Political pressure will force the agency to compensate for wildlife-caused damages resulting from the program. The Chase Lake Prairie Project in central North Dakota is an example of such a situation. The project is an ambitious multiagency effort to restore waterfowl populations across a vast area of public and private lands. Yet the project spends a lot of time and money to compensate or prevent wildlife damage on the private lands intermingled among the public lands. The government thus uses enormous amounts of money to restore wildlife populations and then turns around and compensates landowners damaged by that same wildlife.

An endless progression of other issues and conflicts soon dilutes the effectiveness of the private-lands conservation effort. By the time all these issues and concerns are taken into account, the ecosystem approach to grassland biodiversity conservation is for the most part business as usual.

Financial incentives can convince more landowners, but not all, to cooperate in biodiversity conservation. The practice is already widely used by wildlife management agencies. Ostensibly, many of these private lands incentive programs are designed to foster conservation practices that then become self-perpetuating as landowners see firsthand how the measures can benefit them. But they do not always succeed. Erickson and De Young (1993, 235) reported in a study of farmers' attitudes toward incentive-based conservation practices that "at best, in the absence of other motives, monetary rewards have proven to have a limited and transient effect." Aldo Leopold recognized early on that many incentive-based private lands efforts were a bottomless pit that conservationists and government agencies would do well to avoid (Brown and Carmony 1990, 174).

Federal and state agencies now acknowledge that biodiversity conservation can best be ensured on public lands. For example, the black-footed ferret recovery plan (U.S. Fish and Wildlife Service 1988a) acknowledges that private lands cannot guarantee the successful recovery of the ferret when it states that a national wildlife refuge for grassland ecology should be established (task 6222) and that habitat acquisition ensures legal control over management activities (task 2442). A U.S. Forest Service (1989c, 105) study reported that state wildlife agencies had concluded that "threatened and endangered species management could not be effective on private lands, citing landowners' lack of concern for the species, limited regulatory authority, and inadequate public understanding about the basis for the states' concern for these species."

In summary, grassland biodiversity conservation, as defined in the more comprehensive sense (genetic, taxonomic, and community processes), cannot be ensured on private lands. Only on very large tracts, the type typically associated with public ownership, can many of these species and processes continue unfettered.

But having heard that biodiversity conservation cannot be ensured on private lands, readers should not construe these statements to mean that we should ignore private-lands conservation efforts. Ecological generalists (species that live in many habitats) such as white-tailed deer, ring-necked pheasant, and cottontail rabbit (*Sylvilagus floridanus*) will continue to prosper on private lands with minimal habitat. And more important, well-managed private lands are necessary for supplementing the conservation of grassland biodiversity. Private lands managed in a sustainable and natural fashion can serve as buffer areas around public lands and as corridors connecting natural areas (Noss and Cooperrider 1994). The more the private lands replicate natural conditions, the more effectively they can fill these roles. Sound grazing remains one of the most benign commercial uses of western lands and would work well in this capacity. Technical assistance to ranchers and other private landowners who want to enhance their lands for wildlife should always be offered.

Meanwhile, society needs to accept the candid truth that if comprehensive grassland biodiversity protection is to occur, it will happen on large tracts of contiguous public lands. Society also needs to be aware that nowhere in the nation is there as much potential for restoring such tracts as in the Great Plains.

The Waning Rural Economy

In a national policy of directing land settlement due consideration should
be given to the needs, both national and local, for land to be devoted to
crops, pasture, and forests. . . . Another important consideration is the
economic value of wild life . . . [the land's] value in the natural state as
breeding places of fish, birds, and fur-bearing animals should be adequately considered. The recreational value of wild lands, as well as their
direct economic value in the wild state, should not be overlooked.

Clearly, the interests involved are too great to be left to chance. . . .
Nor can such interests be left entirely to the individual States, for it frequently appears to be to the interest of a particular State to attract settlers
from other States, with little reference to the bearing of such action on the
national needs for the various uses of land or to whether the change is for
the better from the standpoint of welfare and efficiency of the settlers.

Lewis Gray et al., *Agriculture Yearbook, 1923*

Americans pride themselves on "winning the West," but the final outcome may
not yet be determined, at least in the rural Great Plains. The government keeps
pouring resources into the arid region, yet people keep leaving, and those who
remain tend to have a standard of living below the national average.

The 625 Great Plains counties (see appendix A) have always been more
sparsely populated than the rest of the country. The most recent census (1990)
found 19.1 residents per square mile in the grassland biome compared with 65.7
for the rest of the United States and 77 when Alaska and Hawaii are excluded
(U.S. Bureau of Census 1992: see preface, "Sources and Methods Used in

105

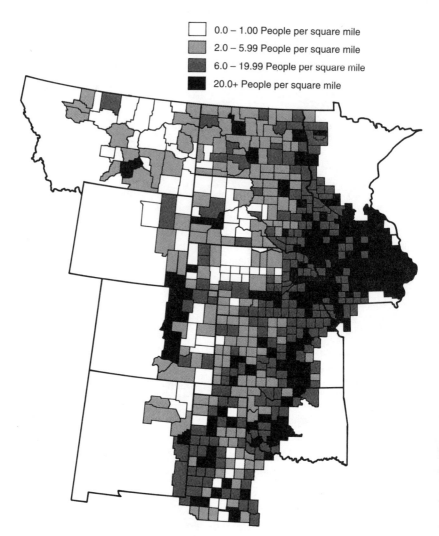

Map 5. Population density in 1990, by county. Data from U.S. Bureau of Census (1994).

Analysis"). But it is outside the region's metropolitan areas—for example, Denver, Minneapolis–St. Paul, Omaha, Des Moines, Sioux Falls, Lubbock, Fargo, and others—that the sparseness of the Great Plains is most striking.

As of 1990, 228 counties in the grassland biome (36 percent) had a population of fewer than six people per square mile (map 5). The significance of that value is that over one hundred years ago the 1890 census defined *frontier* as

Table 3. Characteristics of Rural and Urban Great Plains and National Totals

	450 Least Densely Populated Great Plains Counties	175 Most Densely Populated Great Plains Counties	National Totals
Total population (1990)	3,242,527	9,756,722	248,709,873
Land area (square miles)	542,801	136,471	3,787,425
Human density per square mile (1990)	6.0	71.5	65.7
Rate of population change, 1960–90	0.843	1.270	1.387
Median age (1990)	35.8	32.2	33.0
Percentage of persons 65 and older (1990)	17.9	12.2	12.6
Per capita money income (1987)	$9,032	$11,297	$11,923
Percentage of persons below poverty level (1989)	16.9	12.0	13.1
Direct federal payments for individuals per capita (1989)[a]	$1,971	$1,663	$1,808

[a]Population total from 1990 census.

areas with fewer than six people per square mile (Lang, Popper, and Popper 1994). Even more dramatic is that 68 counties (11 percent) had fewer than two people per square mile in 1990, the criteria the 1890 census used to identify *wilderness*. (The irony is that the pre-Columbian human populations may have ranged from one to three people per square mile in the region.)

Another way of looking at the region's human distribution is that the cumulative density of the 450 least densely populated counties, an area of over 540,000 square miles, is fewer than six people per square mile. This huge "frontier" is almost the size of Alaska, and only six times as densely populated. But unlike Alaska, the rural Great Plains are declining economically and demographically. The Great Plains, especially the 450 least densely populated counties, are arguably the largest economically and demographically distressed region in the United States and also among those most dependent on the federal government (table 3).

Trends suggest that the human sparseness of the region will continue. Although the United States population increased 38.7 percent between 1960 and 1990, the entire Great Plains population, including the metropolitan areas, grew only 12.7 percent. More pertinent, during the same period the 450 least densely populated counties lost 15.7 percent of their population (over 600,000 people).

Table 4. Characteristics of 450 Least Densely Populated (Rural) Great Plains Counties, by Ecoregion

	Tallgrass Ecoregion	Mixed-Grass Ecoregion	Shortgrass Ecoregion
Number of "rural" counties	68	226	156
Total population (1990)	681,969	1,521,313	1,039,245
Land area (square miles)	48,372	227,813	266,616
Human density per square mile (1990)	14.1	6.7	3.9
Rate of population change 1960–90	0.808	0.905	0.933
Median age (1990)	37.4	36.8	33.2
Percentage of persons 65 and older (1990)	20.2	19.4	14.2
Per capita money income (1987)	$9,534	$8,991	$8,770
Percentage of persons below poverty level (1989)	13.8	16.4	19.6
Direct federal payments for individuals per capita (1989)[a]	$2,120	$2,090	$1,700

[a]Population total from 1990 census.

All told, 72 percent of the Great Plains counties lost population between 1960 and 1990, and 83 percent of the 450 least densely populated counties did so.

The decline of Great Plains communities seems to be accelerating. Between the 1980 and 1990 censuses, 82 of Nebraska's 92 counties lost population, and in Iowa 92 of 99 counties did. Overall, 81 percent of the Great Plains counties (and 90 percent of the 450 least densely populated ones) lost population between 1980 and 1990, compared with only 51 percent in 1970–80. Platte County, Wyoming, in the shortgrass plains, led the nation in population decline between 1980 and 1990 (32 percent).

The distressed social conditions in the rural Great Plains occur across all three grassland zones. Although the tallgrass region has had the most dramatic population decline, the shortgrass region continues to have some of the highest poverty rates and lowest population densities in the nation (table 4).

The peak of settlement in the grassland biome occurred around the turn of the century. Consider that Kansas had less frontier (fewer than six people per square mile) a century ago than it does now. Likewise, North Dakota in 1890 was 86 percent frontier, in 1920 the well-settled state was only 21 percent frontier, and in 1990 the frontier was back up to 62 percent (Lang, Popper, and Popper 1994). Other trends also reflect severe long-term decline. Nebraska has at least five thousand to ten thousand deserted farmhouses (P. Brown, cited in

Popper and Popper 1994a), and Kansas has over six thousand ghost towns (D. Fitzgerald, cited in Burns 1982). Every year more and more rural schools are boarded up in the Dakotas because of shrinking enrollment.

Government forecasts suggest that the population decline will continue well into the next century. By the year 2010 populations in Iowa, North Dakota, and Nebraska are projected to be only 81, 94, and 97 percent, respectively, of what they were in 1980 (Wetrogan 1988). More significant, most if not all of the decline will take place in the rural regions, especially away from interstate highways and larger towns (Baltensperger 1991), whereas populations in urban areas will likely continue to grow.

Burns (1982) gave a brief review of why she believed small towns and rural communities in the Great Plains have collapsed. She pointed out that many towns were historically associated with railroads, and their fortunes rose or fell with the industry (towns were established every seven to ten miles along the tracks to provide water and other supplies for steam locomotives). According to Burns, other towns were eliminated in part by the creation of rural mail delivery, and the establishment of the county agricultural agent at the county seat led to the demise of still more small towns. Burns also thought internal factors—a loss of community due in part to technology and government—played a larger part than most people recognized. Granted these factors may have contributed, but the main reason for the collapse of rural communities in the Great Plains is indisputable; the region's inhospitable climate, lack of economically valuable natural resources, high transportation costs, and other factors meant that it was simply never capable of supporting numerous vibrant economies with high human densities.

Because of these and other factors the grassland states, and more specifically the rural regions of those states, have always been heavily dependent on federal subsidies to stimulate and maintain settlement. The historian Walter Prescott Webb (1931, 277) noted that as early as the 1860s "it was the West that was sucking up the capital of the nation," in reference to the subsidizing of railroads throughout the Great Plains. And 130 years later five of the top fifteen states in ratio of federal dollars received to federal revenues paid were Great Plains states (New Mexico, North Dakota, Montana, Oklahoma, South Dakota). More pertinent to the subsequent discussion, a large portion of the federal dollars paid out to state residents are farm payments. For example, almost half of the federal income taxes paid by North Dakotans go right back to the state as farm subsidies (table 5).

Table 5. Federal Income Taxes Paid and Federal Funds Received in 1992

	Approximate Federal Income Tax Revenues Paid (millions of $)	Direct Farm Subsidies Received (millions of $)	Direct Federal Funds Received (millions of $)	Ratio of Federal Farm Subsidies Received to Federal Income Taxes Paid (National Rank)
Colorado	7,400	203.2	17,332.5	0.027 (17)
Iowa	4,500	662.3	11,521.1	0.147 (5)
Kansas	4,600	592.1	11,413.0	0.129 (7)
Minnesota	9,100	422.0	17,032.8	0.046 (11)
Missouri	9,000	293.6	26,221.0	0.033 (15)
Montana	1,200	298.8	4,140.9	0.249 (2)
Nebraska	2,700	478.7	6,940.5	0.177 (4)
New Mexico	2,100	60.3	10,504.0	0.029 (16)
North Dakota	1,000	443.2	3,499.5	0.443 (1)
Oklahoma	4,600	248.3	14,502.5	0.054 (10)
South Dakota	1,100	271.9	3,380.4	0.247 (3)
Texas	32,900	1162.0	71,084.5	0.035 (14)
Wyoming	900	36.7	2,127.7	0.041 (13)

Source: Tax and farm subsidy data from Internal Revenue Service and U.S. Dept. of Agriculture (in World Almanac 1994). Federal funds received from U.S. Bureau of Census (1994).

Because of the wide open spaces, harsh climate, distance to ocean ports, scarcity of water, and other factors, business and industry, the cornerstones of America's modern economy, have always been reluctant to locate in the Great Plains. Consider that in 1987 the region had only one large manufacturing plant (defined as one hundred or more employees) for every 9,530 residents, whereas the United States average was one for every 6,721 people.

Hence the hopes of grassland economies, especially the rural economies, have always depended on agriculture. But farming has always been unpredictable and economically marginal in the region, especially compared with the moister corn belt states of Illinois, Indiana, and others. Mooers (1987) identified five wheat "booms" since the Great Plains were first settled but noted that each was followed by a bust. Owing to frequent droughts, insect plagues, hail, violent winds, and other calamities, farmers in the Great Plains consider themselves fortunate if they have three profitable years out of five. And even when they have a productive year, their output per acre is typically less than that of farmers from other parts of the country. On top of that, they are also burdened by high materials, transportation, and processing costs.

Compounding the problem of the high cost of doing business in the Plains is the declining market value of agricultural commodities. Significant excess capacity in crop production in the United States is projected to continue well into the future (Ray and Frederick 1994), meaning there is little likelihood of an increasing demand for Great Plains farmland (see below, "The Farm Program"). Agricultural exports, which once accounted for 40 percent of the United States' crop production (U.S. Forest Service 1989d), may continue to fall or remain sluggish as other countries make agricultural advances (Ray and Frederick 1994). Similarly, a worldwide decline of 0.5 percent annually in real food prices has been projected for the next several decades owing to increased yields (Waggoner 1994). The U.S. Office of Technology Assessment (1992, 147) concluded that "the emergence of biotechnology and computer technologies will most likely spur on the decline of many small farms and agriculturally dependent rural communities."

Had it not been for government subsidies to farmers, it seems certain that much less of the Great Plains would have been plowed in the first place (Huszar and Young 1984) and thus a significantly higher proportion of the region would have remained in range, a wiser and more sustainable use of the grassland ecosystem. Consider that 76 percent of the farms in Arapahoe County, Colorado, 72 percent of those in Ector County, Texas, and 63 percent of those in Thomas County, Kansas, had operating expenses that exceeded their gross sales in 1992; in other words, were it not for government payments, cultivators in many parts of the arid region would lose money. In 1992 over half the farms in forty-nine grassland counties (thirty from the shortgrass region, eighteen from the mixed-grass region, and one from the tallgrass region) were "deficit farms" when government payments are excluded from income (map 6). Heimlich and Kula (1991) observed that when government payments were excluded and fallow land was accounted for, the profits per acre for cow-calf enterprises in the Great Plains were similar to the returns for wheat production. Government programs, not the market, are largely responsible for the overcultivation of the Great Plains.

Great Plains ranching, the other leg of the region's rural economy, has generally been only marginally profitable to the individual rancher and is less significant to the country than commonly believed. This was true even during the latter part of the 1800s and early 1900s, when western cattle drives were at their peak. At that time Great Plains cattle represented only about 27 percent of the nation's herd, and when Texas was excluded, only about 15 percent (Webb

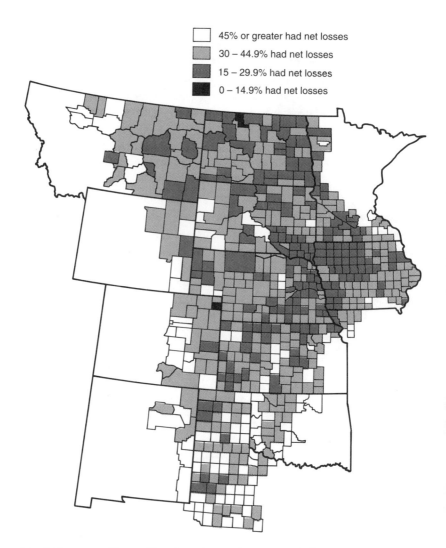

Map 6. Percentage of farms with net losses in 1992, by county, excluding government payments. Data from U.S. Bureau of Census (1995).

1931). Even today the arid shortgrass and mixed-grass Plains, the region most famous for ranching, contain less than 24 percent of the nation's beef cows.

The future of ranching, especially in the arid grasslands, appears stable at best and may even experience a gradual decline. One reason is decreasing demand. Consider that between 1976 and 1989 per capita beef consumption in the United States declined 27 percent. Even considering the expected growth in the

United States population, the projected number of beef cows in the year 2030 is only 16.6 percent greater than in 1976, and it may decline from 1976 numbers if consumption continues to fall (Gee, Joyce, and Madsen 1992).

Other changes will continue to occur in the livestock industry, possibly to the detriment of Great Plains ranchers. In the future, more cattle may be raised in feedlots rather than on the range. The size and potential of some of these operations can be staggering. Mather (1972, 257) reported one feedlot near Greeley, Colorado, that produced enough beef to feed "every man, woman, and child in the states of North Dakota, South Dakota, Wyoming, Montana, and Idaho."

Nationwide, the projected increase in rangeland between 1987 and 2040 is estimated to be only 5 percent, and most of that will occur on private lands as landowners convert cropland back to range. Rangeland in the "North and Great Plains" region of the country is predicted to decrease from 91 million acres in the year 2000 to 86 million acres in 2040 (U.S. Forest Service 1989a). Although grazing will always occur in the Great Plains simply because it is one of the best commercial uses of much of the land, it will probably not be as profitable, nor will it support numerous thriving rural economies. If rural regions of the Great Plains are to survive at anywhere near their present level, they will need economies besides traditional agriculture and ranching.

In parts of the grassland biome petroleum has supported local economies, but often in boom-and-bust cycles accompanied by social unrest and personal misery. Once-thriving oil towns from Pawhuska, Oklahoma, to Belfield, North Dakota, are now mere shells of what they were in the 1980s, with boarded-up storefronts and empty main streets as testimony to the vagaries of the industry. Long-term prosperity for oil towns in the region does not look good. As reported in a U.S. Forest Service (1989b) assessment, most of the easily recovered supplies of petroleum have been depleted.

The demand for coal, oil shale, and other hard fuels may increase in the future, bolstering some grassland economies. Large coal deposits underlie the western Dakotas–eastern Montana area and the southern tallgrass region from eastern Oklahoma–Kansas to southern Iowa and northwestern Missouri. But large-scale coal mining is an expensive proposition that may profit local communities but not the region as a whole.

The United States military has had a significant presence in parts of the Great Plains. Major bases are located in Grand Forks and Minot, North Dakota, and in Rapid City, South Dakota. But as the Department of Defense continues to downsize, its role in Great Plains economies will be reduced, adding to the economic strain of the region.

Only in the major cities of the grassland biome does the future look prosperous. Cities like Sioux Falls (computers) and Rapid City (tourism), South Dakota, Bismarck, North Dakota (government), Lincoln, Nebraska (education), Des Moines, Iowa (manufacturing), and Denver, Colorado (everything), are economically and socially vibrant. The larger cities in the grassland biome, especially those with diversified economies, will continue to see their populations increase as they attract young people from rural areas. But outside the major cities, in the small towns and rural regions, the economies and populations will likely continue to falter. The hopes and dreams of idyllic lifestyles on the prairie will continue to be refuted by the same harsh realities that have been driving homesteaders off the prairies ever since they first settled there (Popper and Popper 1994a). These lessons will be intensified as the United States government, in an effort to reduce federal deficits, cuts federal payments and benefits to the region. Describing western Oklahoma, Frank Popper says, "Like every other Plains state, this is a subsidized, exporting economy. People, oil, farm products stream out, federal subsidies for petroleum, lead and zinc, welfare, agriculture, and defense pour in. It all used to work, but not anymore" (Matthews 1992, 105).

Several states in the grassland biome now acknowledge that they need to diversify their economies, and they all claim that tourism is an untapped market. But most attempts by rural grassland communities to garner the tourism dollar are poor at best. For example, near Lander, Wyoming, local authorities are supporting an effort to create a herd of buffalo as a tourist attraction—one thousand bronze buffalo. Implicit in this proposal is the recognition that tourists want the Old West, but locals do not want to make the full commitment. Meanwhile, North Dakota is also trying to promote the Old West aura. But while it heavily advertises the wildness of the scenic Badlands, the petroleum industry is busily carving that wildness up in an attempt to drain the last drops of oil from the region.

If tourism is ever to play a significant role in reversing the economic decline of these states, the states will have to think big, they will have to think differently, and they will have to think natural. People on vacation are looking for escape, something dramatically different from their everyday civilized experience. Leopold (1966, 272) stated that "recreation is valuable in proportion to the intensity of its experiences, and to the degree to which it differs from and contrasts with workaday life." Ulrich (1983, 109), in a review of recreational preferences, noted that "one of the most clear-cut findings . . . is the consistent tendency to prefer natural scenes over built views. . . . several studies have [shown] that even unspectacular or subpar natural views elicit higher aesthetic preference . . . than do all but a very small percentage of urban views.'' The best way for Great Plains communities to entice tourists may be to promote the Great Plains themselves.

Buffalo Commons

In *The Fate of the Plains* Frank and Deborah Popper (1987a, 2) wrote, "We believe that over the next generation the Plains will, as a result of the largest, longest-running agricultural and environmental miscalculation in American history, become almost totally depopulated. Then a new use for the suddenly-empty Plains will emerge, one that is in fact so old that it predates the American presence.'' That premise summarizes their controversial prophecy of the "buffalo commons'' (Popper and Popper 1994a).

Most of the Poppers' work has concerned the area between the ninety-eighth meridian (an imaginary north-south line passing through San Antonio, Texas, and Jamestown, North Dakota) and the Rocky Mountains. This area, which many scholars consider the Great Plains or High Plains, comprises all the short-grass and most of the mixed-grass regions of the North American grasslands.

The Poppers concluded, based on an analysis of economic, demographic, and geopolitical trends, that portions of the Great Plains would gradually become depopulated. They identified 110 of the 436 counties in their study area as economically, demographically, and socially distressed and predicated that the ultimate conclusion of this emptying of the rural High Plains would be a return to a more compatible and environmentally friendly use: the Great Plains would become a buffalo commons. The Poppers envisioned 139,000 square miles of wildlife refuges in the region, making it the world's largest restoration project (Matthews 1992). All states—Montana, Wyoming, North Dakota, South Dakota, Nebraska, Kansas, Colorado, New Mexico, Oklahoma, and Texas—would be affected. The distressed counties include an estimated 413,000 of the region's 6.5 million inhabitants.

The Poppers' predictions were instantly and loudly challenged by many Great Plains residents. From Texas to Montana, Plains citizens, especially rural people, reacted with denial, hostility, derision, confusion, concern, and finally despair. The Poppers' scenario made national headlines. Yet they were only repeating and elaborating on what others had been saying since the turn of the century. In the early 1900s Vernon Bailey (1926) suggested that an elk industry was more appropriate for the state of North Dakota than raising domestic stock.

Frederick Kraenzel wrote in 1955 that "the majority of the people must leave the region, and the few who remain will have one of two choices—to live a feast-and-famine type of existence or to have, year in and year out, a standard of living considerably lower than most other parts of the nation" (283). The geographer Bret Wallach (1985) argued that large blocks of land should be taken out of agricultural production and restored to prairie to correct the chronic problem of crop surpluses. He thought the federal government should have an active role in the process. The Institute for the Rockies in Missoula, Montana, proposed that fifteen thousand square miles of eastern Montana, or about one-tenth of the state, be turned into a preserve called the "Big Open," which would support 75,000 bison, 150,000 deer, 40,000 elk, and 40,000 antelope (Popper and Popper 1987b).

The final outcome of the Poppers' predictions, and their influence on that outcome, is still unknown. But the evidence to date indicates that their forecasts of economic and demographic decline, the abandonment of farming and cattle ranching, and the ultimate revival of the bison have not been inaccurate (Popper and Popper 1994a).

A few decades ago the worldwide bison population numbered only a few thousand animals. There are now upward of 150,000, of which 130,000 are in private hands (Manning 1995). There may be as many as two thousand bison ranches in the country, many in the Great Plains (Callenbach 1996). The North Dakota bison herd alone now numbers over 10,000 animals, and a special bison processing plant has recently been completed. Native Americans have been especially quick to latch on to the new industry. A consortium of twenty-nine tribes calling itself the Intertribal Bison Cooperative is creating a self-supporting bison industry (Popper and Popper 1994b). Callenbach (1996) estimates there may be close to 300,000 bison in North America by the year 2000. Although the Poppers predicted a boom in Great Plains bison ranching, they cannot take credit for its astounding growth (nor do they). Economics have persuaded or forced many Great Plains landowners to abandon the old ways and explore new opportunities.

The notion of a buffalo commons was immediately appealing to environmentalists. But the concept is not necessarily a panacea for conserving grassland biodiversity. The first shortcoming is that only a few grassland ecosystems would be included in the commons. All the counties identified by the Poppers as economically distressed, and therefore appropriate for conversion to wildlife refuges (commons), are in the shortgrass or western mixed-grass zones. A second shortcoming is that a buffalo commons scenario gives little attention to agricultural surpluses. Even if the lands identified as submarginal are converted to other uses, it is likely there will still be tens of millions of acres of surplus agricultural capacity in the Great Plains. Perhaps most important, returning bison to the Great Plains does not complete ecosystem restoration for the area, and bison can be overstocked just as readily as cattle. Also, returning bison to the grassland biome simply to breed, feed, and be fenced in like cattle raises serious health concerns, genetic risks, and ethical questions. The practice also presents serious spiritual problems for Native Americans. A *Tampa Tribune-Times* article (26 December 1993) concerning the growth of commercial bison ranching quoted a Native American member of a bison cooperative as saying, "It has some tribal elders saying we have to ask the buffalo if they want to come back."

The Farm Program

Many years of land-saving technological process in farming, coupled with a long-term stagnation in the demand for food and fibres, means that certain degrees of freedom are now available. These should permit a more spacious and imaginative use of rural land than ever before.

Clive Potter et al., *The Diversion of Land*

In 1862, almost a hundred years after the birth of the nation, Abraham Lincoln founded the U.S. Department of Agriculture. At that time the new department employed 9 people. Today the department employs over 120,000 and operates on a $60 billion annual budget; the Washington DC office alone employs over 13,000 people in a headquarters consisting of twelve buildings and ten miles of hallways (World Resources Institute 1994). But what does the Department of Agriculture have to do with the grassland ecosystem? Or biodiversity? Or outdoor recreation? The answer is, a lot.

Excluding the agencies of the Food and Nutrition Service ($29 billion) and U.S. Forest Service ($3 billion), in 1991 the Department spent about $28 billion on agriculture, either directly or indirectly. This money was used to support about 2 million farmers, only 630,000 of whom might be considered full time (gross annual agricultural sales over $40,000 [U.S. Department of Agriculture 1992]). Most of the support is through the Farm Program, a massive piece of federal legislation reauthorized every five years. The Farm Program is so vast, so expensive, and so complex that its various workings warrant a book of their own (see Cochrane and Runge 1992). Although the program is multifaceted, a large portion of it specifically addresses surplus agricultural capacity, a topic especially relevant here.

Surplus capacity and surplus production have been a problem for the United States since the mid-1800s. Morgan (1979) stated that surpluses were a problem in Minnesota as early as 1860, and Guttenberg (1976, 477) noted that "the 1920s are memorable in the annals of American land policy as the decade in which the idea of limiting agricultural growth first gained wide currency." Smith (1992, 198) cites a 1927 article by J. W. Berry questioning the wisdom of draining the wet prairies to raise more crops: "Berry, perceptively, raised the question of whether Iowa, in particular, and the United States as a whole, really benefited from the drainage. . . . he noted that, with the exception of a few years during World War I, drainage contributed to surpluses that upset farming conditions to the point of threatening the foundations of agriculture." Morgan (1979, 75) suggested that the stock market crash of 1929 occurred in part because there was too much wheat.

The problem of crop surpluses became even greater after World War II. From the mid-1940s to the 1980s farmers doubled, tripled, and sometimes quadrupled their output per acre of land, mostly thanks to technological improvements. For example, powerful tractors and other machinery replaced horses and made farming easier and more efficient (and freed up land originally used for pasture). Pesticides and fertilizers increased yields while new varieties of crops grew faster, larger, and more densely and in climates and soils where they would not naturally grow. Irrigation greatly increased production. Improvements in transportation and storage meant less waste between field and dinner table.

Hence wheat yields increased from 15.3 bushels an acre in 1940 to 38.1 bushels in 1985, while corn went from 28.4 bushels to an amazing 118 bushels an acre over the same period (Cochrane and Runge 1992). The American farmer, who in 1940 produced enough food to feed 10.7 people, was by 1980 producing enough to feed 75.7 people, a 707 percent increase, even though the amount of cropland in the nation remained steady at approximately 400 million acres (U.S. Forest Service 1989d). During that same period the United States population went from 132.2 million to 226.5 million, a comparatively modest 71 percent increase. By the mid-1980s the United States (and Canada) found itself with enormous food surpluses, on a scale never before witnessed. Inevitably farmers saw the demand for their crops fall, and subsequently the price. It was a classic supply and demand situation. Because of surpluses, prices dropped so far that in some cases the harvest did not repay the cost of production, let alone earn a profit.

Congress had at least three options: it could have let the markets dictate how much land should be in production, a generally self-correcting mechanism on which much of American society is based; the government could have acquired failed farmland as it did in the 1930s to 1940s, and such lands could have been used for conservation, outdoor recreation, and such; or it could have paid farmers to limit their crop production or subsidized their sales. The last option was chosen.

The 1985 farm bill (Food Security Act of 1985, PL 99-198) passed by Congress contained numerous subsidies and programs designed to reduce crop production and maintain farm income, one being the Conservation Reserve Program, better known as CRP. CRP essentially used federal dollars to pay farmers not to grow crops. Instead they would plant a cover crop of grass, clover, or such and then idle their cropland for ten to fifteen years, during which they would receive an annual "rental" payment. Although only one of many programs, CRP provides a foundation for discussing improvements in future national cropland retirement strategies.

As of July 1992, 36.4 million acres of cropland were set aside in CRP (U.S. Department of Agriculture 1993). Approximately 73 percent of that, or 26.5 million acres, was in the thirteen grassland states (several of these states also contain nongrassland biomes, but most of the CRP occurs in the prairie region). In all, about 6 percent of the land area of the United States portion of the grassland biome is in CRP. For perspective, this area of surplus cropland in the Great Plains is larger than the state of Kentucky. From an ecological perspective, it is equivalent to 197 times the land area of Isle Royale National Park—a fully functioning, albeit small, ecosystem.

Although created primarily for commodity reduction, CRP has also had secondary advantages such as erosion control and some wildlife benefits. Although several published studies have reported the wildlife benefits of CRP, these studies are generally game oriented (pheasants) and are implicitly comparing CRP with cropland or barren fields (in which case virtually any change is an improvement). Even the nongame studies that report positively on CRP are generally limited to the small grassland bird guild.

Is CRP an improvement over corn, wheat, or fields of dirt in terms of wildlife conservation? Definitely yes. Does it conserve grassland biodiversity commensurate with its cost or scope? Probably not. When "wildlife" is defined in the broad sense (including invertebrates, plants, and so on), it seems reasonable to conclude that CRP has provided relatively few benefits, in large part because it does not reflect many conservation biology principles.

For example, the average CRP contract with a farmer is for 97.1 acres (U.S.

Department of Agriculture 1993), meaning that the typical tract is even smaller (one contract may include several tracts). In Iowa, 80 percent of all CRP tracts were less than 100 acres; in Kansas, 70 percent were less than 100 acres; and in North Dakota, 44 percent were less than that (Osborn, Llacuna, and Linsenbigler 1990). This fact alone greatly diminishes the value of CRP lands to grassland biodiversity. Compounding the problem, CRP fields are typically juxtaposed with an agrarian landscape. Hence such tracts, especially those in the tallgrass and mixed-grass regions, are often driven ecologically by adjacent processes and habitats (e.g., shelterbelts), creating conditions whereby the sites can be ecological traps for many grassland bird species.

In addition to problems of size and juxtaposition, the selection of cover crop for CRP tracts is often left to the landowner, who typically plants what is least expensive or what is recommended by county agriculture agents, who have traditionally recommended exotic species such as brome, crested wheatgrass, timothy (*Phelum pratense*), orchard grass (*Dactylis glomerata*), and sweet clover. The tradition of planting exotics is so ingrained that many landowners are unaware they can use native grasses. According to the U.S. Department of Agriculture (1993), native grasses account for less than 23 percent of all CRP plantings, and the figure is much lower in many Great Plains states. For example, native grass composed only 0.4 percent of North Dakota's CRP acreage (U.S. Department of Agriculture 1993). Essentially the government is promoting the spread of exotic plants even though wildlife benefits more from native grass mixtures. But the most significant shortcoming of CRP in terms of plant conservation may be the most obvious. Even though there are dozens of endemic or indigenous grassland plant species on the federal endangered, threatened, or candidate species list, CRP and other current cropland retirement strategies completely ignore the preservation and restoration of these species.

A fourth shortcoming of CRP, one that is common to all current cropland set-asides, is that it is short term, often expiring just as the biodiversity benefits start manifesting themselves. For example, in North Dakota it was found that representative grassland species such as meadow voles (*Microtus pennsylvanicus*) did not start becoming abundant until late in the life of the contracts (Lysne 1991). Other studies have also observed that recently established grassland plantings were suboptimal habitat for small prairie mammals because of low forb abundance, low diversity, and high phytomass (Schwartz and Whitson 1986). (The irony of CRP is that it is too long to correct annual fluctuations in commodity supplies and too short to provide biodiversity benefits.)

Potential wildlife benefits are also reduced because the privately owned CRP lands are frequently opened for haying, grazing, or other use during drought or flood "emergency" declarations. In the first nine years of the program CRP lands were opened for so-called emergency haying in every year but one. The harm haying inflicts on grassland wildlife is obvious. A less obvious problem is that the contracts stipulate that a certain amount of a CRP field must remain unharvested during emergency declarations, usually 10–25 percent (although Hays and Farmer 1990 stated that the limit was often exceeded). The hayed portions of CRP tracts provide perfect (and highly unnatural) travel avenues for mammalian predators hunting the unmowed portions, so hayed CRP becomes a death trap for many ground-nesting birds (Luttschwager 1991).

In spite of its enormous cost, few Americans receive direct recreational benefits from CRP because it occurs on private lands. Even if public access were stipulated or granted, it seems unlikely there would be much enthusiasm for visiting small patches of exotic grasses. Hunting may be the one tangible recreational use of CRP, but even that benefit is marginal. CRP was expected to create new hunting opportunities, but Langner (1989) found that it recruited few new hunters.

Yet these ecological and recreational shortcomings would be tolerable were it not for the most startling fact of all concerning the program. The federal government pays, on average, $49.67 annually per acre of land enrolled (U.S. Department of Agriculture 1993). In the grassland biome the state weighted averages range from $82.31 per acre in Iowa to $37.24 per acre in Montana. Since CRP contracts are for ten to fifteen years (mostly the former), American taxpayers pay an average of about $500 an acre for CRP land over the life of the program, plus the administrative costs. Yet the value of farmland and the buildings on it in the Great Plains ranges from only $159 an acre in Wyoming (shortgrass prairie) to $335 an acre in North Dakota (mixed-grass prairie) to $1,212 an acre in Iowa (tallgrass prairie). For the region as a whole the average value of farmland and associated buildings is only $433 an acre. The truth is self-evident. American taxpayers could have bought many of these lands (and the buildings on them) for less than the cost of the CRP contract. Further, CRP and other Farm Program components artificially inflate land values; without the government payments, the market value of these lands would be even less (Shoemaker 1989).

Yet another serious failing of CRP and the 1985 farm bill is that the program allows farmers to plow up native prairie (including prairie with endangered plants) to put more land into cultivation at the same time they are retiring their cultivated land into CRP fields of brome and other exotic grasses (provided they have a soil conservation plan). In fact they are implicitly encouraged to do so because the Farm Program makes the forces of supply and demand generally irrelevant.

For example, producers get deficiency payments on crops they sell when the market price (the real price) does not meet the government-established target price. So even if the market is glutted and the selling price of wheat is only $2.10 a bushel while it costs the farmer $2.50 to produce it, the farmer is still encouraged to plant wheat because the government will pay the difference between the market price and an artificially established target price, say $3 a bushel. Therefore, while we are paying farmers to take land out of production, we are also subsidizing them to cultivate more land. The Farm Program has been likened to stepping on the accelerator and the brake at the same time.

Lending institutions have been quick to capitalize on the situation. Throughout the Plains, banks encourage landowners to convert native prairie to (artificially) more valuable farmland in order to obtain operating loans (Huszar and Young 1984). Banks often view farming as low risk, in part because of government subsidies. As a result, even more native prairie is broken.

In 1993 the U.S. General Accounting Office estimated that CRP contracts initiated as part of the 1985 farm bill will cost about $21 billion over their life span. In 1996 President Clinton signed legislation authorizing another round of CRP contracts, whose cost may be comparable to that of the first round. As noted by the U.S. General Accounting Office report, CRP postpones rather than resolves agriculture's problems. In a large sense CRP is not a solution but a continuation of the problem. If the current program were a one-time effort to permanently reduce the nation's surplus capacity, most Americans could probably accept it. But that is not the case. Cropland set-asides, in one form or another, have been a part of American agriculture since early in the century.

Cropland set-aside programs were initiated in 1933 with the Agricultural Adjustment Act, in 1934 with the Cropland Adjustment Act, in 1936 with the Agricultural Conservation Program, and in 1938 with the second Agricultural Adjustment Act. The Soil Bank Program of 1956 set aside 28.7 million acres during its peak in 1960–61. Other more recent set-aside programs include the Emergency Feed Grain Program of 1961, the Wheat Program of 1962, the Water Bank Program, the Cropland Adjustment Program of 1966, and the Payment-in-Kind Program of 1983. With the exception of World War II, the Korean War, and the first few years of the Reagan administration, set-aside programs have generally gotten progressively larger and more costly.

Now the Conservation Reserve Program (technically, the second CRP program; the first was a component of the Soil Bank Program) alone is setting aside 36.4 million acres in addition to the acreage set aside in the other extant programs. As of 1993 those other programs include the Acreage Reduction Program (also known as Acreage Conservation Reserve), Paid Land Diversion Program, and 0-50/92 program.

The Acreage Reduction Program is especially relevant, since it costs as much as $10 billion in some years, or five times the cost of CRP. The program is typically implemented with one-year contracts that do not have nearly the soil conservation benefits of CRP because cover crops are required on only half of the set-aside acres. Yet the advantage of the program is that it is capable of making short-term adjustments to commodity production. Up to 50 million acres have been retired annually in this program. Arguably, even if all the land in one of the other programs (e.g., CRP) was permanently converted to some other use, the nation would still have a considerable surplus of cropland with which to ensure a dependable and stable food supply. The amount of this surplus land is staggering.

In 1992 alone approximately 52 million acres of cropland, an area larger than thirty-six of the fifty states, were idled in federal farm programs. In 1983 American taxpayers paid for a record 80 million acres in either short-term or long-term set-aside programs. Heimlich and Kula (1991, 17) observed that from the mid-1950s to 1989, "except for brief periods from 1974 to 1977 and 1980 to 1981, government programs idled as much as 20 percent of Great Plains cropland." And during the periods when less than 20 percent of the Great Plains cropland was in set-aside programs, the federal expenditures simply shifted to other farm programs. For example, in the first few "cost-cutting" Reagan years set-asides were initially discouraged; the result was that deficiency payments and other Farm Program expenditures soared, prompting a return to off-budget set-asides and commodity price supports (Cochrane and Runge 1992, 52).

Berner (1984) observed that a mean of 15.1 million acres was retired annually during the first twenty-five years (1934–58) of set-asides and that during the second twenty-five years the mean more than doubled to 34 million acres annually. Since publication of Berner's paper, set-asides have greatly increased in size and cost; since 1983 the annual acreage has risen closer to 58 million acres, or about 15 percent of the nation's cropland (fig. 2). Over the past sixty years set-asides have averaged about 30 million acres annually. The sum of the annual set-aside acreage since 1934 is enough to cover over 95 percent of the land

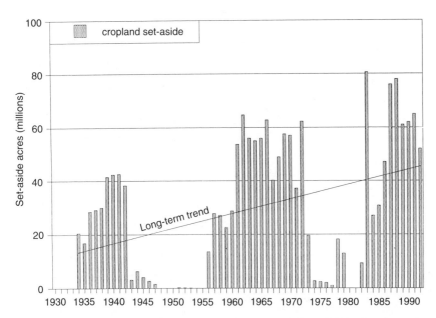

Figure 2. Federal cropland set-aside acreage. Data from Berner (1984) and White, Langley, and Edelman (1994).

area of the lower forty-eight states. The long-term trend has been a 4.2 percent annual increase in the amount of cropland placed in federal set-aside programs, suggesting even larger set-asides in the future.

As staggering as these amounts are, the reality is that they are only a fraction of the acreage that needs to be retired to get supply back in equilibrium with demand. In a study of cropland set-asides, Laycock (1988, 7) found that the 28 million acres retired in the Soil Bank program did "not appear to have resulted in a substantial drop in the acres of wheat planted in the plains." Cochrane and Runge (1992) concluded that even if CRP reaches its ultimate goal of 45 million acres, it will only modestly affect commodity supplies. They found that CRP would reduce corn production by a mere 435 million bushels—only 19 percent of the 2.3 billion bushel surplus!

Great Plains farmers are the recipients of a large portion of the Farm Program benefits. In some cases programs are designed specifically for them. For example, since 1956 the Great Plains Conservation Program has paid for converting 110 million cultivated acres to grass (Dicks and Osborn 1994). Federal crop insurance, a program that pays out two dollars for every dollar collected, is especially costly in areas of marginal farmland such as the western plains. As Guither, Baumes, and Meyers (1994, 232) observed, "In 1990, direct government payments provided 54.9 percent of the net cash farm income in Montana, 55.1 percent in North Dakota, 48.6 percent in Kansas, but only 3.3 percent in North Carolina." Although the market value of the agricultural products sold from the Great Plains was only 20.9 percent of the nation's total in 1992, the region was the recipient of 49.9 percent of the direct Farm Program payments.

Illogically, the arguments supporting some of these programs often pit one program against another. For example, a U.S. Department of Agriculture report argued that CRP produced net "savings" because the costly program reduced the need for income support payments to farmers (Young and Osborn 1990). A pro-CRP pamphlet titled *A Bargain for the U.S. Taxpayer* argues that CRP is good for the nation because without it the farm payments for six Great Plains states would cost $3,179,624,000 instead of only $3,163,236,000. Similarly, a $3.1 billion drought relief package in 1988 and a $900 million package in 1989 were "justified" because the reduced production resulting from the drought had created a "savings" in the Farm Program.

Disturbingly, the problem of surplus agricultural capacity is going to get worse. Food production per acre has been steadily increasing since the turn of the century, far outpacing the increase in the United States population. By the end of the twentieth century wheat, corn, and cotton yields are expected to increase an average of 22, 11, and 18 percent, respectively, from their 1990 levels (U.S. Office of Technology Assessment 1992). Auer (1989, 60) studied the Canadian farm situation and predicted that between 1989 and 2000 total prairie farm output will probably increase by roughly 40 percent.

New technologies such as biotechnology and computer systems threaten to cause an explosion in food production, exacerbating the problem of surpluses (U.S. Office of Technology Assessment 1992). For example, by the early part of the twenty-first century (or possibly even in the late 1990s), varieties of crops may be developed that are resistant to viruses, bacteria, and fungi. Elaborate computer systems will aid in harvesting those crops and getting them to market more efficiently. Already, "master farms" are producing two to five times the average state and world yields per unit area (Waggoner 1994). Farming appears to be on the verge of its third revolution (horse power and machinery power being the first two [Hurt 1994]).

Similarly, livestock commodities are expected to increase owing to science and technology (U.S. Office of Technology Assessment 1992). Beef calves per cow are expected to increase 7 percent between 1990 and 2000 (twinning in cattle may become the norm rather than the exception), and pounds of beef produced per pound of feed consumed are likely to rise about 8 percent during the same period. Swine and poultry are projected to increase 18 and 5 percent, respectively, in terms of pounds of meat produced per pound of feed. New hormones and other technological improvements are predicted to increase milk production per dairy cow by a whopping 35 percent in just ten years, at a time when the country already has milk surpluses.

Meanwhile the United States population is expected to increase only 0.5 percent annually over the next few decades and then level off about the year 2038, when it may begin a gradual decline that might last until 2080 (Spencer 1989). During the same period, agricultural exports are projected to fall or stagnate as other countries make agricultural advancements (Ray and Frederick 1994). It seems likely that the United States will have excess agricultural capacity well into the future.

Ultimately, we may conclude that the Farm Program has not helped typical American farmers but has hurt them. As early as 1924 Lewis Gray, who headed the Division of Economics at the U.S. Department of Agriculture, astutely noted that a farm subsidy "tends to overestimate the expansion of the farming area, and this in turn makes the subsidy increasingly essential. Thus, like a drug addict, we must go on and on increasing the dose" (Gray et al. 1924, 504). Gray et al. observed that government policies that encourage over-expansion were harmful to the nation's resources, to the government, and to established farmers.

Throughout the nation's history the American farmer has been seen as a proud person who exemplifies virtuous values, an industrious work ethic, and independence. Unfortunately, many farmers now harvest as much from the government as from the field. Consider that 40.6 percent of farmers surveyed in North Dakota indicated that CRP income alone exceeded their net cash income from farming (Mortensen et al. 1989). Throughout the Great Plains the average farmer in the federal Farm Program received $10,561 in direct federal subsidies in 1992, a $2.6 billion federal expenditure. And that was a good year for the government. In 1987 each farmer enrolled in the program received on average $16,766 (the entire per capita income—farm and nonfarm—in the grassland biome was $10,779 for the same period). For farmers enrolled in the Farm Program, government payments accounted for 23 percent of farm income received in 1992 and 39 percent in 1987. On average, the amount that has been spent on direct farm payments in the grassland biome since 1933 is enough (in 1992 dol-

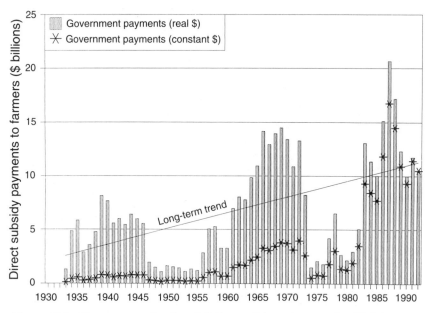

Figure 3. Federal farm payments. Data from U.S. Bureau of Census (1955, 1993) and U.S. Department of Agriculture (1950, 1964, 1978, 1992).

lars) to have bought every single acre of cropland and rangeland in the region and the buildings on it, with $42 billion left over. It is enough to have bought each acre of cropland in the region two times over, and each acre of cropland enrolled in the federal Farm Program three times over. Last, federal farm subsidies have continued to increase at a long-term rate of 5.3 percent annually (in real dollars) since the 1930s (fig. 3).

A similar situation exists in Canada, which is also burdened by commodity surpluses. According to Hjertaas (1993, 351), "Programs such as Gross Revenue Insurance Plan, crop insurance, and transportation subsidies effectively pay a farmer in Saskatchewan $40 [Canadian] for each acre he cultivates." Auer (1989, 59) found that "the total assistance to Prairie farmers amounts to $4 billion [Canadian]. That averages out to roughly $30,000 per farm." In spite of these expensive government efforts, the number of farms in prairie Canada is still expected to decline by 15 percent between 1989 and 2000 (Auer 1989).

The same is true in the United States. Even with enormous subsidies, the number of farms declined 14.7 percent between 1978 and 1992; 17.5 percent in the grassland biome (table 6). Just as significant, the rural farm population declined 31 percent between 1980 and 1990—36 percent in the grassland biome.

Table 6. Agricultural Statistics in Grassland Ecoregions and National Totals

Region	Number of Farms 1978	Number of Farms 1992	Land in Farms 1978 (acres)	Land in Farms 1992 (acres)	Average Value of Farmland and Buildings (acres)[a] 1978	Average Value of Farmland and Buildings (acres)[a] 1992
Tallgrass	201,884	158,508 (−21.5%)	66,221,120	62,269,680 (−6.0%)	$1,195.09	$1,013.62 (−15.2%)[a]
Mixed-grass	193,959	160,766 (−17.1%)	155,750,900	150,918,974 (−3.1%)	$409.23	$400.91 (−2.0%)
Shortgrass	81,071	74,211 (−8.5%)	167,275,568	163,890,353 (−2.0%)	$230.51	$241.30 (+4.7%)[a]
Great Plains subtotal	476,914	393,485 (−17.5%)	389,247,588	377,079,007 (−3.1%)	$466.12	$432.72 (−7.2%)[a]
United States total	2,257,775	1,925,300 (−14.7%)	1,014,777,234	945,531,506 (−6.8%)	$619.00	$727.00 (+17.4%)[a]

[a]Dollars are constant dollars. In real dollars the change from 1978 to 1992 was −60.5 percent for the tallgrass region, −54.4 percent for the mixed-grass region, −51.3 percent for the shortgrass region, −56.8 percent for the Great Plains subtotal, and −45.3 percent for the United States total.

The typical farm household now consists of a husband and wife nearing retirement (the average age of a grassland farmer in 1992 was 51.2) and with no children willing to take over the farm. In many cases government programs such as CRP are simply a golden parachute. For example, the typical CRP contract holder in North Dakota was 57 years old in 1987; over 10 percent of these farmers intended to sell their property once the CRP contracts expired (Mortensen et al. 1989).

In many cases farmers are moving to urban areas but still maintaining control of the land. In other cases they sell their land to nonfarmers who use it for recreation or as an investment. Consider that a North Dakota study found that 27 percent of the state's CRP recipients did not farm at all in 1987 and that 10 percent lived out of state (Mortensen et al. 1989). This trend is becoming increasingly common; landowners live in urban areas and only rarely travel to the country to check on the farm. In 1982, 30 percent of all farmers in the grassland biome were what are commonly known as "suitcase farmers;" in 1992 that figure was up to 35 percent. What disturbs many people is that some of these suitcase farmers are foreigners, a trend that seems to be increasing. Between December 1989 and December 1992 the amount of foreign-owned farmland in the Great Plains went from 1.22 to 1.36 million acres, a 9.7 percent increase. In many other cases the suitcase farmers are insurance companies that have repossessed defaulted properties; between 1980 and 1986 the amount of farmland owned and operated by insurance companies increased tenfold (as cited in Manning 1995).

The negative effects of the current farm situation extend beyond the farm. As large portions of the land base are retired under CRP and other set-asides—up to 60 percent of the cropland in some counties (Dicks and Osborn 1994)—the need for farm implement businesses, farm supply dealers, and grain haulers decreases. As these industries suffer, so do the communities where they are located. North Dakota alone lost $141 million and 2,416 jobs statewide as a result of CRP (Mortensen et al. 1989). One of the consequences of CRP and the current Farm Program is that their negative effects are felt throughout the entire Great Plains rather than limiting the effects of cropland retirement to a few select sites or regions.

Having spent considerable time criticizing the federal Farm Program, I need to clarify that most grassland agriculture is necessary and good. And a certain level of surplus is desirable to balance short-term deficiencies and stabilize price fluctuations. It is chronic and excessive surpluses that are the problem and hence provide society the opportunities for radical land-use adjustments. As

Wuerthner (1994, 907) noted, "Obviously, not all agriculture in the West is unprofitable and undesirable, but if we are to stem the continued decline in biodiversity we should attack the least efficient and most environmentally costly land uses."

What farmers and ranchers in the Great Plains would like is independence from government handouts, a reasonable profit for their products, and vibrant communities and small towns to live in. The current Farm Program fails to deliver these desires. In fact it merely exacerbates the problem and postpones solutions. CRP was found to prolong farming for 20.6 percent of its recipients (Mortensen et al. 1989), exactly what the nation did not need. Yet if a small number of farmers and ranchers had retired and their land had been permanently taken out of production, the remaining farmers and ranchers would have benefited from the reduction in commodity supplies. The greater the number of retirees, the greater the benefit.

The Great Plains were settled on the untested premise that all the land was needed for commodity production, and that if there were surpluses, they could be exported for profit. The premise also assumed that agriculture in the region would be self-supporting. But current realities question that premise.

The nation needs to acknowledge that under the current markets and those predicted for the future, vibrant agrarian communities are not possible across 100 percent of the Great Plains landscape, at least not without massive government subsidies. But they may be possible on 70–90 percent of the region. The question then becomes what to do with the remaining 10–30 percent of the grassland biome.

Exploring the Reserve Concept

If the larger members of the fauna of the Great Plains are to be restored under natural conditions a great acreage is necessary. Bison, antelope and elk need large amounts of forage, which in the short-grass type is not truly abundant. If the bison, particularly, is to be preserved as a wild species in the United States, it must be granted a large natural range free from the domesticating confinement of small fenced parks. From a consideration of all these points, it seems that a million acre tract would be needed.

V. H. Cahalane, "A Proposed Great Plains National Monument"

A Singular Opportunity

If we are serious about conserving naturally functioning ecosystems in the Great Plains—and we should be—then we need to consider radical changes in our conservation strategies. Current efforts, no matter how well funded, no matter how well intended, are often superficial, ephemeral, and anachronistic. New knowledge, along with new values and new aspirations, dictates new approaches.

If we are serious about improving the quality of life for the typical farmer and rancher—and we should be—then we need to consider radical changes in the Farm Program. The current policies and programs will not reverse the falling fortunes of the family operator in the Great Plains. The current programs will not prevent the decline of rural towns throughout the region. American taxpayers, faced with a $5 trillion debt, cannot afford to keep subsidizing rural economies just to keep people on the land. Like the need for radical measures to conserve grassland biodiversity, there is also a need for radical measures to sustain grassland economies.

Mainly because of the singular economic and demographic climate of the arid grasslands, the region presents opportunities not found in any other eco-region in the United States. California's Central Valley, Florida's Everglades, and the Pacific Northwest all present extremely contentious and complex land-use issues. At times it appears that development in these regions is inevitable and that the best one can hope for in terms of conservation may be to slow or alter the process of ecosystem degradation, not stop it. But the Great Plains are different. They provide new economic as well as environmental opportunities for the nation. Some authors and scholars have already sensed these possibilities.

The buffalo commons scenario of the Poppers (1994b) is perhaps the most ambitious and most publicized proposal, arguing for 139,000 square miles of refuges in the shortgrass and mixed-grass prairies. But even if the scenario does come to fruition, it will not necessarily conserve the shortgrass and mixed-grass ecosystems, and it will do nothing for the tallgrass region.

Ernest Callenbach (1996) expanded on the Poppers' work. Callenbach argued that a Great Plains economy of bison, along with wind power, could sustain itself well into the future. He argued that government buyouts could achieve the conversion at little or no cost to taxpayers.

The geographer Bret Wallach (1985) offered some excellent ideas about using Farm Program–like mechanisms to take land out of production permanently and return it to prairie. He proposed giving farmers fifteen-year contracts to restore their land to native prairie. The idea seems especially meritorious in that the average Great Plains farmer is over fifty. However, Wallach also recommended that landowners be able to maintain a forty-acre homestead after the fifteen-year contracts expire. As I have noted, homesteads, shelterbelts, roads, power lines, pets, and other human influences can seriously compromise attempts at restoring grassland biodiversity.

Coffman, Jonkel, and Scott (1990) recommended that bison be restored to a 15,000-square-mile "Big Open" region in central and eastern Montana. They noted that "within its 15,000 square miles lives a human population of less than 3,000. In contrast, Belgium—an area about the same size as the Big Open—has 10 million people. And although the Big Open is mostly rangeland, Belgium produces more than five times as much beef" (40). The authors also noted that cash supports to the region are more than $10 million annually, but in spite of those supports the region is still economically distressed and has had a net outflow of population for fifty years. They recommended a planned transition to a "wildlife-based economy" including bison, elk, and other large herbivores. Privately owned wildlife-based economies are definitely better than the current situation, but they are unlikely to provide all the conservation and recreation values that publicly owned wilderness areas do (Noss 1994).

Bock and Bock (1995) noted the declining agricultural value of national grasslands and their likely increasing value as natural landscapes and suggested that all livestock be permanently removed from them. They noted that ungrazed (or bison-grazed) national grasslands would "re-create the extraordinary habitat mosaic that once composed the North American Great Plains" (219).

The agricultural economists Willard Cochrane and C. Ford Runge (1992) thoroughly examined the federal Farm Program and suggested ways to reform it. They proposed, among other strategies, "support for a national effort to expand wilderness areas, national parks, and the national forests of the nation" (136). They also proposed establishing publicly owned natural areas near urban centers. The economists did not explore biodiversity conservation in detail, but their argument was clear: permanent conversion of excess farmland to natural areas could lessen the need for expensive farm programs, improve the farm economy, and enhance recreational and ecological benefits.

Lewis (1989, 171) reviewed the history of the National Grasslands and observed that conservationists supported setting land aside for conservation whereas farmers on productive land viewed land retirement programs in marginal lands "as a means of reducing the surplus productive capacity of the national agricultural land base." Lewis believed the two groups could form a "coalition" for comprehensive land retirement. Last, he pointed out that the federal Conservation Reserve Program offers no guarantee that the land will stay out of production, and that federal acquisitions made during the 1930s and 1940s "have remained under grass cover for the past half century" (171).

Other researchers have also noted that biodiversity conservation and government frugality can go hand in hand (Licht 1994). Wuerthner (1994, 907) observed that "the savings afforded by termination of land uses currently subsidized by government programs and lax environmental accounting could be used in many parts of the country to provide a foundation for landscape restoration." He believed that in many regions of the West the amount spent on agricultural subsidies could easily cover the cost of land acquisition for wildlife.

For the past several decades land acquisition for wildlife purposes in the Great Plains has been undertaken mainly by the U.S. Fish and Wildlife Service and, to a lesser extent, the Nature Conservancy. Such efforts have operated independent of federal farm policies and programs, and in many cases in competition with them. Yet based on all the available economic, demographic, and ecological data, it does not seem unwise to suggest that a more comprehensive and permanent reallocation of land uses in the grassland biome be considered. A comparatively straightforward strategy might replicate the land utilization projects of the 1930s to 1950s whereby the federal government, as part of its agriculture policy, acquires failing farms. Yet this time around the projects could better incorporate conservation biology principles and the desires of a public oriented to outdoor recreation. In the following chapters I will explore the feasibility of establishing some county-size units in the grassland biome for the sake of biodiversity and outdoor recreation.

Although numerous tracts of public land in the lower forty-eight states are commonly viewed as naturally functioning ecosystems, few of them actually are that. Except for select areas in the northern Rocky Mountains (e.g., Bob Marshall Wilderness), none of the national forests and none of the Bureau of Land Management properties are naturally functioning ecosystems. They are multiple-use areas where the system functions in response to human operations such as logging, mining, and livestock grazing as much as it does from natural processes. Although the approximately five hundred national wildlife refuges in the lower forty-eight states are not compromised to the same degree by commercial interests, they are generally too small to sustain natural processes and the full complement of indigenous species and processes. The same is true for the fifty national parks administered by the National Park Service. Especially prominent among the missing species are the large carnivores. Wide-ranging, celebrated, and controversial, they also happen to be at the top of the food chain, the cogs whose behavior resonates down to the smallest microbes (and vice versa).

So the truth of the matter is that there are few naturally functioning ecosystems in the lower forty-eight states and absolutely none in the vast grasslands in the center of North America. From Alberta to Texas and from Iowa to Colorado there are no grassland ecosystems unfettered by human activities.

For purposes of this book an ecological reserve can be described as a functioning ecosystem within a socially delineated boundary. It contains the most complete possible assemblage of native flora and fauna and the abiotic features and processes that sustain them, and it implies the capacity for these entities to exist and interact in a generally natural, self-regulating, self-evolving, and self-sustaining environment. Although I will use the term "reserve" in describing these hypothetical sites, they could just as easily be called refuges, parks, preserves, or any of other numerous administrative designations.

The Importance of Size

The larger a nature reserve, the more species it is likely to contain. Ecologists have understood this principle for years and have recently refined their knowledge of it with the study of *island biogeography* (see Shafer 1990). Island biogeography predicts that larger islands (and reserves) generally contain more species, in part because they are more likely to include a variety of soil types, topography, microclimates, hydrological features, successional stages, and disruptive processes, but also in part because they have greater species persistence (how long a species survives at a particular site).

If a reserve (i.e., an island) is to successfully sustain a species, it needs enough individuals of that species to allow it to survive catastrophic events such as a disease, flooding, drought, and harsh winters. These factors, also known as stochastic factors because they appear random and unpredictable, are more likely to cause extinction when a population has already been reduced or weakened by other causes (e.g., reduction in habitat area, habitat fragmentation, change in predator composition).

Consider the heath hen (*Tympanuchus cupido cupido*), a close relative of the prairie chicken, which originally inhabited the Atlantic coast. The heath hen declined rapidly in the late 1800s owing in part to overhunting. Conservation efforts, including the establishment of a small refuge, were put in place to protect the last one hundred birds. Although the population experienced a brief rebound, the refuge was not large enough to survive natural variation (e.g., harsh winters) and outside influences. The species finally went extinct in 1932, twenty-five years after the protective refuge was established and hunting was banned. The population had fallen below a minimum viable level and was vulnerable to stochastic events (Shaffer 1981).

The minimum number of individuals needed in a wild population for long-term survival is an elusive value. Only recently have scientists begun devoting serious effort to learning what constitutes a minimum viable population, defined by at least one scientist as "the smallest isolated population having a 99% chance of remaining extant for 1,000 years despite the foreseeable effects of demographic, environmental, and genetic stochasticity, and natural catastrophes" (Shaffer 1981, 132). Other definitions have used different time spans and probabilities but have been generally consistent with the interpretation.

Minimum viable populations, based on simulation models, can be quite large. For example, Belovsky (1987) developed a mammalian minimum viable population model that predicts that grassland species such as the black-footed ferret, swift fox, and gray wolf would need populations of approximately 8,000, 5,000, and 2,000 animals, respectively, to have a 95 percent probability of surviving one hundred years, and populations of 100,000, 60,000, and 20,000 to have a 95 percent probability of surviving one thousand years (assuming a midpoint environmental variance). Species that are especially susceptible to environmental change—for example, invertebrates and many small-bodied vertebrates—typically require populations much larger than those predicted for bigger animals. Noss and Cooperrider (1994, 60) thought that "with few exceptions, populations on the order of thousands of individuals appear necessary for long-term persistence."

Other models have been developed that deal specifically with the genetic element. In regard to sustaining genetic variability and vigor within a species, conservation biologists often use an admittedly unrefined and untested standard known as the 50/500 rule. Inbreeding depression is thought to occur when the breeding population falls below fifty individuals; genetic drift may be a concern below five hundred. The recovery strategies for several grassland species make use of the larger figure. For example, a recovery objective for both the Neosho madtom and the American burying beetle is to protect several distinct populations comprising at least five hundred individuals (U.S. Fish and Wildlife Service 1991a, 1991c). Likewise, the recovery strategy for the threatened prairie bush clover (*Lespedeza leptostachya*) calls for seed banks of at least five hundred seeds from selected populations (U.S. Fish and Wildlife Service 1988b). As pointed out by Soule (1980), however, larger populations may be needed to preserve long-term evolutionary potential.

With a cursory understanding of genetics and minimum viable populations, we can go on to consider the land area needed to maintain grassland species. By some arguments the amount of land needed to conserve biodiversity, and hence naturally functioning ecosystems, can be staggering. For example, Wilson (1992) suggested that 10 percent of a biome or other land surface should be in reserves, and Noss and Cooperrider (1994, 168) stated that "most regions will require protection of some 25 to 75 percent of their total land area in core reserves and inner buffer zones.'' Odum (1994, 20) thought a landscape that was ''two-thirds 'semi-natural' '' was desirable for biodiversity conservation. Although ideal, such scenarios are unlikely in the grassland biome in the near future, especially in the tallgrass region.

More modest estimates can be derived from the Belovsky (1987) mammalian model mentioned earlier. The model predicts that species such as the black-footed ferret, swift fox, and gray wolf would require areas of 150, 300, and 2,000 square miles, respectively, to have a 95 percent probability of surviving one hundred years, and areas of 1,000, 2,000, and 15,000 square miles to have a 95 percent probability of surviving one thousand years (assuming a midpoint environmental variance). However, these estimates are useful only in the proper context; for example, ferrets and swift foxes have evolved in the presence of wolves and may require that presence for their long-term survival.

Soule and Simberloff (1986, 19) took a simpler autecological approach to identifying reserve sizes needed. They believed the best way to estimate the minimum acceptable size of reserves would be to ''(1) identify target or keystone species whose disappearance would significantly decrease the value or species diversity of the reserve; (2) determine the minimum number of individuals in a population needed to guarantee a high probability of survival for these species; (3) using known densities, estimate the area needed to sustain the minimum number.'' Such an approach has been proposed many times, including for the establishment of tallgrass reserves specifically designed for grassland birds (Samson 1980). But as Soule and Simberloff pointed out, the keystone species of many ecosystems are often the largest herbivores and carnivores—which are typically the species with the highest territorial needs.

The two grassland species with the highest territory needs are both extirpated from the Great Plains. (It is often suggested that bison and the other grazers historically migrated across the grassland biome and therefore utilized larger areas, but populations of these species appear to be sustainable on relatively small tracts.) Those two species are the gray wolf and grizzly bear. Fortunately both species are still extant, although in ecosystems radically different from the grasslands. Can they be reintroduced to the grassland biome, assuming restoration of suitable habitat? The answer is a definite yes for wolves. For grizzly bears the answer is much less clear.

It is important that wolves be established in larger grassland reserves, but their presence would serve more as a system functionary (in the words of Aldo Leopold, a ''cog'') than for the preservation of the species per se. There are an

138

estimated fifty-five thousand wolves in North America, many living in remote regions of Canada and Alaska; the species is in no danger of extinction.

Even though the survival of the species is not in danger, the wolf that was historically endemic to the Great Plains has been extirpated. For years this wolf was considered a different species or subspecies and known commonly by names such as buffalo wolf, lobo, loafer, or Plains wolf, but recent and more advanced taxonomic work suggests that it was not significantly different morphologically from the animals that currently exist in the forests of northern Minnesota (Nowak 1995). Grassland wolves may have behaved differently than forest wolves do (e.g., more nomadic, larger packs), but these differences were probably learned strategy adjustments to the prey they hunted and the environment they inhabited, not genetic traits.

Either way, it seems reasonable to assume that wolves from nearby forested regions can readily adapt to living in a grassland ecosystem as long as adequate prey is available. A more pressing problem is establishing grassland reserves large enough to sustain wolves at population levels even close to five hundred animals. Theoretically, reserves as large as eight thousand square miles may be needed. Fortunately, a reserve of that size is probably not necessary to maintain a functioning simulacrum of a grassland ecosystem. Wolves are needed in grassland ecosystems for their role, not for the conservation of the species per se. Hence a population of fifty individuals at any one site should more than suffice in most cases. Therefore functioning grassland reserves could be designed that adequately meet the life requirements of species with the largest territory needs (wolves) and are large enough to sustain minimum viable populations of most or all other species (e.g., swift foxes, ferrets).

A functioning ecological reserve with a small number of wolves already exists in the lower forty-eight states. That closed ecosystem is Isle Royale National Park in Lake Superior, an 894-square-mile forested island about 22 miles from Grand Portage, Minnesota. Only 210 square miles of the island are terrestrial, yet these 210 square miles have sustained an average of 19.6 (SD=10.5) wolves from the winter of 1979–80 to 1992–93 while at the same time sustaining 1,160.8 moose (SD=394.3). Essentially, Isle Royale is a closed ecosystem that still has a functioning predator-prey relationship between a large carnivore and a large herbivore, even though it has only a small amount of land. The relationship is functioning so well that the site was designated an International Biosphere Reserve in 1981.

Granted, there may be problems with such small wolf populations, such as inbreeding, but that would not be a serious concern in grassland reserves, since the presence of wolves is not to protect the species per se, but to fill a role in the ecosystem, much as they do on Isle Royale. Should inbreeding depression or population survival become a concern, humans could transport animals between reserves or import them from a nongrassland population. The professional organization the Wildlife Society, recognized this possibility when it stated that "if national parks and other protected areas cannot provide large enough areas for self-perpetuating populations of wolves, systematic and periodic reintroduction of wolves from outside may ensure population survival" (Wildlife Society 1991, 8). The same paper stated that populations that are "ecologically functional" may be a more suitable goal in some cases than those that are "minimally viable."

Therefore it seems reasonable to contemplate establishing a series of Isle Royale–type ecological reserves in the grassland biome. Such a thought is less intimidating than it might first seem. The 210 square miles of land in Isle Royale would fit 197 times into the amount of CRP (excess cropland) in the grassland states alone. Similarly, the land area of Isle Royale would fit 27 times into the current national grasslands acreage in the Great Plains, 65 times in the BLM land, 12 times in the Fish and Wildlife Service land, and twice in the National Park Service land. Based on these figures, restoring wolves to the grassland biome seems like a modest proposal.

But what about grizzly bears? They too were once present on the vast contiguous prairies, and they too were extirpated by European settlers. Should they be restored to the grassland ecosystem? The question here is much more complex. Granted, grizzly bears were historically present in the grassland biome, but their density was never as great as that of wolves. To maintain a self-sustaining or even functional grizzly bear population would require an enormous amount of land (Shaffer 1981), especially in an arid grassland environment. There is also the question whether the grizzly can be reacclimated to the prairie environment. The indigenous grizzly was probably an opportunist that had learned to take advantage of ephemeral food sources unique to the Great Plains. Can grizzlies taken from forest and alpine ecosystems adapt to a grassland environment? The answer is uncertain. Last, as I shall discuss later, functioning county-size (or larger) reserves with bison and wolves can probably be created even within agrarian states like Kansas. But forcing grizzlies into such relatively small reserves would not only present an enormous political and management challenge, it might also be viewed as unethical. Having said that, however, I should state that there may be opportunities to restore grizzlies in shortgrass reserves, especially where the Plains meet the Rocky Mountains. Whenever feasible, such a bold undertaking should be pursued.

Just as important as the question of how large grassland reserves need to be to support functional numbers of wolves and maintain viable populations of other species is the question of how large they must be to contain bison in a fashion that reasonably simulates historical patterns. The use of the word "contain" rather than "sustain" is deliberate, for even small reserves can sustain bison. For instance, Theodore Roosevelt National Park in North Dakota, Badlands National Park in South Dakota, and the Nature Conservancy's Niobrara River Preserve in Nebraska, Tallgrass Preserve in Oklahoma, Ordway Prairie in South Dakota, and Cross Ranch in North Dakota all support bison. So do many other small pastures throughout the Great Plains, both public and private. But containing bison in a naturally functioning ecological reserve along with wolves and other predators will undoubtedly require a much larger land unit. As evidence of that, one bison herd in the Wood Buffalo National Park area in Canada traveled fifty-three miles when fleeing wolves, even though the wolves had long given up the pursuit (Carbyn, Oosenbrug, and Anions 1993). That of course does not mean that all bison will run fifty-three miles to flee wolves; indeed, most will not flee at all. And those that do would likely turn when faced with a fence or other barrier. Still, a larger reserve would reduce the likelihood of problems and would more closely replicate natural predator-prey dynamics. One reason that bison in Wood Buffalo National Park in northern Canada seem to be suffering unnaturally high levels of wolf predation is that the available sedge meadow habitat has been reduced as a result of massive water projects (Carbyn, Oosenbrug, and Anions 1993). The reduced habitat increases the likelihood that wolves will locate bison, reduces the amount of escape habitat available, and results in smaller herds that are more susceptible to predation. Larger reserves also allow bison bulls to wander away from their parental herd and encounter unrelated herds for breeding. Such processes replicate natural genetic and social patterns, an especially valuable service as more and more commercial operations manipulate the species' natural makeup. As Meagher (1978, 133) pointed out, "A Great Plains population [of bison], free-ranging on mixed prairie habitat and subject only to natural influences—including predation by wolves . . . would help maintain the species' full genetic variability. . . . small relict and remnant prairies are not enough to restore a free-ranging wild population."

There are of course many other arguments for creating large grassland reserves. Most (e.g., fragmentation, exotics, metapopulations, administration) have been discussed repeatedly throughout this book. Yet this does not mean that small reserves are without value. Many of these tracts contribute important benefits by providing recreational and educational opportunities near urban areas, and some are critical to preserving endemic species with limited distributions. A comprehensive vision for the grassland landscape should include small as well as large tracts of public land, a combination of both sides of the SLOSS (single large or several small) debate that has been ongoing in the scientific community. That said, it should be a cause for concern when the proliferation of small tracts jeopardizes the potential for someday establishing large functional ecological reserves.

Although we may not have a thorough understanding of minimum viable populations and minimum areas, we do know enough not to put all our eggs in one basket. That is to say, we should not establish a population of five hundred ferrets at a site in South Dakota and feel confident about the long-term survival of the species. Rather, we should have at least three distinct populations of ferrets, each of at least five hundred animals. This ensures with a high level of certainty that the species can sustain itself well into the future. Should a plague, drought, harsh winter, or other catastrophe eliminate the population from one reserve, animals could recolonize or be reintroduced from another site.

Reclaiming Lost Land

The drought-resistant, fire-tolerant, sod-forming grasses of the tallgrass, mixed-grass, and shortgrass prairies did not naturally blanket the landscape overnight, and we should not expect to restore the land to its original condition overnight. Reconstructing a semblance of the prairie ecosystem, especially in the drier parts of the grassland biome, is an expensive, frustrating, and trying experience that relies as much on patience and timely rains as on money and technology.

Whenever possible, grassland reserves should be where there are existing tracts of native prairie. In the shortgrass region reserves could be established that are already mostly native prairie. But in the tallgrass region, especially in Iowa, Minnesota, and Missouri, remnant prairie composes less than 1 percent of the landscape. A significant investment will be needed to restore these sites to a functioning facsimile of historical conditions.

Restoring native grasslands costs about $80 an acre for a grass-only mixture, a third of the cost being for seed (native grass seed costs about $1.50 to $8.50 per pound; an acre will require six to eight pounds). Most of the cost goes to seedbed preparation, seeding, and maintenance. Interseeding native forbs among the grasses can increase the price another $20 to $30 an acre (seed only) but may be necessary in some areas. Without forbs, the resulting animal diversity would be limited (Schwartz and Whitson 1986).

Yet just as important as reestablishing native vegetation is restoring the structural integrity of the prairie landscape—in other words, removing everything that is not prairie, such as buildings, rock piles, old machinery, wells, shelterbelts, and other human-made features.

Of course there is more to reconstructing a prairie ecosystem than planting seed and removing anthropogenic structures: restoring a prairie requires the full complement of flora and fauna. But because of fragmentation and isolation, many prairie species are incapable of naturally reoccupying restored lands. Public agencies have long recognized this. The state of Missouri is reintroducing the western smooth green snake (*Opheodrys vernalis*) into tallgrass prairies, and the U.S. Fish and Wildlife Service is reintroducing the threatened prairie bush clover to the newly established Walnut Creek National Wildlife Refuge. Similar efforts, involving myriad species, may be necessary for grassland reserves. But once again an advantage of large reserves is that they benefit from economies of scale. Rather than having to rely on dozens or even hundreds of small restoration sites, many with low potential for long-term species persistence, large reserves would require restoration on only a few sites. Such a scenario would be an improvement ecologically, logistically, economically, administratively, and perhaps most important, politically.

Functional prairie restoration can be done. It simply requires patience and realistic expectations. We need to constantly remind ourselves that most prairie plants evolved to survive droughts and fires, not to colonize cultivated lands. As Mlot (1990) pointed out, prairie restorations are often dominated by weeds the first few years because the true prairie plants are doing most of their growing belowground, in preparation for the inevitable droughts and fires. If the prairie plants can be patient, then surely we can, especially when the rewards will accrue for generations to come.

Nor should we become obsessed with restoring prairies to postcard beauty. Even some conservationists are guilty of this mentality. The original prairie ecosystem did at times include pristine and picturesque panoramas, but in many cases the land looked ravaged. Consider that John James Audubon (1969,

1:513) found some prairies in the northern plains "so completely trodden by Buffaloes that it was next to impossible to walk." Successful reserves will contain both apparent purity and apparent despoilment.

Critics will argue that we can never truly restore prairie. To a certain extent they are right, but that should not prevent us from trying for the best possible simulacrum (even if it requires more "creation" than "restoration"). We know that many prairie birds respond positively to restored prairies within a couple of years (Higgins, Arnold, and Barta 1984), especially when forbs are planted along with the grasses (Volkert 1992). We know that even cultivated prairie soils can return to some of their natural characteristics in just a few years after prairie restoration (Mlot 1990). We also know that many native species can naturally revegetate formerly cultivated land (Tilman 1987) and that over time native plants can sometimes displace exotics (Inouye et al. 1987). Throughout the arid Great Plains there are numerous areas known as "go-backs," sites that were cultivated early in the century but allowed to go back to grass during the Dust Bowl period. To the untrained eye, and in some cases to the trained eye, these sites now look as if they had never been plowed.

Management

Many readers may have concluded by now that large grassland ecological reserves can sustain themselves without human intervention, or that I am implying that. The assumption is wrong. There are simply too many external influences of human origin to assume that even large prairie reserves can sustain themselves in perpetuity without human assistance. (The irony, of course, is that humans must guard these sites against human impact.) Management of all public lands, including large reserves, is necessary in this age of ozone depletion, global warming, acid rain, exotic species, and other worldwide environmental degradation. Even wilderness areas need active management to ensure the conservation of biological diversity. Management of large reserves will for the most part consist of two phases.

The first and, one hopes, most extensive phase will be monitoring. The most obvious form will be monitoring of species diversity, that is, the number of species, their abundance, and their distribution in the ecosystem. But monitoring should also include the most basic level of biodiversity—genetic diversity. For instance, rather than simply monitoring the distribution and abundance of black-footed ferrets, we should also monitor their genetic variability. This information provides us with valuable insight about individual movements, the existence of metapopulations, and the long-term viability of the species. Continuous monitoring of the biotic community should be complemented by continuous monitoring of the abiotic components of the reserves. Measures of water quality, soil erosion, and air quality can provide valuable databases of normality from which we can assess human activities and determine whether environmental changes are natural or human caused (Landres 1992). Such determinations are beneficial not only for preserving grassland biodiversity, but also for ensuring human health and sustainability.

The second phase of reserve management would be more conventional wildlife management. As monitoring detects abnormalities and malfunctions in the reserves—for example, invasion by exotic species—remedial actions will become necessary. Such management may consist of relatively straightforward techniques ranging from eliminating exotic animals to implementing prescribed burns that favor native grasses to controlling the spread of exotic diseases. For example, it would probably be necessary to monitor bison for exotic diseases such as tuberculosis, brucellosis, and anthrax. To simply let these diseases run their course may compromise the biotic integrity of the reserves (but native diseases should be allowed to affect bison populations).

There will of course be many other management needs in the reserve. One of the most significant would be maintaining the boundaries. By now readers have probably questioned how ecological reserves, with bison, wolves, and other beasts, can peacefully coexist with private farmland and rangeland. One option that is workable and pragmatic, albeit not aesthetically pleasing, is to fence the sites.

Large grassland reserves with bison, elk, and wolves will probably never become a reality without fences, especially in the tallgrass and mixed-grass regions. Farmers will never tolerate bison ranging onto their lands, nor will ranchers tolerate wolves roaming through their pastures. Nor should they have to. The burden on landowners near the reserves would be disproportionate and unfair. Hence fencing appears necessary. Cahalane (1940, 133) observed this fifty years ago when he proposed a million-acre Great Plains National Monument: "Restoration of bison, elk and antelope presupposes the construction of a fence sufficient to prevent the animals from wandering to agricultural areas." He also recognized the value of restoring wolves and the need for wolfproof barriers.

The idea of putting up a bison- and wolfproof fence around a twenty-five-hundred-square-mile reserve at first seems ludicrous. Only after careful analysis and deliberation does it begin to sound plausible. Consider that a fence around a reserve of this size would cost about $8 million to build (at $40,000 per mile—a generous amount), including both labor and materials. That amount, though large, is a pittance compared with present government expenditures for grassland conservation, cropland set-asides, farm subsidies, and wildlife damage programs. Indeed, the strongest argument against establishing fences (other than aesthetics) is that they may alter the nomadic nature of bison. This concern seems minor and tolerable, especially in light of the values large reserves would provide.

There is little doubt that adequate barriers can be constructed that would prevent bison from charging through them or elk from jumping over. Fences costing $10,000 to $20,000 a mile are already used throughout the Great Plains to contain these animals within national parks and private pastures. To contain wolves, the fences would have to be enhanced. The fencing material would have to be sunk into the ground to keep wolves from digging under it, and the mesh would have to be of a size that prevented their getting through. Such a fence could easily be built for about $40,000 a mile.

Perhaps the biggest obstacle to containing bison, elk, and wolves within grassland reserves would be the rivers that flow through the region. Grassland rivers are notorious for their wild fluctuations in flow. Still, it seems reasonable to assume that modern technology can design workable barriers that will not disrupt river flows while still containing larger animals.

Last, the fences should be designed so they are porous to species that are not perceived as harmful to adjacent land uses. For example, swift foxes and black-footed ferrets should be able to traverse the reserve boundary. If the landscape outside the reserves is seminatural (a buffer zone [Noss and Cooperrider 1994]), then a permeable fence would greatly expand the available habitat for such species. If the seminatural landscape connects with another reserve (a corridor), then genetic exchange and genetic diversity would be enhanced. Such a condition is desirable and is especially feasible in the shortgrass and mixed-grass regions, where grazing is the most sustainable and profitable land use (when government payments are excluded). Porous fences can also help reduce the "inside/outside" mindset that can alienate people from nature.

Having discussed the feasibility of fences for grassland reserves, I must emphasize that such structures are inappropriate or unnecessary in most other regions. Parks such as Yellowstone, Glacier, and North Cascades have the benefit of extensive buffer zones of national forests and other public lands outside their boundaries. In addition, they are in regions of rugged topography, unsuitable soils, or humid climate where constructing and maintaining hundreds of miles of fence is impractical. It is fair to say that of all the large ecoregions in North America, the grassland biome and the desert Southwest are the only ones that are conducive to such a strategy.

One last comment needs to be made concerning bison- and wolfproof fences around grassland reserves. Even if fences were not constructed by the government or other managing entity, bison would still be effectively fenced within the proposed reserve boundaries by the vast network of existing barbedwire fences that litter the Great Plains. This is true even in the Poppers' buffalo commons scenario. No matter what the scale, bison that are restored to the grassland biome are going to be fenced in.

How far humans need to intervene within grassland reserves will also depend on how we define a natural ecosystem. Although even today's urban ecosystems could be considered natural in the sense that humans are simply another species, that would be inconsistent with the conventional use of the term. Natural ecosystems are usually defined as ecosystems that are comparable to what existed on the site before European settlement. By that definition, humans are a part of natural ecosystems in North America—and apparently a very significant part. An estimated 10 million Native Americans lived in North America before European settlement, a surprisingly large 3 percent of the current United States population (Noss and Cooperrider 1994). In the Great Plains Native Americans are known to have intentionally set fires for wildlife management (Dodge 1989). They also hunted the great herds of bison, often killing great numbers by driving them over cliffs. Similarly, tribes along the major rivers, such as the sedentary Mandans and Hidatsas, planted crops such as corn, squash, and beans that may have had local, although minor, influence on wildlife.

Hence, if we want to simulate and conserve as best we can a "natural" grassland ecosystem, we should be willing to incorporate a human presence. To adequately mimic a pre-Columbian human presence will require the input of anthropologists and historians as well as ecologists and biologists. Such acceptance also justifies the occasional footprint left by managers, recreationists, and hunters.

Tourism

A detailed analysis of the human use—and the associated economics—of hypothetical grassland reserves is beyond the scope of this book, but several conceptual points are worth noting.

147

A survey by the United States government revealed that 108.7 million U.S. residents sixteen years and older, or 57 percent of that age group, participated in some form of wildlife-related recreation in 1991 (U.S. Fish and Wildlife Service 1993a). Of those, 76.1 million participated in nonconsumptive recreation such as viewing, photographing, and feeding wildlife, while 35.6 million fished and 14.1 million hunted. The amount of nonresidential, nonconsumptive wildlife-related recreation is especially noteworthy, since it increased 63 percent between 1980 and 1990 (Aiken 1994).

Total expenditures on wildlife-related activities in 1991 were $59 billion, including $22.8 billion spent on trips (U.S. Fish and Wildlife Service 1993a). One study estimated that the total dollar value of the nonconsumptive wildlife resource, measured as willingness to pay, was as high as $164.5 billion (in 1980 dollars [Rockel and Kealy 1991]). The researchers even suggested the figure may have been an underestimate when one considers the loss of alternative wildlife sites. The value of wildlife to the nation's economic and spiritual well-being cannot be denied.

The government study also found that at least 84 percent of those who traveled farther than one mile to take part in nonconsumptive wildlife-related activities did so on public lands (U.S. Fish and Wildlife Service 1993a). Public lands represent our best, and for some people our only, source of wildlife-related recreation. Public lands are especially valuable where the supply is the least—that is, the midwestern United States.

According to the U.S. Forest Service (1990), open space is the primary outdoor recreation resource. The same report found that the rate of wilderness recreation has continued to increase over the past several decades. Clearly society is pursuing not only wildlife, but also solitude and spiritual renewal. But in the past twenty years the amount of land in the United States farther than half a mile from a road has declined almost 1 percent annually (U.S. Forest Service 1990). (In the Great Plains the largest protected roadless area is a sixty-four-thousand-acre unit in South Dakota's Badlands National Park, a mere three-hour hike from one end to the other.) By the year 2040, the amount of roadless area is expected to decrease 31 percent from 1987. The same study also found that of thirty-one common outdoor pursuits, the largest gaps between demand and supply in the year 2040 will involve backpacking, wildlife observation, and camping in primitive campgrounds. Another study found that by the year 2040 each potential recreationist will face a 32 percent decline in available wildlife and

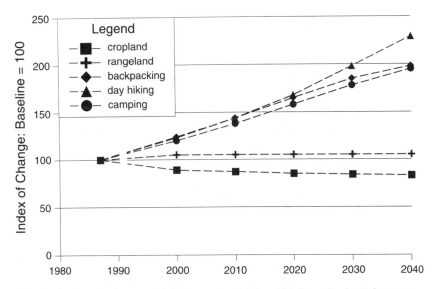

Figure 4. Projected land-use needs to the year 2040. Data from U.S. Forest Service (1989c, 1990).

fish resources (U.S. Forest Service 1989c). Yet during this same period the na-tion will have no additional need for rangeland or cropland (fig. 4); in fact, it will probably still have the current level of excess agricultural capacity.

These and other studies provide convincing evidence that the public's desire for more wildlife-related outdoor opportunities is great and that the desire will continue to increase. Already the demand is so great that many national parks, such as Grand Canyon National Park, are considering adopting a reservation system. To many Americans this borders on unconstitutional, but the only solu-tion to overcrowding is either to adopt such drastic restrictions or to create more parks and wild areas. Surely there is a need for more public wildlands, if for no other reason than to provide outdoor experiences for the nation.

As I have said repeatedly throughout this book, the presence of bison, prairie dogs, and wolves is crucial to the establishment of fully functional ecological reserves, especially in the mixed-grass and shortgrass prairies. From a tourism perspective, bison and wolves are the most important. Wolves deserve addi-tional discussion because they are the most controversial and the most studied. The social and economic analyses of the reintroduction of wolves into Yellow-stone National Park provides a starting point for drawing inferences about the recreational and economic benefits of establishing grassland reserves that con-

149

tain wolves. In spite of vocal opposition to reintroducing wolves into Yellow-stone, surveys showed that a great majority of park visitors, and even most residents of Montana, Idaho, and Wyoming, have positive perceptions of wolves and support wolf reintroductions (Bath 1992). Other surveys showed that the typical Yellowstone visitor was willing to make a one-time donation of $23 to support wolf recovery in the park, whereas those against it were willing to pay only $2 to oppose reintroductions (Duffield 1992). The regional net economic impact of establishing wolves in the park was estimated to be on the order of $43 million annually (after deducting for livestock losses and reduced hunting opportunities due to wolf predation on ungulates). Last, Kellert (1985, 532) makes an interesting observation: "Experience has demonstrated the ability to rationalize the protection of these culturally familiar animals [wolves] and, in the process, obtain public support for establishing habitat preserves. In this manner, the preservation of all species party to the same food webs as the target species can be accomplished."

In summary, Americans love their wildlife and spend considerable time and money on wildlife-related activities. A Times Mirror Magazines Conservation Council (1992) survey found that most Americans were willing to pay for wildlife conservation. They were also willing to divert funds from other federal programs for conservation efforts. From that it seems reasonable to suggest that a portion of the money currently spent on temporary cropland set-asides, with only marginal wildlife and recreational value, be considered for the permanent creation of large natural areas in the grassland biome.

Hunting

Whether hunting should be allowed in grassland reserves—or anywhere, for that matter—can be viewed as a moral question. I will not address that question other than to say that at least one survey found that 64 percent of the public approves of hunting if the meat is eaten (Kellert 1980). But if the question of hunting in reserves is viewed from almost any other perspective, then the answer must be yes. Managed hunting should be allowed in grassland reserves.

The first argument for hunting can be made from an anthropological and evolutionary perspective. Wildlife on the Great Plains has been subjected to hunting for the past twelve thousand years. Thousands of generations of bison, elk, deer, and antelope have evolved in response to human-caused mortality. Indigenous people on the Great Plains may have harvested a million bison annually, or fifteen to twenty bison per capita (Barsh 1990). Although the techniques and goals of Native American hunters were radically different from those of modern sport hunters, this concern can be adequately addressed by wildlife managers when they establish hunting seasons and regulations. Last, whatever unnaturalness would result from modern hunting is probably insignificant in light of the political support that will be needed from the hunting community to establish reserves.

Of course any hunting in the reserves should be carefully managed, with only surplus animals taken. Once again the goal of the reserve managers should be to replicate natural conditions; that is, the proportion of animals taken by Native Americans (harvest strategies should allow for winter mortality in harsh winters, a natural and important process). Even with these moderate levels of human harvest, hypothetical grassland reserves could provide substantial amounts of food. The bison and elk alone could produce an annual harvestable surplus of at least seven thousand pounds of biomass per square mile in the tallgrass reserves, four thousand per square mile in the mixed-grass regions, and three thousand per square mile in the shortgrass regions.

The Politics

Towards evening, on rising a hill, we were suddenly greeted by a sight which seemed to astonish even the oldest amongst us. The whole plain, as far as the eye could discern, was covered by one enormous mass of buffalo. . . . It was truly a sight that would have excited even the dullest mind to enthusiasm.

John Townsend, in Thwaites, *Early Western Travels, 1748–1846*

By now it should be evident that creating large grassland ecological reserves would benefit grassland conservation as well as farmers and ranchers, rural communities, outdoor recreationists, American taxpayers, and future generations. However, the obstacles to such public reserves are formidable and entrenched. Dramatic changes in government policy and programs do not occur overnight. As Wooten (1965, 1) noted in his comprehensive review of the successful land redistribution programs of the 1930s and 1940s, "Public policy and plans seldom spring full-grown into being, but develop gradually as the result of public support of certain programs and public rejection of others."

Politics, emotions, special interest groups, and government inertia may seem impossible to overcome, but they are not. Many people will quickly see the substantial benefits of retiring excess cropland in the Great Plains and using it for conservation and recreation. The biggest impediment will be simply getting the discussions to the table. If the issues and concepts are discussed in an open forum, with all the facts laid out honestly and clearly, it will become self-evident that prairie restoration is in the best interest of the country. As Bret Wallach (1985, 5) said, "A prairie-restoration proposal, in other words, sounds outrageous until it is compared with what we've already got."

Even the most vehement antienvironmentalist could find positive benefits from a series of reserves. For example, after the creation of these areas a great number of endangered and threatened grassland species could be removed from the endangered species list. The rancher in Wyoming would no longer experience hassles and perceived infringement of property rights because of the potential presence of black-footed ferrets. The livestock owner in eastern North Dakota would not be prosecuted for shooting an endangered wolf that dispersed into the agrarian region from the forests of northern Minnesota. Property values would not decline because an endangered bird established a nest. All these concerns are real, and all are cases where private landowners pay, or may pay, a disproportionate share to protect and conserve a public resource. (Conversely, conservationists would not be as likely to have their efforts thwarted by private entities [see Westemeier 1988].)

Also, the retirement of a few producers would decrease agricultural capacity and hence increase the prices farmers and ranchers get at the market. This would also reduce their dependency on the federal government and American taxpayers. Still, the thought of taking land out of "production" may be too much for some people to bear. To counter that, the sobering economic realities of the conventional uses of the Great Plains will need to be repeated over and over.

As I explained in previous chapters, agricultural capacity in the United States is increasing much more rapidly than population growth, resulting in a costly surplus of cropland. Traditionally the nation has tried to address the problem of excessive surpluses via expensive farm programs. Yet the $5 trillion national debt has forced the nation to reevaluate such tactics. In 1996 President Clinton signed legislation that phases out deficiency payments and many other farm subsidies over a seven-year period (but not land set-asides). If carried out, the legislation will likely result in many bankrupt farmers and ranchers, especially the smaller operators and those in the arid portions of the Great Plains.

There are some who argue that the best way to solve the farm crisis is to practice more sustainable farming practices (smaller fields, fewer pesticides, less plowing). They believe society should return to an agrarian lifestyle more similar to that at the turn of the century. Although some of these arguments have merit, they ignore capitalism, technology, and human nature. Few producers have demonstrated a self-initiated willingness to sacrifice short-term profits for the sake of long-term environmental or economic sustainability (at least without government incentives or penalties). And even if farmers do adopt more sustainable practices, there may still be surpluses. Indeed, high productivity and sustainability may go hand in hand (Waggoner 1994).

Although it is true that existing rangeland would likely make up a large portion of many grassland reserves, functionally there is little difference between rangeland and cropland from a national economic and food-producing perspective. Approximately half of our harvested crops are used for livestock feed; conversely, a great percentage of our rangeland has recently been converted to cropland. Indeed, a tract of land may regularly revert from one use to the other. And prices for rangeland commodities—beef—are also depressed because of surplus production.

Rangeland currently constitutes 34 percent of the United States land area and is especially prevalent in the western United States (U.S. Forest Service 1989a). For the sake of argument, assume that a series of grassland reserves are established solely from rangeland and that they total 7.5 million acres. That is less than 1 percent of the nation's total. This amount of retired rangeland could easily be compensated for by using excess cropland to produce livestock feed (or by restoring it to rangeland). For example, a typical acre of Iowa farmland can produce about 3 tons of hay annually, or 140 bushels of feed corn, or 16 tons of corn silage. Assuming that a cow needs 3 tons of hay annually and that a series of grassland reserves will displace 400,000 beef cows, then the displaced cattle could theoretically be maintained on only 400,000 Iowa acres, or 18 percent of the CRP acreage in the state as of July 1992 (U.S. Department of Agriculture 1993). In fact, if all the CRP in the United States was used for livestock forage it could support about 20 million cattle, compared with the 2 million head that are sustained on all the currently grazed public lands in the United States. Likewise, CRP in the grassland biome alone could support 8 million head of cattle; compare that with the 9 million beef cows supported in the region in 1992. These analyses admittedly are crude, but the argument that any potential reduction in the nation's beef supply could be countered by utilizing surplus cropland remains sound. Noss and Cooperrider (1994, 258) noted this possibility when they stated, "As a society we need to ask if it is wise to subsidize destructive grazing practices on arid and semiarid lands in order to export meat to areas with greater precipitation (and thus productivity), particularly since the latter produce the vast majority of the nation's meat anyway."

Although the reduction of agricultural outputs would arguably be beneficial to the nation, the loss to local economies could be harmful and therefore should not be ignored. But these losses could be mitigated in whole or in part by business associated with the establishment of ecological reserves. For instance, entrance fees to the public reserves could be used to compensate local economies, and profits from wholesale harvests of surplus bison could also be targeted toward nearby communities. Not only would the harvests yield large amounts of revenue (bison for slaughter sell for about $1.25 to $1.35 per pound—15–45 percent more than beef), the roundups or hunts could provide employment for local residents. Local residents could also find new opportunities in providing tourist accommodations, working at visitor facilities, reserves, or guiding services, or in other outdoor-associated employment. Many of these same people would continue to farm and ranch outside the reserve boundaries; hence the reserves would provide new opportunities without affecting their way of life.

The Clinton administration chose in the early 1990s to compensate Pacific Northwest loggers and rural communities $1.2 billion for relief from logging restrictions to protect the northern spotted owl (*Strix occidentalis caurina*). Much of the money went for job retraining. Surely Congress could consider a comparatively modest effort to retrain agricultural producers, especially when such expenditures would ultimately lessen the need for Farm Program expenditures. The U.S. Office of Technology Assessment (1992) made such a recommendation when it suggested providing retraining to help farmers leave farming.

Although many skeptics will question the likelihood of the government's purchasing large tracts of land, there are numerous precedents for extensive public land acquisition, including those for reservoir construction, military uses, and highways. In one extremely successful case in the 1930s to 1940s, large tracts of land in the Great Plains were acquired for soil conservation, economic relief, commodity reduction, and wildlife restoration. Many of the private individuals who sold land to the government "welcomed the federal land-use program" (Hurt 1986, 96). Those lands now constitute much of our national grasslands and Bureau of Land Management land, available to all Americans. The current situation begs for a phase 2 of those extremely successful efforts.

There are also more recent analogues of the federal government's assisting landowners who have made dubious land-use decisions. After the great Mississippi and Missouri River floods in the summer of 1993, the federal government actively assisted and subsidized six thousand landowners who were willing to relocate out of floodplains. In addition, many floodplain farm fields were purchased by the federal government and restored to natural areas. The situation is analogous to that of the farmers who try to farm the arid Great Plains. Not only do the Plains get flooded, the region is also parched by droughts, plagued by locusts, cursed by poor crop prices, and burdened by logistics.

It is worth repeating that grassland reserves could be created in large part from existing public lands. Such a strategy was used as recently as 1994 when Congress passed the California Desert Protection Act. The act created a 3.3-million-acre national park (the largest in the lower forty-eight states), a 1.4-million-acre national preserve, and an 0.8-million-acre national park out of existing federal and private lands. (The national preserve designation is especially relevant because it allows for hunting.) Skeptics of public land acquisition strategies should not dismiss the significance of these events.

The next argument may be one of the more important factors in determining whether a Great Plains land retirement program becomes a reality. Society should consider paying more than the conventional market value of the lands in question. There are several reasons for this: society is already paying the market value of these lands many times over in the form of Farm Program payments and other subsidies; the ecological value of these lands has no real relation to the conventional market value, which typically is measured only by commercial or residential value; there should be an economic benefit to the people who are being asked to relocate; establishment of reserves can reduce the need for other grassland conservation measures (e.g., endangered species management); and sellers will be more cooperative if they feel they are coming out ahead rather than "failing." A precedent for high prices has been set in Canada, where the government paid "good prices" for land to create a grasslands national park (Popper and Popper 1994a). The Poppers report that Canadian ranchers and farmers now criticize the government for moving too slowly to create the park. Likewise, the United States dairy cattle buyout of the 1980s succeeded because the prices the federal government offered were higher than the free market prices (U.S. Office of Technology Assessment 1992). Offering attractive prices in conjunction with a capital gains tax break would make such offers even more appealing.

Many of these tracts could be purchased with federal dollars already earmarked for land acquisition. The Land and Water Conservation Fund Act of 1964 created a fund from offshore oil leases, motorboat fuel taxes, proceeds of surplus government property, and certain types of user fees. About $900 million is collected annually. Unfortunately, appropriation of these funds has slowed to a trickle ever since the Reagan years. However, if Congress elected to use these funds as intended (to acquire land for outdoor recreation and wildlife conservation), grassland reserves could be acquired with no additional cost to American taxpayers. Of course redirecting current Farm Program expenditures would have the same effect.

Economically minded people may conclude that the government could acquire many of the lands in question at the current market value by simply stopping subsidies to the landowners. Without Farm Program payments many Great Plains farmers would soon face bankruptcy and hence be willing to sell or would default on their FHA loans. Such an approach seems malicious and is probably politically impossible in the United States. As Kraenzel (1955) noted, a planned approach would be a more humane and rational way to address the Great Plains' economic woes.

There will undoubtedly be a public outcry from many residents of the grassland states, especially those in rural areas, against any proposals for government acquisition. The most frequent protest will be that people should mind their own business. But all Americans have a stake in the future of the Great Plains. Cochrane and Runge (1992, 29) agreed when they stated that "in the national economy of the 1990s it is inconceivable that the political universe for formulating and executing policies for the food, farm and rural sectors be limited to the farming community."

Unfortunately, in American politics parochial interests often supersede national needs. Even the wisest and most necessary of programs and initiatives can fail because of this propensity. It is especially true when the political representation is heavily skewed. Consider that the states of North Dakota, South Dakota, Nebraska, Montana, and Wyoming have a combined population of 4.2 million people, or 1.7 percent of the entire United States population, yet they have 10 percent of the senators in the United States Senate. Compare that with a state like California that has a population over 29.7 million yet is represented by only two senators. All the grassland counties combined, both rural and urban, have a population of only 13 million, half that of California, yet they are represented by twenty-four more senators. From an environmental perspective these inequalities would be irrelevant if Great Plains senators and representatives voted comparably to their colleagues, but they do not. Western politicians have traditionally opposed pro-environment legislation. Consider that the League of Conservation Voters (1994) gave the twenty-six grassland senators a combined score of 33, while the score for the remaining seventy-four United States senators was 52 (100 represents a perfect environmental record while 0 means the person voted against every major environmental initiative). Likewise, the twenty-five United States representatives that have more than half of their districts in the grassland biome had a combined score of 44 compared with a score of 56 for the rest of the United States House of Representatives. More telling, when the representatives from Denver, Minneapolis–St. Paul, and Omaha are removed from the grassland group, the score for grassland representatives falls to a dismal 39 compared with 56 for the rest of the nation.

However, the political clout of grassland counties will continue to decline as their population declines. For example, after the 1990 census the grassland states (excluding Texas) experienced a net loss of three representatives (Montana, Kansas, Iowa) and three electoral college votes. Trends suggest that this decline will continue well into the next century. Yet it could be decades before the decline is great enough that the nation can rationally address the huge subsidies being spent in the region. Therefore other legislative and administrative mechanisms may be needed if grassland reserves are ever to become a reality.

One such mechanism would be an independent government commission to address the issue. Once again a precedent has been set. The closing of over 160 surplus military bases in the early 1990s was successfully accomplished in large part by a commission of eight people. Realizing that it was incapable of tackling the necessary evil, Congress created the base-closure commission as part of the fiscal year 1991 defense authorization. The law required three rounds of military base closings—1991, 1993, and 1995. Needless to say, every single closing was stubbornly fought by local communities and their politicians. Fortunately the commission members had no political affiliations that compromised their impartiality or integrity. Hence they were able to overcome the hurdles of parochial politics while objectively looking at the big picture and the long-term needs of the country. The overhaul of the Farm Program and the establishment of several large grassland reserves as a by-product of that process could be implemented by a comparable commission. A similar recommendation was made by the economists Cochrane and Runge (1992) after they exhaustively analyzed the existing federal farm program.

The following may be the most important element in determining whether grassland reserves ever come to fruition. Landowners within the reserves need to have input into the process. The input could be in a variety of forms. For example, a process could be set up whereby a site would be converted if a majority (or some other predetermined percentage) of landowners voted to sell. (Land condemnation is unlikely under any strategy for sociopolitical reasons; hence some landscape fragmentation may be unavoidable in the immediate future.) Another strategy would be to leave the delineation of reserves up to the individual states. States that wanted to continue receiving farm subsidies would solicit input from their residents, then identify reserve sites. The actual acreage of the reserves in each state could be calculated based on the state's historical crop production, past set-aside acreage, total amount of farm subsidies, or other criteria. There are probably a great number of other strategies that could be debated.

Additional enticements could be offered to make the program more salable. The government might enter into term contracts (e.g., five-year) with the sellers to plant native grasses and remove unnatural vegetation (shelterbelts), vacant buildings, and so on. Most farmers already have the equipment and expertise to plant grasses, so they would be ideal contractors for grassland restoration. Such contracts would also sustain many farmers until retirement.

But before such strategies can be considered, there has to be a general public consensus that the system is broken. Public sentiment must force typically fainthearted politicians that drastic measures are needed. The prerequisite for such sentiment is public education and awareness. Cochrane and Runge (1992, 27) also saw this need: "Urbanites and their representatives in Congress have the votes to write the farm legislation, if they knew what they wanted. But they don't. They are so deeply mired in a set of false and misleading images about farmers, farming and rural America, that they cannot take the effective legislative action." Urbanites witness the conversion of hundreds of acres of farmland to suburban residential sites, and they perceive food shortages. What they do not see are the tens of millions of acres of Great Plains farmland being retired because of surplus capacity, and that they are paying for it.

Hypothetical Reserves

And what a splendid contemplation too, when one imagines them as they
might in future be seen, (by some great protecting policy of government)
preserved in their pristine beauty and wildness, in a magnificent park,
where the world could see for ages to come. . . . What a beautiful and
thrilling specimen for America to preserve and hold up to the view of her
refined citizens and the world, in future ages! A nation's park.

George Catlin, *Letters and Notes on the Manners, Customs, and
Conditions of the North American Indians*

The location of potential ecological reserves in the grassland biome should be
determined only after reasonable investigation by ecologists, hydrologists,
economists, agriculturalists, sociologists, and others. But we should not spend
too much time and money on deliberations. Every day means another $30 mil-
lion spent on agricultural subsidies and species closer to extinction.

I have taken the liberty of delineating several hypothetical grassland reserves, in part because I believe these sites have potential and in part because I
think they can illustrate the economic, ecological, and social effects of implementing such actions. Although such a scenario is subject to ridicule, it would
be a disservice not to provide some elucidating examples. The major criteria I
used to select the sites were ecological value, amount of public land present,
potential to reduce farm surpluses, social impact, and potential for tourism.

Although the hypothetical reserves described here may seem extremely ambitious, they are actually quite modest, especially in terms of reducing agricultural capacity. For example, the total amount of cropland (including unharvested land) contained within the hypothetical reserves amounts to only 4.8

million acres, just 1.1 percent of the nation's total and 2.6 percent of the Great Plains total. More significant, the amount of cropland is only 13.1 percent of that placed in CRP (excess cropland), while all the land within the hypothetical reserves, public and private, crop and range, is just 48.2 percent of the CRP total. Obviously, even more ambitious efforts would be needed to make serious and lasting inroads in our surplus agricultural capacity. Yet the examples presented here provide a useful working reference.

For each hypothetical reserve the technical information concerning location, cost, agriculture, and so on can be found in map 7 and tables 7 and 8. The following text will briefly discuss some unique opportunities and considerations associated with each site.

One obstacle to establishing large unfragmented, publicly owned grassland reserves is the anxiety of state governments about the prospect of more federal lands within their boundaries. Yet surprisingly, some large grassland reserves could be established with no net increase in federal ownership within the states where they occur. Consider a hypothetical Western Dakotas reserve in western North Dakota and eastern Montana.

Over 650,000 acres of fragmented federal lands already exist within the hypothetical reserve boundary in the form of the Little Missouri National Grasslands. Therefore only 1.3 million more acres would be needed to complete a 3,080-square-mile reserve. Such a large land acquisition by the federal government would be challenged by the states of North Dakota and Montana. Yet within the six counties that the hypothetical reserve is a part of and the nine counties adjacent to them, the federal government (Forest Service, BLM, Fish and Wildlife Service, National Park Service) already owns 2.1 million acres. Theoretically the federal government could exchange the public lands outside the reserve boundary for the private lands within and still have 150,000 acres left over. For the government such an arrangement would be an improvement ecologically and administratively. For the state it would be beneficial in increasing tourism. (Of course such an approach does nothing to reduce commodity surpluses.)

A large Western Dakotas reserve could contain shortgrass, badlands, and riverine ecosystems and would in many ways rank alongside Yellowstone, the Everglades, the Grand Canyon, and some of the nation's other magnificent natural areas. The rich topography of the region is conducive to numerous microcommunities including mixed-grass prairie, Rocky Mountain juniper (*Ju-*

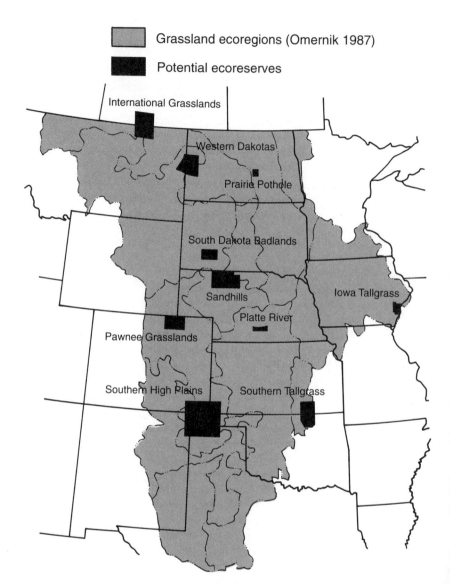

Map 7. Hypothetical reserves. Modified from Licht 1994.

Table 7. Attributes of Hypothetical Reserves

Reserve	Area (square miles)	Percentage of Public and Nature Conservancy Land[a]	Human Population within Reserve	Mean Value of Land and Buildings in 1992 (per acre)	Approximate Cost to Acquire at Appraised Value (millions of $)
Western Dakotas	3,080	33%	1,400	$185	$235
Southern Tallgrass	2,820	2%	16,800	$315	$545
Prairie Pothole	1,290	2%	1,900	$255	$200
South Dakota Badlands	2,450	38%	2,200	$140	$130
Sandhills	5,409	6%	3,100	$180	$575
Pawnee Grasslands	1,274	31%	900	$245	$135
International Grasslands[b]	1,800	33%	1,000	$180	$135
Iowa Tallgrass	400	0%	11,100	$1,100	$275
Southern High Plains	8,379	9%	16,700	$265	$1,265
Platte River	550	1%	3,800	$1,100	$375
Total	27,452	15%[c]	58,900	X=$265[c]	$3,870

Note: See also map 7 and preface, "Sources and Methods Used in Analysis."

[a]Public lands include only U.S. Forest Service, U.S. Fish and Wildlife Service, Bureau of Land Management, and National Park Service lands.

[b]U.S. portion only.

[c]Weighted mean.

niperus scopulorum) shrubland, cottonwood floodplain, deciduous woody draws, and sagebrush prairie. The shallow Little Missouri River is typical of many Great Plains rivers and is a likely home for several unique and threatened fish species including the sicklefin chub (*Hybopsis meeki*), sturgeon chub (*H. gelida*), and blue sucker (*Cycleptus elongatus*). (Water quality deterioration, apparently due to overgrazing, currently threatens these fish.) Because of the diversity of habitats, such a reserve could theoretically support 25,000 bison, 300 wolves, 100 mountain lions, 10,000 elk, 700 bighorn sheep, 15,000 mule deer, 1,000 white-tailed deer, 15,000 antelope, 3,000 swift foxes, 1,200 black-footed ferrets, 1.2 million prairie dogs, and countless other components of the northern Great Plains ecosystem. Because of its large size and the variety and abundance of species it could conserve, such a reserve could become North America's Serengeti, a site to rival anything found in Africa.

163

Table 8. 1992 Farm Statistics within Hypothetical Reserves

Reserve	Number of Farms	Change in Number of Farms 1978–92	Net Cash Return for Agricultural Sales per Farm	Percentage of Deficit Farms[a]	Total Cropland (thousands of acres)	Percentage of Cropland Not Harvested	Percentage in CRP, WRP, and Commodity Set-Aside	Number of Beef Cows	Government Farm Payments (millions of $)
Western Dakotas	530	−17%	$17,240	30%	280	32%[b]	32%	40,620	$3.9
Southern Tallgrass	1,730	−10%	$9,940	46%	330	46%	10%	69,200	$2.0
Prairie Pothole	550	−17%	$20,600	32%	525	33%	26%	24,260	$5.7
South Dakota									
Badlands	175	+18%	$17,140	39%	115	49%	19%	34,960	$1.0
Sandhills	550	0%	$35,160	30%	335	14%	4%	152,580	$0.7
Pawnee									
Grasslands	310	−21%	$11,410	37%	300	60%	32%	18,840	$4.5
International									
Grasslands[c]	250	−14%	$13,480	37%	305	59%	29%	14,020	$3.6
Iowa Tallgrass	700	−28%	$17,210	43%	215	14%	12%	2,730	$4.9
Southern									
High Plains	2,180	−11%	$72,200	36%	2,110	53%	34%	61,120	$34.1
Platte River	540	−12%	$50,220	31%	270	18%	6%	12,790	$6.4
Total or average	7,515	−13%	$35,060	38%	4,785	43%	25%	431,120	$66.8
Percentage of U.S. total	0.39%	—	—	—	1.10%	—	—	1.32%	1.28%

Note: See also map 7 and preface, "Sources and Methods Used in Analysis."

[a]Defined as farms with net income less than zero when government payments are excluded.

[b]U.S. Bureau of Census (1995) data indicated 24 percent of cropland not harvested, while set-aside data suggest that at least 32 percent of the cropland was not harvested. I used the higher figure. The discrepancy is likely due to absentee landowners, who place large amounts of cropland in government set-aside programs but are not considered farmers (owing to sales less than $1,000); hence they are not included in the Bureau of Census data.

[c]U.S. portion only.

164

Thanks to shallow soils with layers of bedrock just below the surface, a comparatively large amount of Chautauqua, Elk, and Greenwood Counties in Kansas and Osage County in Oklahoma escaped the plow, making the region ideal for a Southern Tallgrass reserve. Already a recently established Tallgrass Prairie Preserve, owned and managed by the Nature Conservancy, provides a 36,950-acre seed source for a larger reserve. The nonprofit group will eventually restore nineteen hundred head of bison. Although a modest acreage when compared with many national parks, and having only limited accommodations and publicity, the site received approximately twelve thousand visitors in 1992, with substantial increases expected once the bison herd is fully established.

Although the Nature Conservancy's efforts are commendable, they are inadequate to meet the public's demand for outdoor recreation and education. The nonprofit group's overriding mission is to conserve biological diversity, with education and recreation secondary. Therefore to realize the full benefits that can be derived from such a reserve, the area needs to be publicized and made available for public use to a much greater extent than the Conservancy can accommodate.

A second argument can be made for establishing a large grassland reserve in the region. If a system of reserves is established as part of a concerted effort to reduce the nation's agricultural capacity, then it is only fair that all states in the grassland biome accept reductions in the amount of land in production (the same could be argued for the other thirty-seven states). It would be unfair, and perhaps politically impossible, to expect the Dakotas, Montana, Nebraska, and other states to reduce their commodity output while Kansas and Oklahoma do not. Although the proposed site is as much rangeland as cropland, the retirement of the former effectively reduces the surpluses of the latter, as I have already noted.

Of all the locales in the two states, the site described here would make the greatest contribution to the conservation of grassland biodiversity. The lush vegetation and mild winters in the southern tallgrass region are conducive to large numbers of grazing animals. It is reasonable to assume that seventy-five thousand bison could be sustained on the site, and elk, which have been absent from Oklahoma and Kansas since the turn of the century (except for a few token herds), could be reestablished, perhaps ten thousand or more.

The most significant beneficiaries of a Prairie Pothole reserve in east-central North Dakota would be waterfowl and other wetland-related species. Though waterfowl are not threatened with extinction, it is quite evident that current efforts to stem their precipitous decline are often short term, marginally successful, and aesthetically unappealing.

In the absence of naturally functioning ecosystems, wildlife managers have often resorted to gimmicks and gadgets to produce ducks. A search of the scientific literature reveals that at least 263 scientific papers have been published since 1935 concerning artificial nesting structures, predator exclosures, captive propagation, and other technological solutions to waterfowl conservation. The cost-benefit ratio of some of these techniques is disheartening. One study in the Prairie Pothole Region estimated that the annual cost per fledged duck in 1982 dollars ranged from $2 per duck for predator management (elimination of predators) to $8.54 per duck for nest baskets to $223 per duck for human-made nesting islands (Lokemoen 1984). Such practices raise not only cost-benefit questions but also aesthetic and evolutionary concerns. How many generations of mallards can be raised in concrete nesting culverts and plastic tubs before the ancestral grassland nesting duck is bred out of the population? Another artificial solution to our waterfowl woes is equally disturbing. It has been suggested that pen-raised waterfowl be released to replenish wild populations. Over twenty thousand captive-raised mallards have already been released into the wild in central North Dakota, and seven thousand wood ducks, a nongrassland species, have been released in the northern plains.

A large grassland reserve in the Prairie Pothole Region would give waterfowl an opportunity to breed in an environment without shelterbelts, farmsteads, croplands, rock piles, or roads. A large grassland reserve in pristine condition, consisting mainly of grasses and wetlands, would become an invaluable laboratory for biologists as well as a duck factory for waterfowl. In ecological terms, the site would be a *source* population producing surplus animals that could colonize low-quality habitats (agrarian regions).

Granted, such a reserve is not going to single-handedly restore Great Plains waterfowl populations. Efforts on private lands and small public tracts, although less efficacious, should continue. Still, compared with present management efforts, a large Prairie Pothole reserve would be a great improvement over a comparable acreage of small, scattered sites.

In addition to waterfowl, other wetland species would benefit. The threatened piping plover and rare white pelican (*Pelecanus erythrorhynchos*) already use many of the wetlands in the area. Even whooping cranes could benefit from such a reserve. Both whooping cranes and sandhill cranes (*Grus canadensis*) originally nested in the Dakotas. There is no reason to assume that nesting colonies of both could not be reestablished if a suitable ecosystem was present.

The Chase Lake Project is the official name for a land acquisition, protection, and management effort currently under way at the site by government and nongovernment organizations including the U.S. Fish and Wildlife Service, North Dakota Game and Fish Department, Ducks Unlimited, and the Nature Conservancy. The project, initiated in September 1989, will consist of 130,000 acres within the hypothetical reserve boundaries by the year 2000, of which 34,000 acres are owned in fee title and another 96,000 are in government easements. Since an additional 190,000 acres in Kidder and Stutsman Counties are in CRP or WRP (Wetlands Reserve Program), it does not seem unreasonable to consider permanently retiring some of these lands from cultivation.

Situated within an hour of Rapid City, the Black Hills, and Mount Rushmore, a South Dakota Badlands reserve would prove invaluable not only for conserving Great Plains biodiversity but also for tourism and education. Just as important, the reserve could be a source of material and spiritual prosperity for a group of Americans who desperately need both.

Over 37 percent of all Native Americans live in ten grassland states (excluding Missouri, Iowa, and Wyoming [1990 census, cited in World Almanac 1994, 434]). Those same states also contain some of the largest tribal reservations in terms of area. For example, South Dakota has almost 2.4 million acres of tribally owned lands and another 2.1 million acres owned by individual Native Americans, while Montana has over 2.6 million acres of tribally owned lands and almost 3 million acres of individually owned lands.

Yet the lands within the reservations are some of the most marginal farmland in the country, and probably would not have been farmed were it not for government subsidies. Consider that when government payments are excluded, ninety-two farms in Shannon County (containing the Pine Ridge Reservation) had net losses in 1992 while only ninety-eight had net gains. Still, the federal government pours almost $1 million annually into the county in agricultural subsidies.

There is simply no benefit to the country in continuing to use these lands for agriculture. It would be in the best interest of all Americans, including the local residents, to look for new and more sustainable use for them.

The present condition of the people who live on the Pine Ridge Reservation is deplorable. In 1989, 66 percent of the Native Americans in the two counties encompassing the reservation were living below the poverty level. Shannon County, which contains most of the reservation, had the nation's lowest money income per capita in 1989 ($3,417). The high rate of economic as well as emotional poverty is the result of generations of well-chronicled injustices against Native Americans. Unfortunately, many of these wrongs are irreversible, but efforts should be made to address the destitute condition of the people. Fundamentally, the root of much of the despair and impoverishment is that they see no reason for their existence. Current welfare approaches only exacerbate the sense of helplessness and insignificance.

A South Dakota Badlands reserve administered cooperatively between the United States government and the people of the Pine Ridge Reservation could alleviate many of the problems facing the reservation's residents. While the nation would benefit because of the ecological, educational, and recreational values of such an arrangement, the Native Americans would benefit materially as well as spiritually. Employment as technicians, guides, wildlife managers, and in the tourism industry would give them economic independence, while restoring a large, naturally functioning grassland ecosystem, with all its indigenous flora and fauna, would revive a spirituality that has been missing from Native Americans since the last bison disappeared. That the reserve encompasses the Stronghold Table plateau, a site of historic ghost dances, and is also just north of the town of Wounded Knee, the infamous massacre site, makes the area even more appropriate for a real and permanent restitution.

Just about every species associated with the shortgrass region of the Great Plains could exist at a Badlands reserve. A population of 250 wolves could exist in the area, fulfilling their role as regulators of the Great Plains ecosystem. Perhaps 25,000 bison would prosper there. Bighorn sheep, elk, antelope, and mule deer would also be present. Black-tailed prairie dogs could flourish in large complexes as they historically did, in contrast to the present situation where the towns are isolated, restricted, and persecuted. A quarter of a million acres of prairie dog towns could be sustained, 15 percent of the reserve's area, an amount large enough to theoretically support 1,500 ferrets (Stromberg, Rayburn, and Clark 1983). Other rare species such as Townsend's big-eared bat (*Plecotus townsendii pallescens*), the fringed-tailed myotis (bat) (*Myotis thysanodes pahasapensis*) and western small-footed myotis (*M. ciliolabrum*) could also be conserved.

The Sandhills of west-central Nebraska are a unique grassland ecosystem within the Great Plains and therefore warrant special attention. Underlain by soils that are 96 percent sand by volume, this 23,300-square-mile region is generally regarded as the largest sand dune area in the Western Hemisphere.

The Sandhills ecosystem can carry about one bison per forty acres, meaning a 5,400-square-mile Sandhills reserve could sustain approximately 86,500 animals. Although only half the current livestock density, bison could be sustained without intensive labor, supplemental feed, or groundwater pumpage. At a conservative 20 percent of the herd, about 17,500 could be harvested annually, about 10 million pounds of edible meat. That equates to $20 million a year, about equal to the current net value of agricultural products produced within the hypothetical reserve. Moreover, hunters currently pay about $1,500 for a chance to hunt a bison bull. Of course if wolves were reintroduced to the site the figures would be slightly less, but even then the human harvest would still be enormous. Barsh (1990) estimated that Plains Indians took up to 10 percent of the bison population annually, even in the face of wolf predation. In fact, as Barsh pointed out, men and wolves were historically copredators on the Great Plains; hunting by indigenous people may have even produced more food for wolves in the form of carrion and wounded bison.

Another possible site for a Sandhills reserve would include the counties of Brown, Rock, and Keya Paha. The merits of this site include the middle reach of the Niobrara River and a variety of ecological communities. This area has been called the "biological crossroads of the nation" because it includes relicts of six vegetation types (eastern deciduous forest, northern boreal forest, Rocky Mountain pine forest, mixed-grass prairie, tallgrass prairie, and Sandhills prairie). The site also includes a spectacular and canoeable stretch of the Niobrara River that provides tens of thousands of recreational hours each year.

Of all the large ecotypes in the grassland biome, the Sandhills may be as close as any to its pre-Columbian condition. This is in part because of the sandy soil and arid climate, which make cultivation unwise in the region, and in part because of sound grazing practices implemented in recent decades. Therefore establishing a Sandhills ecological reserve seems less compelling than conserving many other sites. Still, like many other regions in the Great Plains, the Sandhills are an economically and demographically distressed region. Having said that, I need to clarify that arguments for grassland reserves do not imply that all of a region should be returned to bison range. Indeed, there are strong social and cultural reasons not to do that, especially in the Sandhills. Ranching is an integral part of Nebraska's heritage and deserves its own piece of the Sandhills, just as the region's biodiversity does. The question becomes, Is there room for both?

Situated only twenty-five miles east of Fort Collins, Colorado, and sixty miles northeast of Denver, the Pawnee National Grasslands are one of the best examples of High Plains shortgrass prairie left in public ownership. The sparse grasses, lack of water, and flat topography make the area an archetype of the once vast plains that ran from southwestern South Dakota to just short of Mexico. The existing national grasslands could constitute the core of a Pawnee Grasslands reserve that would potentially receive great human use.

The Pawnee National Grasslands comprise 193,060 acres of public land intermingled with private land. A hypothetical boundary could encompass 93 percent of the Grasslands as well as another 71,000 acres of state and federal land. The remaining 564,814 acres is private. All told, the site would contain 1,274 square miles of classic High Plains prairie.

In addition to endangered and threatened species (black-footed ferret, whooping crane, bald eagle, peregrine falcon, and Eskimo curlew), the Pawnee National Grasslands are home to other rare species such as the mountain plover (2,600 of the remaining 4,360–5,610 occur on the national grasslands), ferruginous hawk, black tern (*Chilidonias niger*), white-faced ibis (*Plegadis chihi*), and loggerhead shrike. Rare mammal species include the swift fox and fringed-tailed myotis. Insects include the regal fritillary butterfly (*Speyeria idalia*), lost ethmiid moth (*Ethmia monarchella*), Albarufan dagger (*Acronia albarufa*), and Colorado burrowing mayfly (*Ephemera compar*). A rare fish, the Plains topminnow (*Fundulus sciadicus*), and a rare plant, the Colorado butterfly weed (*Gaura neomexicana coloradoensis*), can also be found in the area. In addition to these species approximately 410 plant and 324 vertebrate species occur on the site (U.S. Forest Service 1992), many of them endemic to the Great Plains shortgrass prairie.

Canada has already taken the initiative and established approximately half of what will eventually be a 350-square-mile Grasslands National Park abutting the United States. The ambitious Canadian effort is commendable, but it is not enough. The acreage is so small that even bison may not be restored to the site. The United States should complement the Canadian effort by collaborating on a large International Grasslands reserve. Such an undertaking would conserve a common resource as well as further strengthening the bonds between the two countries.

Their history of cooperative wildlife conservation efforts is rich with landmark accomplishments. The Migratory Bird Treaty of 1918, signed by Canada and the United States, was one of the first pieces of legislation in the world to acknowledge the need for international cooperation to conserve migratory wildlife. The collaborative efforts have carried over to the conservation of endangered species. For example, whooping cranes, which breed in the Northwest Territories and winter in Texas, are monitored and protected by both countries. Black-footed ferret offspring from the last remaining wild population found near Meeteetse, Wyoming, are now raised and bred at the Toronto Zoo.

Unfortunately the two countries also have a history of competition in selling farm commodities (Morgan 1979). A cooperative effort to establish an International Grasslands reserve would be an admission by both that they need to reduce crop surpluses. The escalating trade wars, especially in wheat, threaten to harm what has historically been one of the strongest friendships in the world.

A three thousand-square-mile reserve, of which eighteen hundred square miles are in the United States, could contain 30,000 bison, approximately 300 wolves, perhaps 1,200 black-footed ferrets, and 3,000 swift foxes. The reserve would also be home to antelope, mountain plovers, burrowing owls, eastern short-horned lizards (*Phrynosoma douglassii brevirostre*), and many other shortgrass prairie species.

Because of its proximity to the metropolitan areas of Chicago, Kansas City, St. Louis, Minneapolis–St. Paul, and Des Moines, an Iowa Tallgrass reserve would likely receive more human use than any of the other hypothetical reserves described in this book. The significance of this should not be dismissed. According to the U.S. Forest Service (1990, 25), "Close-to-home open space, which is the most heavily used and demanded recreation source, is most severely threatened by development." Iowa, with only about 0.4 percent of its land in federal and state ownership and only 0.02 percent (seventy-seven hundred acres) of the state dedicated to biodiversity conservation (in the state preserve system), arguably has less open space than any state in the nation and hence relatively few outdoor opportunities. The comparatively trivial Walnut Creek National Wildlife Refuge being developed near Des Moines is expected to draw an astounding two hundred thousand people a year once it is completed.

A sizable reserve with camping, backcountry hiking, canoeing, and big-game hunting would draw many times that number.

Creating a wildlife reserve in Iowa's "sea of cropland" would pose interesting ecological questions. For example, it is often speculated that pre-Columbian bison herds summered throughout the entire grassland biome yet overwintered only in the southern and central shortgrass prairies. The basis for this argument is that tallgrass species such as big bluestem do not retain their nutritional value over winter, whereas shortgrass species do, and that central and southern shortgrass regions typically have less snow cover than other parts of the grassland biome. However, such assertions remain debatable. Consider that the journals of Alexander Henry (1897), who traded in the tallgrass region along the North Dakota–Minnesota border, describe great herds of bison in the region all winter long. Likewise, bison stayed in the northern shortgrass plains all winter rather than migrating south (Coffman, Jonkel, and Scott 1990). Dary (1974) made a comprehensive review of the records of early explorers and rejected the notion of migratory bison herds.

Still, suppose a reserve cannot be designed in Iowa that meets all the bison's needs. This presents an interesting management dilemma. In such cases an elevated level of management may be necessary. In designing reserves, two precepts need to be considered: the smaller the site, the more human manipulation is necessary to conserve biodiversity; and the more the surrounding landscape differs from the managed site, the more human manipulation is necessary.

The suggestion that thousands of square miles of settled farmland and rangeland in the southern High Plains be returned to the bison and wolves is not made lightly. The mere idea invites ridicule and scorn. Nevertheless such a scenario can be argued based on one of the most profound of denominators—water.

In addition to a declining rural population (the rural farm population in the hypothetical reserve declined 49 percent between 1980 and 1990) and a depressed economic climate (the poverty rate in 1989 was 16 percent), the residents of the hypothetical reserve are facing a grave environmental crisis. Over 58 percent of the harvested cropland within the reserve boundaries was irrigated in 1992, with almost all of the water coming from the Ogallala aquifer. Yet government forecasts predict that by the year 2020 the aquifer will contain only half the drainable water it had in 1980 (Luckey et al. 1988). In some areas groundwater levels may fall by as much as 150 feet, making pumpage economically infeasible. When that happens, much of the region's agriculture will be decimated.

The depletion of the Ogallala is a tragedy not only for people within the hypothetical reserve, but for all Great Plains residents who live over the 174,000-square-mile bed of underground water. Sometime soon the users of the aquifer are going to have to reduce their collective withdrawal. There are two strategies. First, every user can reduce the amount currently withdrawn. Such a measure will not be easy, since many are already operating at or near top efficiency. Also, it would probably require some level of legislation and enforcement. A second strategy would be to completely eliminate water withdrawals in selected regions of the aquifer, thereby allowing other sites to maintain their current level. In the latter case retiring a vast block of land from agricultural production (for a reserve) would benefit residents living over a much greater area.

Last, it is worth noting that the site of the hypothetical reserve was the epicenter of the last great environmental tragedy in the Great Plains; the 1930s Dust Bowl. Without corrective actions, it might also be the epicenter of the next.

In June 1793 the French explorers Paul and Pierre Mallet explored a broad, grassy river that wound its way through what would later become Nebraska. The brothers named the river La Rivière Plate, which means flat river. English-speakers eventually changed the name to Platte River or, more commonly, the Platte. To the early explorers the Platte seemed timeless and unspoilable. By 1993 it was listed by the conservation group American Rivers as one of the ten most endangered rivers in the United States.

The beginning of the end for the historic Platte occurred when a series of dams and reservoirs were built between 1909 and 1957 (Schalles 1994). The reservoirs inundated large portions of the river, directly eliminating miles of riverine and riparian habitat. And the associated water releases, which differed from natural hydrographs, degraded and destroyed the rest. The unvarying flows from the dams have channelized, straightened, narrowed, and dulled the once spirited river. For example, where the Platte was historically half a mile wide or wider in some spots, it is now down to less than a couple of hundred yards (Krapu, Reinecke, and Frith 1982). Without fluctuations in the river's level, and in the absence of fire, trees have invaded what was historically a mostly treeless riparian zone (Krapu, Reinecke, and Frith 1982). The invasion of trees and channelization of the river have resulted in a significant loss of habitat for sandhill cranes, least terns, piping plovers, and other species associated with a grassland riverine ecosystem.

The subjugation of the Platte was done in large part for irrigation. As much

173

as 70 percent of the river's water is now used to produce crops (U.S. Fish and Wildlife Service 1981), commodities of which the United States has enormous and costly surpluses. From a national perspective, a strong argument can be made to return some of the irrigated cropland to grassland, thereby reducing the nation's excess agricultural capacity (generally speaking, irrigated acreage has twice the capacity of nonirrigated land) while reducing the need for impoundments and artificial hydrographs. To date, Farm Program programs such as CRP have done very little to reduce the stress agriculture places on Great Plains water resources (Schaible 1989).

Of course the predictable local response to proposals for converting irrigated cropland to grassland is that such a scenario would devastate local economies. Yet that is not necessarily so. In 1991 alone an incredible $15 million was invested in the economy of Grand Island, Nebraska, by the eighty thousand visitors to the river (Lingle 1992). Many were there to witness the cranes and other migratory birds that use the Platte. Although the significance of agriculture to the region's economy continues to wane, the value of the river continues to grow, even with minimal marketing.

For ten thousand years the Platte has been a staging area for some of the continent's greatest bird migrations, including those of Canada geese (*Branta canadensis*), pintail ducks, semipalmated plovers (*Charadrius semipalmatus*), semipalmated sandpipers (*Calidris pusilla*), greater and lesser yellowlegs (*Tringa melanoleuca* and *T. flavipes*), common snipe, black terns, willets, and most spectacular and famous of all, the cranes (see U.S. Fish and Wildlife Service 1981). Half a million cranes—mostly sandhills but also the occasional whooping crane—still use the Platte. Although these are impressive numbers, they are only a fraction of the pre-Columbian densities. The sounds of the birds in an agrarian landscape are one thing, but the timeless sounds of great clamorous flocks against an endless prairie backdrop are quite another.

Other Sites

Of course creating of a handful of large reserves throughout the grassland biome does not guarantee conservation of all grassland biodiversity, nor would it diminish the ecological value of the numerous other natural areas in the region. Indeed, it is important that many of these other sites be protected and enhanced because of their biodiversity (and heritage) value. These sites can range from small fens in North Dakota to pluvial lakes in Texas.

Some of the more noteworthy sites are the John E. Williams Preserve (the

Nature Conservancy) near the town of Turtle Lake, North Dakota, the Lost-wood National Wildlife Refuge near the town of Kenmare, North Dakota, and the Salt Plains National Wildlife Refuge in Alfalfa County, Oklahoma. All these sites contain saline wetland complexes that are characteristic of the arid Great Plains and critical to shorebirds and other wildlife. All would benefit by enlargement and habitat enhancement that discourages the presence of rac-coons, skunks, and other predators (e.g., removing buildings, rock piles, and brush piles and converting nearby cropland to native grassland).

Of all the wetland sites in the grassland biome, the most important may be the Cheyenne Bottoms near Great Bend, Kansas. Indeed, it may be the single most important wetland complex in the Western Hemisphere. It has been esti-mated that no other site in the Great Plains gets even 10 percent as much shore-bird use as the Bottoms (Zimmerman 1990). And the Manomet Bird Observa-tory in Massachusetts estimates that up to half of all shorebirds that migrate through the interior United States use the Bottoms. One reason the Bottoms is so critical to migratory shorebirds is that it is fifteen hundred miles from both the Gulf Coast and the Prairie Pothole Region of Canada, making it a perfect resting and refueling site. Its value is so great that it is the only Great Plains wet-land on the Ramsar List (wetlands of international importance) and one of only ten wetlands selected from the United States.

Another site that warrants consideration as a large grassland reserve is the area that encompasses the Sheyenne National Grasslands in southeast North Dakota. The grasslands consist of seventy thousand acres of fragmented public lands intermingled with sixty-five thousand acres of private land. The site can best be described as tallgrass prairie savanna with a smattering of other unique and valuable ecological communities including sand dunes, fens, and the Shey-enne River.

The remnant tracts of prairie in the Loess Hills in western Iowa constitute much of what is left of Iowa's once vast prairie (loess is windblown dust that ac-cumulates during periods of glaciation). The Hills generally parallel the Mis-souri River, being most pronounced from Council Bluffs, Iowa, to Sioux City. The region is especially valuable because of the diversity of grasslands. Al-though mixed-grass species such as little bluestem predominate, tallgrass spe-cies such as big bluestem and shortgrass species such as buffalograss are also common.

Society should also look closely at the states of Illinois, Wisconsin, Indiana, and even Ohio for potential grassland ecological reserves. Although not part of the contiguous grassland biome, these states did have significant amounts of savanna, especially Illinois (known as the Prairie State). Land in these states is much more expensive and agriculturally productive; therefore it appears to be more difficult to economically justify grassland restoration. However, as I have stressed repeatedly, one of the main reasons for establishing such reserves is to reduce agricultural capacity. These states are also in dire need of more public recreational lands for hiking, hunting, and other outdoor uses. Last, reserves in these states would instill a sense of fairness by having all the grassland states lessen their agricultural production.

Ideology, Reality, Morality,

and the Future of the Great Plains

> There is, after all, the possibility of a richer future. That is the promise of
> grass, and I mean this literally. The grass can live again.
>   Richard Manning, *Grassland: The History, Biology, Politics, and*
>   *Promise of the American Prairie*

A fresh breeze appears to be blowing across the nation concerning the protection of native grasslands. A new awareness and appreciation of the most profound of all of North America's ecosystems seems to be developing (see Manning 1995). The Nature Conservancy's ambitious Tallgrass Prairie Preserve in Oklahoma is a shining example. So are the scattered tracts, albeit small, of remnant tallgrass prairie being acquired and protected by government agencies, nongovernment organizations, local communities, and even private citizens. Even Congress appears to be getting serious about grassland conservation as discussions of a grasslands national park arouse renewed interest. Yet we still have a long way to go (Samson and Knopf 1994). Compared with other ecosystems and natural resource issues, grasslands are underrepresented and underappreciated.

A review of a national conservation directory (National Wildlife Federation 1993) reveals that there are still no organizations that deal solely with the conservation of the grassland ecosystem. Meanwhile there are nine organizations working solely with forest issues, four with Great Lakes issues, five with coastal areas, six with rivers, two with caves, three with deserts, and two with polar regions. In addition, there are three organizations working solely with cranes, five with wolves, five with turtles and tortoises, ten with birds of prey, and one with billfish. Obviously there needs to be a greater organized effort to preserve and restore grasslands.

The subtlety and serenity of grasslands defines their character, but those same traits engender a lack of focus compared with jagged peaks and cascading waters. Grasslands require familiarity before appreciation, not the other way around. Unfortunately we never had a chance to develop that familiarity. Therefore restoring and protecting grassland ecosystems remains considerably more difficult than doing so for our other natural resources.

If America is serious about conserving and restoring grassland biodiversity—and it should be—then it needs to acknowledge that the status quo is unacceptable. Ultimately our ability to conserve viable populations of many grassland species will depend on our willingness to preserve the integrity of the grassland ecosystem where the species evolved. We will have to forgo the idea of *habitat* in favor of the concept of *ecosystem*. We will have to restore processes as well as grasses.

Will the concepts presented here ever be implemented? Certainly not immediately, but perhaps in time. Even if large grassland reserves with a full assemblage of native flora and fauna never come to fruition, much of the information synthesized here can still be put to good use. Grassland managers can, when appropriate, increase efforts to eliminate nongrassland features on the landscape. Government agencies can emphasize landscape management and land consolidation. And national agriculture programs can better incorporate national conservation and recreation needs.

If we do not permanently correct the problem of excess agricultural capacity, the result will be an increasing burden on American (and Canadian) taxpayers, more dying grassland towns, more foreign ownership, more abandoned fields of exotic grasses, and more bankrupt farmers and ranchers. Perhaps most important, the integrity, self-esteem, and reputation of farmers and ranchers will continue to erode. Those traits are inversely proportional to dependence on the federal government: the concepts discussed in this book have the potential to reduce that dependency. When farmers and ranchers are prosperous and secure, they are more likely to develop and practice a land ethic. When they see a healthy and comfortable future, they are more likely to conserve soil, protect water resources, and enjoy wildlife. When they are poor and desperate, with bill collectors pounding on the door, they worry only about the coming year's profit margin.

There will undoubtedly be several opportunities in the near future for the

178

country to seriously consider establishing ecological reserves in the grassland biome. Another drought will soon hit the region; that is inevitable. The last one, from 1987 to 1991, cost American taxpayers over $5.4 billion in agricultural disaster payments alone. Without government succor, many farmers and ranchers will not survive the next one. But the ballooning national debt is making politicians and society question habitual and unwise government spending. Continually subsidizing cultivation in the arid Great Plains while the nation is burdened with huge crop surpluses fails the test of common sense. In contrast, permanently retiring portions of the Great Plains benefits taxpayers, the failing producers, the remaining producers, and future generations.

Critics will point out, and rightly so, that the world's population is skyrocketing and that starvation is rampant in Third World countries. Therefore, they will argue, we will need to produce even more food in the future. But the billion dollar question is, Who's going to pay for it? The hungry poor in these countries cannot afford the prices that American and Canadian farmers demand. American and Canadian taxpayers, already deeply in debt, cannot be expected to shoulder the burden forever.

Developed nations such as the United States and Canada have both moral and self-serving reasons to assist less developed nations. But distributing free food is not the solution. If anything, it exacerbates the problem. A persuasive argument can be made that it is better to subsidize the Third World hoe maker, teacher, and doctor. In the long run these handouts to other nations would be more efficient, wiser, and kinder. As Waggoner (1994) suggested, the world may be able to sustain 10 billion people, almost twice the 1990 population, on the current amount of cropland if certain conditions are met (although the quality of life may not be as high). Rather than subsidizing excessive cultivation in the United States and fostering Third World dependence on American taxpayers, it would be far wiser to promote sustainable and productive agriculture in the poorer nations.

Furthermore, it is hypocritical for us to preach conservation to less developed countries when we cannot maintain species in our own backyard. While countries like Ecuador set aside 38 percent of their land area for conservation and communist countries like China create hundreds of new reserves totaling 150,000 square miles, we are unable to maintain even one naturally functioning grassland ecosystem. And the challenge of restoration should not deter us. For example, Costa Rica has established a 125,000-acre tropical forest reserve that will be (re)created on land used for cattle ranches (Wilson 1992).

Nowhere in the United States, or anywhere in North America for that matter, is there a similar opportunity for fully restoring a fragmented and destroyed ecosystem. Only in the rural Great Plains, with their faltering economy and declining human population, can the argument for ecosystem restoration be made from both an environmental and an economic perspective.

Other critics will argue that we should keep people on the land, as if land needed people to make it worthwhile. But the truth is that when we subsidize 500 producers and encourage them to stay on the land, we are at the same time excluding 241 million other Americans from experiencing their grassland heritage. And only a small portion of the Great Plains would be needed to make significant advances in grassland conservation. For example, the total of the ambitious hypothetical reserves described in this book amounts to only 4 percent of the grassland biome in the United States–3.1 percent when savanna regions are included. So people will still be living on 96 to 96.9 percent of the region. Essentially the great grasslands will remain settled.

Although the available scientific information argues that biodiversity conservation can best occur on large, contiguous tracts of habitat, with the full assemblage of native species and processes, the conservation of biodiversity ultimately becomes an issue of values. There are no doubt many who deem a Great Plains wholly composed of shelterbelts, roads, and cropland a better place. And there are others who would argue that anthropogenic influences are themselves a natural event and therefore species that fail to adapt should be allowed to go extinct. These are personal tenets and should not be confused with the facts and hard logic presented here in support of how grassland biodiversity conservation might occur. Indeed, this information was based on the premise that conserving grassland biodiversity and wilderness areas is a worthy societal goal and that conservation is most effective when it allows nature to proceed and evolve (mostly) unfettered by human interference. Without such a premise, all the arguments become moot.

The concept of reserves to protect grassland ecosystems does not imply that we should ignore wildlife conservation on private lands. Nor should we accept reserves as a Noah's ark panacea for all our biodiversity problems. For example, a scattering of reserves throughout the grassland biome will not prevent the mixing of eastern forest biota with that of western forests. And the reserves themselves will need to be protected from exotic species, pollution, and other harmful effects. But scientists now recognize and appreciate the value, efficacy, and necessity of large, unfragmented tracts of habitat. Only in such areas can we preserve the integrity of native ecosystems. Ambitious new conservation efforts such as the Wildlands Project, an energetic mix of science and activism, and its affiliated magazine *Wild Earth* are mapping conservation strategies that think big both spatially and temporally. Such bold undertakings are needed to help guide us into the next century.

Do we really need large reserves, with wolves and bison running free, to conserve grassland biodiversity? The answer is unclear. It is quite possible that black-footed ferrets, mountain plovers, swift foxes, and ferruginous hawks can survive without these large reserves, especially with modern techniques and management. Then again, they may not. That is one reason we need large, functioning ecosystems. Because we know so little about how natural grassland systems work, it behooves us to create the necessary classrooms. As Leopold so astutely pointed out, "A science of land health needs, first of all, a base datum of normality, a picture of how healthy land maintains itself as an organism" (Leopold 1966, 274). To Leopold the most perfect norm was wilderness.

Even if large protected areas are not needed or desired for the sake of grassland fauna and flora, a compelling argument can be made that such areas are important for the nation's well-being. Such areas can provide desperately needed recreational opportunities, immeasurable existence values, and even spiritual renewal. In the final analysis, the conservation of the grassland ecosystem is not for the critters and plants, but for humans.

From Aristotle to Thoreau to Leopold, philosophers have argued in favor of the intangible benefits humans derive from wild creatures and wild areas. Ehrenfield (1988) felt that the aesthetic value of wildlife provided a psychological well-being to humans beyond its tangible value. Even the science of economics now recognizes that the "existence value" of wildlife "may be quite large relative to the use value" (Stevens et al. 1991, 399). Ryan (1986, 123) observed that large prairie tracts not only provide "substantial benefits to prairie wildlife, but preserve the spiritual feeling of the wide-open prairie that is an integral aspect of the human experience."

It is not hyperbole to say that land, the foundation of all human life, means more to our nation than acres, bushels, or dollars. It is inextricably woven throughout our culture, our past, and our future. Land is the strongest link between generations–stronger than books, stronger than legends. It is said that the Iroquois treated the land as a gift to the seventh generation to come. We would do well to carry that morality with us. If we can see what Black Elk saw, or relive what Lewis and Clark lived, even for a day, then we can relate to them in ways that modern technology can never replicate. And so will the seventh generation to come. Some will object to "wasting" this land. But the question to ask is, Where is it going to go? Indeed, seven generations from now the land set aside in grassland reserves may be some of the best and most productive land still available.

One need never visit a grassland reserve to profit from its existence. Just as visitors to Yellowstone National Park said they benefited from simply knowing that wolves would be reintroduced (Duffield 1992), many Americans would value simply knowing that grassland reserves are there (Stevens et al. 1991). Whether they read about it in a newspaper, watch a documentary on television, or gaze down on it from thirty thousand feet, they will profit from just knowing there is still room for wilderness.

For too many Americans the word "wilderness" has become synonymous with the tundra and the Arctic, those inhospitable regions to the north. For too many true wilderness can be found only a couple of thousand miles and a couple of thousand dollars away. For too many wilderness is no longer defined as an opportunity or an adventure but rather, a frozen block of ice near the North Pole.

Having wilderness at the North Pole is not good enough. Leopold (1966, 277) said that "relegating the grizzlies to Alaska is about like relegating happiness to heaven; one may never get there." The same is true for wilderness. We need a place nearby where the soles of our boots get worn, where wisdom and instinct matter more than technology, where discovery and mystery are the norm, where the spirits of the past can connect with those of the future. We need for ourselves, as much as for the beasts, places where the bison's beard gets soaked in the morning dew, where courting fritillaries can dance their aerial fights above dazzling fields of wildflowers, and where ferrets can peek out of their burrows and see wolves trotting by. We need a place where the distant horizon leads to another distant horizon, and that horizon leads to another, and that horizon leads to . . .

Appendix A
Counties Used for Analyses

Colorado
Adams S
Arapahoe S
Baca S
Bent S
Cheyenne S
Crowley S
Denver S
Douglas S
Elbert S
El Paso S
Huerfano S
Kiowa S
Kit Carson S
Las Animas S
Lincoln S
Logan S
Morgan S
Otero S
Phillips S
Prowers S
Pueblo S
Sedgwick S
Washington S

Weld S
Yuma S

Iowa
Adair T
Adams T
Audubon T
Benton T
Black Hawk T
Boone T
Bremer T
Buchanan T
Buena Vista T
Butler T
Calhoun T
Carroll T
Cass T
Cedar T
Cerro Gordo T
Cherokee T
Chickasaw T
Clarke T
Clay T
Clayton T

Clinton T
Crawford T
Dallas T
Decatur T
Delaware T
Des Moines T
Dickinson T
Dubuque T
Emmet T
Fayette T
Floyd T
Franklin T
Fremont T
Greene T
Grundy T
Guthrie T
Hamilton T
Hancock T
Hardin T
Harrison T
Henry T
Howard T
Humboldt T
Ida T

Note: T = tallgrass; M = mixed-grass; S = shortgrass. See map 1 for further information.

Iowa T	Taylor T	Graham M
Jackson T	Union T	Grant S
Jasper T	Warren T	Gray M
Jefferson T	Washington T	Greeley S
Johnson T	Wayne T	Greenwood T
Jones T	Webster T	Hamilton S
Keokuk T	Winnebago T	Harper M
Kossuth T	Winneshiek T	Harvey M
Linn T	Woodbury T	Haskell S
Louisa T	Worth T	Hodgeman M
Lucas T	Wright T	Jackson T
Lyon M		Jewell M
Madison T	**Kansas**	Kearny S
Mahaska T	Atchison T	Kingman M
Marion T	Barber S	Kiowa M
Marshall T	Barton M	Lane S
Mills T	Brown T	Lincoln M
Mitchell T	Butler T	Logan S
Monona T	Chase T	Marion T
Montgomery T	Chautauqua T	Marshall T
Muscatine T	Cheyenne S	McPherson M
O'Brien T	Clark S	Meade S
Osceola T	Clay M	Mitchell M
Page T	Cloud M	Morris T
Palo Alto T	Comanche S	Morton S
Plymouth T	Cowley T	Nemaha T
Pocahontas T	Decatur M	Ness M
Polk T	Dickinson M	Norton M
Pottawattamie T	Doniphan T	Osborne M
Poweshiek T	Edwards M	Ottawa M
Ringgold T	Elk T	Pawnee M
Sac T	Ellis M	Phillips M
Scott T	Ellsworth M	Pottawatomie T
Shelby T	Finney S	Pratt M
Sioux T	Ford M	Rawlins M
Story T	Geary T	Reno M
Tama T	Gove M	Republic M

184

Rice M
Riley T
Rooks M
Rush M
Russell M
Saline M
Scott S
Sedgwick M
Seward S
Sheridan M
Sherman S
Smith M
Stafford M
Stanton S
Stevens S
Sumner M
Thomas S
Trego M
Wabaunsee T
Wallace S
Washington M
Wichita S

Minnesota
Big Stone M
Blue Earth T
Brown T
Chippewa M
Clay T
Cottonwood T
Dakota T
Dodge T
Faribault T
Fillmore T
Freeborn T
Goodhue T
Grant M

Jackson T
Kandiyohi T
Kittson T
Lac qui Parle M
Lincoln M
Lyon M
Marshall T
Martin T
McLeod T
Mower T
Murray T
Nicollet T
Nobles T
Norman T
Olmsted T
Pennington T
Pipestone M
Polk T
Pope M
Red Lake T
Redwood T
Renville T
Rock M
Sibley T
Steele T
Stevens M
Swift M
Traverse T
Wabasha T
Waseca T
Watonwan T
Wilken T
Yellow Medicine M

Missouri
Andrew T
Atchison T

Clinton T
De Kalb T
Gentry T
Harrison T
Holt T
Nodaway T
Worth T

Montana
Big Horn S
Blaine S
Carter S
Chouteau S
Custer S
Daniels M
Dawson M
Fallon S
Fergus S
Garfield M
Golden Valley S
Hill S
Liberty S
McCone M
Musselshell S
Petroleum S
Phillips S
Pondera S
Powder River S
Prairie S
Richland M
Roosevelt M
Rosebud S
Sheridan M
Stillwater S
Teton S
Toole S
Treasure S

Valley S
Wheatland S
Wibaux S
Yellowstone S

Nebraska
Adams M
Antelope M
Arthur M
Banner S
Blaine M
Boone M
Box Butte S
Boyd M
Brown M
Buffalo M
Burt T
Butler M
Cass T
Cedar M
Chase S
Cherry M
Cheyenne S
Clay M
Colfax T
Cuming T
Custer M
Dakota T
Dawes S
Dawson M
Deuel S
Dixon M
Dodge T
Douglas T
Dundy M
Fillmore M
Franklin M
Frontier M

Furnas M
Gage M
Garden M
Garfield M
Gosper M
Grant M
Greeley M
Hall M
Hamilton M
Harlan M
Hayes M
Hitchcock M
Holt M
Hooker M
Howard M
Jefferson M
Johnson T
Kearney M
Keith S
Keya Paha M
Kimball S
Knox M
Lancaster T
Lincoln M
Logan M
Loup M
Madison M
McPherson M
Merrick M
Morrill S
Nance M
Nemaha T
Nuckolls M
Otoe T
Pawnee T
Perkins S
Phelps M
Pierce M

Platte M
Polk M
Red Willow M
Richardson T
Rock M
Saline M
Sarpy T
Saunders T
Scotts Bluff S
Seward M
Sheridan M
Sherman M
Sioux S
Stanton M
Thayer M
Thomas M
Thurston T
Valley M
Washington T
Wayne M
Webster M
Wheeler M
York M

New Mexico
Curry S
Harding S
Lea S
Mora S
Quay S
Roosevelt S
San Miguel S
Union S

North Dakota
Adams M
Barnes M
Benson M

Billings M

Bottineau M

Bowman M

Burke M

Burleigh M

Cass T

Cavalier M

Dickey M

Divide M

Dunn M

Eddy M

Emmons M

Foster M

Golden Valley S

Grand Forks T

Grant M

Griggs M

Hettinger M

Kidder M

La Moure M

Logan M

McHenry M

McIntosh M

McKenzie S

McLean M

Mercer M

Morton M

Mountrail M

Nelson M

Oliver M

Pembina T

Pierce M

Ramsey M

Ransom M

Renville M

Richland T

Rolette M

Sargent M

Sheridan M

Sioux S

Slope M

Stark M

Steele M

Stutsman M

Towner M

Traill T

Walsh T

Ward M

Wells M

Williams M

Oklahoma

Alfalfa M

Beaver S

Beckham M

Blaine M

Caddo M

Canadian M

Cimarron S

Comanche M

Cotton M

Custer M

Dewey M

Ellis S

Garfield M

Grady M

Grant M

Greer M

Harmon M

Harper M

Jackson M

Kay M

Kingfisher M

Kiowa M

Major M

McClain M

Noble M

Osage T

Roger Mills S

Texas S

Tillman M

Washita M

Woods M

Woodward M

South Dakota

Aurora M

Beadle M

Bennett S

Bon Homme M

Brookings M

Brown M

Brule M

Buffalo M

Butte S

Campbell M

Charles Mix M

Clark M

Clay M

Codington M

Corson S

Custer S

Davison M

Day M

Deuel M

Dewey S

Douglas M

Edmunds M

Fall River S

Faulk M

Grant M

Gregory M

Haakon S

Hamlin M

Hand M	**Texas**	Hemphill S
Hanson M	Andrews S	Hockley S
Harding S	Armstrong S	Howard S
Hughes M	Bailey S	Hutchinson S
Hutchinson M	Baylor M	Irion M
Hyde M	Borden M	Jones M
Jackson S	Briscoe S	Kent S
Jerauld M	Carson S	King S
Jones M	Castro S	Knox M
Kingsbury M	Childress M	Lamb S
Lake M	Cochran S	Lipscomb S
Lincoln M	Coke M	Lubbock S
Lyman M	Coleman M	Lynn S
Marshall M	Collingsworth S	Martin S
McCook M	Concho M	McCulloch M
McPherson M	Cottle S	Midland S
Meade S	Crane S	Mitchell M
Mellette S	Crosby S	Moore S
Miner M	Dallam S	Motley S
Minnehaha M	Dawson S	Nolan M
Moody M	Deaf Smith S	Ochiltree S
Pennington S	Dickens S	Oldham S
Perkins S	Donley S	Parmer S
Potter M	Ector S	Potter S
Roberts M	Fisher M	Randall S
Sanborn M	Floyd S	Reagan S
Shannon S	Foard S	Roberts S
Spink M	Gaines S	Runnels M
Stanley S	Garza S	Scurry M
Sully M	Glasscock S	Sherman S
Todd M	Gray S	Sterling M
Tripp M	Hale S	Stonewall S
Turner M	Hall S	Swisher S
Union M	Hansford S	Taylor M
Walworth M	Hardeman M	Terry S
Yankton M	Hartley S	Tom Greene M
Ziebach S	Haskell M	Upton S

Wheeler M	**Wyoming**	Johnson S
Wichita M	Campbell S	Laramie S
Wilbarger M	Converse S	Niobrara S
Winkler S	Crook S	Platte S
Yoakum S	Goshen S	Weston S

Appendix B
Endangered, Threatened, and Candidate
Species in the Great Plains, 1994

Mammals

Black-footed ferret (*Mustela nigripes*) E
Gray wolf (*Canis lupus*) E,T
*Grizzly bear (*Ursus arctos horribilis*) T
Indiana bat (*Myotis sodalis*) E

Cave myotis (*Myotis velifer*) C
Colorado hog-nosed skunk (*Conepatus mesoleucus figginsi*) C
Fringed-tailed myotis (*Myotis thysanodes pahasapensis*) C
*Lynx (*Felis lynx canadensis*) C
New Mexico jumping mouse (*Zapus hudsonius luteus*) C
*North American wolverine (*Gulo gulo luscus*) C
Occult little brown bat (*Myotis lucifugus occultus*) C
Plains spotted skunk (*Spilogale putorius interrupta*) C

Note: E = endangered; T = threatened; C = candidate. Candidate species from U.S. Fish and Wildlife Service 1991b, 1993c. In the summer of 1996 the U.S. Fish and Wildlife Service revised its candidate list. The revised list includes only species for which there are data to warrant listing them as endangered or threatened. Still, the list above is useful as an indicator of rare or threatened grassland species.

*Species not (or no longer) strongly associated with the grassland biome, but listed by the U.S. Fish and Wildlife Service as possibly occurring in a grassland county (typically because the county also contains nongrassland habitats).

**Possibly extinct.

Prebles meadow jumping mouse (*Zapus hudsonius preblei*) C
Small-footed myotis (*Myotis ciliolabrum*) C
*Southwestern otter (*Lutra canadensis sonorae*) C
Spotted bat (*Euderma maculatum*) C
Swift fox (*Vulpes velox*) C
Texas kangaroo rat (*Dipodomys elator*) C
Townsend's big-eared bat (*Plecotus townsendii pallescens*) C

Birds

*Arctic peregrine falcon (*Falco peregrinus tundrius*) T
Bald eagle (*Haliaeetus leucocephalus*) E,T
Black-capped vireo (*Vireo atricapillus*) E
Eskimo curlew (*Numenius borealis*) E
Least tern (*Sterna antillarum*) E
*Mexican spotted owl (*Strix occidentalis lucida*) T
*Northern aplomado falcon (*Falco femoralis septentrionalis*) E
Peregrine falcon (*Falco peregrinus anatum*) E
Piping plover (*Charadrius melodus*) T
Whooping crane (*Grus americana*) E

*Apache northern goshawk (*Accipiter gentilis apache*) C
Bachman's sparrow (*Aimophila aestivalis*) C
Baird's sparrow (*Ammodramus bairdii*) C
Black rail (*Laterallus jamaicensis*) C
Black tern (*Chilidonias niger*) C
Cerulean warbler (*Dendroica cerulea*) C
Ferruginous hawk (*Buteo regalis*) C
Henslow's sparrow (*Ammodramus henslowii*) C
Loggerhead shrike (*Lanius ludovicianus*) C
Mountain plover (*Charadrius montanus*) C
*Northern goshawk (*Accipiter gentilis*) C
Southwestern willow flycatcher (*Empidonax traillii extimus*) C
Western snowy plover (*Charadrius alexandrinus nivosus*) C
White-faced ibis (*Plegadis chihi*) C

Reptiles

Concho water snake (*Nerodia harteri paucimaculata*) T

Alligator snapping turtle (*Macroclemys temmincki*) C
Blanding's turtle (*Emydoidea blandingii*) C
Texas garter snake (*Thamnophis sirtalis annectans*) C
Texas horned lizard (*Phrynosoma cornutum*) C

Fish
Neosho madtom (*Noturus placidus*) T
Pallid sturgeon (*Scaphirhynchus albus*) E

Arkansas darter (*Etheostoma cragini*) C
Arkansas River shiner (*Notropis girardi*) C
Arkansas River speckled chub (*Hybopsis aestivalis tetranemus*) C
Blue sucker (*Cycleptus elongatus*) C
Flathead chub (*Platygobio gracilis*) C
Lake sturgeon (*Acipenser fulvescens*) C
Paddlefish (*Polyodon spathula*) C
Plains minnow (*Hybognathus placitus*) C
Plains topminnow (*Fundulus sciadicus*) C
Sicklefin chub (*Hybopsis meeki*) C
Speckled chub (*Extrarius aestivalis tetranemus*) C
Sturgeon chub (*Hybopsis gelida*) C
Topeka shiner (*Notropis tristis [=topeka]*) C
Western silvery minnow (*Hybognathus argyritis*) C

Clams
Higgin's eye pearly mussel (*Lampsilis higginsi*) E

Elktoe (*Alasmidonta marginata*) C
Neosho mucket (*Lampsilis rafinesqueana*) C
Ouachita kidneyshell (*Ptychobranchus occidentalis*) C
Snuffbox mussel (*Epioblasma triquetra*) C
Western fanshell (*Cyprogenia aberti*) C

Insects
American burying beetle (*Nicrophorus americanus*) E
Pawnee mountain skipper (*Hesperia leonard [=pawnee] montana*) T

[No common name] (*Schinia indiana*) C

Albarufan dagger (*Acronicta albarufa*) C
**Colorado burrowing mayfly (*Ephemera compar*) C
Dakota skipper (*Hesperia dacotae*) C
Powesheik skipper (*Oarisma powesheik*) C
Prairie mole cricket (*Gryllotalpa major*) C
Regal fritillary (*Speyeria idalia*) C
Scott optioservus riffle beetle (*Optioservus phaeus*) C
Tawny crescent (*Phyciodes batesii*) C

Crustaceans
*Iowa Pleistocene snail (*Discus macclintocki*) E

Clanton's cave amphipod (*Stygobromus clantoni*) C

Plants
Blowout penstemon (*Penstemon haydenii*) E
Eastern prairie fringed orchid (*Platanthera leucophaea*) T
Mead's milkweed (*Asclepias meadii*) T
*Northern monkshood (*Aconitum novaboracense*) T
Prairie bush clover (*Lespedeza leptostachya*) T
Texas poppy mallow (*Callirhoe scabriuscula*) E
Ute's ladies tresses (*Spiranthes diluvialis*) T
Western prairie fringed orchid (*Platanthera praeclara*) T

Arapien stickleaf (*Mentzelia argillosa*) C
Arkansas River feverfew (*Parthenium tetraneuris*) C
Bell's twinpod (*Physaria bellii*) C
Brandegee milkvetch (*Astragalus brandegei*) C
Brandegee wild buckwheat (*Eriogonum brandegei*) C
Cleft sedge (*Carex fissa*) C
Colorado butterfly weed (*Gaura neomexicana coloradoensis*) C
Colorado green gentian (*Frasera coloradensis*) C
Cooper's milkvetch (*Astragalus neglectus*) C
Dakota wild buckwheat (*Eriogonum visheri*) C
Dwarf burhead (*Echinodorus parvulus*) C
Dwarf milkweed (*Asclepias uncialis*) C
Earleaf foxglove (*Tomanthera auriculata*) C

Engelmann's goldenweed (*Oonopsis engelmannii*) C
Fameflower (*Talinum rugospermum*) C
Hall's bulrush (*Scirpus hallii*) C
Handsome sedge (*Carex formosa*) C
Hayden's yellow-cress (*Rorippa calycina*) C
Hill's thistle (*Cirsium hillii*) C
Holy Ghost ipomopsis (*Ipomopsis sancti-spiritus*) C
Purple false-foxglove (*Tomanthera skinneriana*) C
Roundleaf four-o'clock (*Oxybaphus [=Mirabilis] rotundifolius*) C
Sandhill goosefoot (*Chenopodium cycloides*) C
Skinner's purple false foxglove (*Agalinus skinneriana*) C
Slender dodder (*Cuscuta attenuata*) C
Smith whitlow-grass (*Draba smithii*) C
Spellenberg's groundsel (*Senecio spellenbergii*) C
Spring gentian (*Eustoma grandiflorum*) C
Streaked ragweed (*Ambrosia linearis*) C
Wolf's spike-rush (*Eleocharis wolfii*) C

Works Cited

Agnew, W., D. W. Uresk, and R. M. Hansen. 1986. Flora and fauna associated with prairie dog colonies and adjacent ungrazed mixed-grass prairie in western South Dakota. *J. Range Manage.* 39 (2): 135–39.

———. 1988. Arthropod consumption by small mammals on prairie dog colonies and adjacent ungrazed mixed grass prairie in western South Dakota. In *Eighth Great Plains wildlife damage control workshop proceedings.* Gen. Tech. Rep. RM-154. Fort Collins CO: U.S. Forest Service.

Aiken, R. 1994. *1980–1990 fishing, hunting, and wildlife-associated recreation trends.* Rep. 91–92. Washington DC: U.S. Fish and Wildlife Service.

Albertson, F. W., G. W. Tomanek, and A. Riegel. 1957. Ecology of drought cycles and grazing intensity on grasslands of central Great Plains. *Ecol. Monogr.* 27:27–44.

Albertson, F. W., and J. E. Weaver. 1945. Injury and death or recovery of trees in prairie climate. *Ecol. Monogr.* 15:393–433.

———. 1946. Reduction of ungrazed mixed prairie to short grass as a result of drought and dust. *Ecol. Monogr.* 16:449–63.

Angermeier, P. L., and J. R. Karr. 1994. Biological integrity versus biological diversity as policy directives. *BioScience* 44:690–97.

Audubon, M. R. 1969. *Audubon and his journals.* Vols. 1 and 2. 1897. Reprint, New York: Dover.

Auer, L. 1989. *Canadian prairie farming, 1960–2000: An economic analysis.* Ottawa: Economic Council of Canada.

Bailey, V. 1926. *North American fauna no. 49: A biological survey of North Dakota.* Washington DC: Bureau of Biological Survey.

Baltensperger, B. H. 1991. A county that has gone downhill. *Geogr. Rev.*, Oct., 431–42.

Barker, W. T., K. K. Sedivec, T. A. Messmer, K. F. Higgins, and D. R. Hertel. 1990. Effects of specialized grazing systems on waterfowl production in southcentral North Dakota. *Trans. N. Am. Wildl. Nat. Resour. Conf.* 55:462–74.

Barsh, R. L. 1990. The substitution of cattle for bison on the Great Plains. In *The struggle for the land: Indigenous insight and industrial empire in the semiarid world*, ed. P. Olson. Lincoln: Univ. of Nebraska Press.

Basore, N. S., L. B. Best, and J. B. Wooley Jr. 1986. Bird nesting in Iowa no-tillage and tilled cropland. *J. Wildl. Manage.* 50:19–28.

Bath, A. J. 1992. Identification and documentation of public attitudes toward wolf reintroduction in Yellowstone National Park. In *Wolves for Yellowstone? A report to the United States Congress*, vol.4, *Research and analysis*, ed. J. D. Varley and W. G. Brewster. Yellowstone National Park WY: National Park Service.

Belovsky, G. E. 1987. Extinction models and mammalian persistence. In *Viable populations for conservation*, ed. M. E. Soule. New York: Cambridge Univ. Press.

Berger, J. 1990. Persistence of different-sized populations: An empirical assessment of rapid extinctions in bighorn sheep. *Cons. Biol.* 4:91–98.

Berner, A. H. 1984. Federal land retirement program: A land management albatross. *Trans. N. Am. Wildl. Nat. Resour. Conf.* 49:118–31.

Bernstein, N. P., K. K. Baker, and S. R. Wilmot. 1990. Changes in a prairie bird population from 1940 to 1989. *J. Iowa Acad. Sci.* 97:115–20.

Best, L. B. 1978. Field sparrow reproductive success and nesting ecology. *Auk* 95:9–22.

Betz, R. F., and H. F. Lamp. 1992. Flower, pod, and seed production in eighteen species of milkweeds (*Asclepias*). In *Proceedings of the twelfth North American prairie conference*, ed. D. D. Smith and C. A. Jacobs. Cedar Falls IA: Univ. of Northern Iowa.

Blockstein, D. E. 1994. U.S. policies to conserve biodiversity. In *Biological diversity: Problems and challenges*, ed. S. K. Majumdar, F. J. Brenner, J. E. Lovich, J. F. Schalles, and E. W. Miller. Easton PA: Pennsylvania Academy of Science.

Bock, J. H., and C. E. Bock. 1995. The challenges of grassland conservation.

In *The changing prairie: North American Grasslands*, ed. A. Joern and K. H. Keeler. New York: Oxford Univ. Press.

Boettcher, J. F., and T. B. Bragg. 1989. Tallgrass prairie remnants of eastern Nebraska. In *Proceedings of the eleventh North American prairie conference*, ed. T. B. Bragg and J. Stubbendieck. Lincoln NE: Univ. of Nebraska.

Bohning-Gaese, K., M. L. Taper, and J. H. Brown. 1993. Are declines in North America insectivorous songbirds due to causes on the breeding range? *Cons. Biol.* 7:76–86.

Botkin, D. B. 1995. *Our natural history: The lessons of Lewis and Clark*. New York: G. P. Putman's Sons.

Bradbury, 1986. *Travels in the interior of America in the years 1809, 1810, 1811*. 1911. Reprint. Lincoln: Univ. of Nebraska Press.

Bragg, T. B. 1982. Seasonal variations in fuel and fuel consumption by fires in a bluestem prairie. *Ecology* 63:7–11.

Brewerton, G. D. 1993. *Overland with Kit Carson: A narrative of the Old Spanish Trail in '48*. Lincoln: Univ. of Nebraska Press

Brown, D. E., and N. B. Carmony, eds. 1990. *Aldo Leopold's wilderness*. Harrisburg PA: Stackpole Books.

Brown, M., and J. J. Dinsmore. 1986. Implications of marsh size and isolation for marsh bird management. *J. Wildl. Manage.* 50:392–97.

Brown, M. H., and W. R. Felton. 1955. *The frontier years: L. A. Huffman, photographer of the plains*. New York: Bramhall House.

Buffington, L. C., and C. H. Herbel. 1965. Vegetational changes on a semi-desert grassland range from 1858 to 1963. *Ecol. Monogr.* 35:139–64.

Burger, L. D., L. W. Burger Jr., and J. Faaborg. 1994. Effects of prairie fragmentation on predation on artificial nests. *J. Wildl. Manage.* 58:249–54.

Burnett, J. A., C. T. Dauphine Jr., S. H. McCrindle, and T. Mosquin. 1989. *On the brink: Endangered species in Canada*. Saskatoon, Saskatchewan: Western Producer Prairie Books.

Burns, N. 1982. *The collapse of small towns on the Great Plains: A bibliography*. Emporia KS: Emporia State Research Studies.

Burroughs, R. D. 1961. *The natural history of the Lewis and Clark expedition*. East Lansing: Michigan State Univ. Press.

Cahalane, V. H. 1940. A proposed Great Plains National Monument. *Sci. Month.* 51 (July-Dec.): 125–39.

Callenbach, E. 1996. *Bring back the buffalo! A sustainable future for America's Great Plains*. Washington DC: Island Press.

Carbyn, L. N. 1982. Coyote population fluctuations and spatial distribution in relation to wolf territories in Riding Mountain National Park, Manitoba. *Can. Field Nat.* 96:176–83.

———. 1986. Some observations on the behaviour of swift foxes in reintroduction programs within the Canadian prairies. *Alberta Nat.* 16(2): 37–41.

———. 1989. Status of the swift fox in Saskatchewan. *Bluejay* 47(1): 41–52.

Carbyn, L. N., S. M. Oosenbrug, and D. W. Anions. 1993. *Wolves, bison and the dynamics related to the Peace-Athabasca Delta in Canada's Wood Buffalo National Park.* Edmonton: Canadian Circumpolar Institute, Univ. of Alberta.

Catlin, G. 1973. *Letters and notes on the manners, customs, and conditions of the North American Indians.* Vol 1. 1844. Reprinted. New York: Dover.

Chilgren, J. D. 1979. Drowning of grassland birds in stock tanks. *Wilson Bull.* 91:345–46.

Clark, F. E. 1975. Viewing the invisible prairie. In *Prairie: A multiple view*, ed. M. K. Wali. Grand Forks: Univ. of North Dakota Press.

Clark, T. W., T. M. Campbell III, D. C. Socha, and D. E. Casey. 1982. Prairie dog colony attributes and associated vertebrate species. *Great Basin Nat.* 42:577–82.

Cochrane, W. W., and C. F. Runge. 1992. *Reforming farm policy.* Ames: Iowa State Univ. Press.

Coffin, B., and L. Pfannmuller. 1988. *Minnesota's endangered flora and fauna.* Minneapolis: Univ. of Minnesota Press.

Coffman, D. C. 1991. William Hornaday's bitter mission. *Montana Mag.*, Feb., 58–66.

Coffman, D., C. Jonkel, and R. Scott. 1990. The Big Open: a return to grazers of the past. *West. Wildlands*, fall, 40–44.

Coleman, J. S., and S. A. Temple. 1993. Rural residents' free-ranging domestic cats: A survey. *Wildl. Soc. Bull.* 21:381–90.

Coleman, R. A., N. Fuller, J. P. Mazzoni, R. Berry, J. Davis, D. Adams, D. G. Young, R. Fries, and T. Heuer. 1990. *Report to the director: A review of secondary uses occurring on national wildlife refuges.* Washington DC: U.S. Fish and Wildlife Service.

Collins, A. R., J. P. Workman, and D. W. Uresk. 1984. An economic analysis of black-tailed prairie dog (*Cynomys ludovicianus*) control. *J. Range Manage.* 37(4): 358–61.

Cooperrider, A. Y. 1990. Conservation of biological diversity on western rangelands. *Trans. N. Am. Wildl. Nat. Resour. Conf.* 55:451–61.

Coppock, D. L., J. K. Detling, J. E. Ellis, and M. I. Dyer. 1983. Plant-herbivore interactions in a North American mixed-grass prairie: I. Effects of black-tailed prairie dogs on intraseasonal aboveground plant biomass and nutrient dynamics and plant species diversity. *Oecologia* 56:1–9.

Cowardin, L. M., D. S. Gilmer, and C. W. Shaiffer. 1985. Mallard recruitment in the agricultural environment of North Dakota. *Wildl. Monogr.* 92:1–37.

Crouch, G. L. 1984. Wildlife habitat on a western Plains stream: Past, present and future. In *Wooded draws, characteristics and values for the northern Great Plains*, ed. D. L. Noble and R. P. Winokur. Symposium proceedings, 12–13 June.Rapid City: South Dakota School of Mines and Technology.

Dahl, T. E. 1990. *Wetland losses in the United States, 1780's to 1980's.* Washington DC: U.S. Fish and Wildlife Service.

Dary, D. A. 1974. *The buffalo book.* Chicago: Sage Books, Swallow Press.

Davis, S. K. 1993. Impact of cowbird parasitism and predation on avian productivity in fragmented grassland of southwestern Manitoba. North American research workshop on the ecology and management of cowbirds, 4–5 November. Austin TX.

De Smet, K. D. 1993. Status of ferruginous hawk and loggerhead shrike recovery efforts. In *Proceedings of the third prairie conservation and endangered species workshop*, ed. G. L. Holroyd, H. L. Dickson, M. Regnier, and H. C. Smith. Natural History Occasional Paper 19. Edmonton: Provincial Museum of Alberta.

Dicks, M. R., and C. T. Osborn. 1994. Land use issues. In *Food, agriculture, and rural policy into the twenty-first century*, ed. M. C. Hallberg, R. G. F. Spitze, and D. E. Ray. Boulder CO: Westview Press.

Dinsmore, J. 1994. *A country so full of game: The story of wildlife in Iowa.* Iowa City: Univ. of Iowa Press.

Dodge, R. I. 1989. *The plains of North America and their inhabitants.* Newark: Univ. of Delaware Press.

Duffield, J. W. 1992. An economic analysis of wolf recovery in Yellowstone: Park visitor attitudes and values. In *Wolves for Yellowstone? A report to the United States Congress*, vol. 4, *Research and analysis.* ed. J. D. Varley and W. G. Brewster. Yellowstone National Park WY: National Park Service.

Duncan, D. C. 1987. Nest–site distribution and overland brood movements of northern pintails in Alberta. *J. Wildl. Manage.* 51:716–23.

Ehrenfield, D. 1988. Why put a value on biodiversity? In *Biodiversity*, ed. E. O. Wilson and F. M. Peters. Washington DC: National Academy Press.

Elliot, P. F. 1978. Cowbird parasitism in the Kansas tallgrass prairie. *Auk* 95:161–67.

Erickson, D., and R. De Young. 1993. Management of farm woodlots and windbreaks: Some psychological and landscape patterns. *J. Environ. Syst.* 22(3): 233–47.

Fannin, T. E., and B. J. Esmoil. 1993. Metal and organic residues in addled eggs of least terns and piping plovers in the Platte Valley of Nebraska. In *Proceedings, the Missouri River and its tributaries: Piping plover and least tern symposium/workshop*, ed. K. F. Higgins and M. R. Brashier. Brookings: South Dakota State Univ.

Fisser, H. G., K. L. Johnson, K. S. Moore, and G. E. Plumb. 1989. Fifty-one-year change in the shortgrass prairie of eastern Wyoming. In *Proceedings of the eleventh North American prairie conference*, ed. T. B. Bragg and J. Stubbendieck. Lincoln: Univ. of Nebraska.

Flather, C. H., L. A. Joyce, and C. A. Bloomgarden. 1994. *Species endangerment patterns in the United States*. Gen. Tech. Rep. RM-241. Fort Collins CO: U.S. Forest Service.

Frankel, O. H. 1974. Genetic conservation: Our evolutionary responsibility. *Genetics* 78:53–65.

Freeman, S., D. F. Gori, and S. Rohwer. 1990. Red-winged blackbirds and brown-headed cowbirds: Some aspects of a host-parasite relationship. *Condor* 92:336–40.

French, N. R., W. E. Grant, W. Grodzínski, and D. M. Swift. 1976. Small mammal energetics in grassland ecosystems. *Ecol. Monogr.* 46:201–20.

Fritzell, E. K. 1978. Habitat use by prairie raccoons during the waterfowl breeding season. *J. Wildl. Manage.* 42:118–27.

Fuller, T. K. n.d. *Guidelines for gray wolf management in the northern Great Lakes region*. Tech. pub. no. 271. Ely MN: International Wolf Center.

Fuller, T. K., and L. B. Keith. 1981. Non-overlapping ranges of coyotes and wolves in northeastern Alberta. *J. Mammal.* 62:403–5.

Gaines, E. P., and M. R. Ryan. 1988. Piping plover habitat use and reproductive success in North Dakota. *J. Wildl. Manage.* 52:266–73.

Gaines, M. S., G. R. Robinson, J. E. Diffendorfer, R. D. Holt, and M. L. Johnson. 1992. The effects of habitat fragmentation on small mammal populations. In *Wildlife 2001: Populations*, ed. D. R. McCullough and R. H. Barrett. London: Elsevier Applied Science.

Gee, C. K., L. A. Joyce, and A. G. Madsen. 1992. *Factors affecting the demand for grazed forage in the United States.* Gen. Tech. Rep. RM-210. Fort Collins CO: U.S. Forest Service.

Gese, E. M., O. J. Rongstad, and W. R. Mytton. 1988. Home range and habitat use of coyotes in southeastern Colorado. *J. Wildl. Manage.* 52:640–46.

Gibson, D. J. 1989. Effects of animal disturbance on tallgrass prairie vegetation. *Am. Mid. Nat.* 121:144–54.

Gilmer, D. S., and R. E. Stewart. 1983. Ferruginous hawk populations and habitat use in North Dakota. *J. Wildl. Manage.* 47:146–57.

Goodson, N. 1983. Effects of domestic sheep grazing on bighorn sheep populations: A review. *Proceedings of the third biennial symposium of the Northern Wild Sheep and Goat Council* 3:287–313.

Gray, L. C., O. E. Baker, F. J. Marschner, B. O. Weitz, W. R. Chapline, W. Shepard, and R. Zon. 1924. The utilization of our lands for crops, pasture and forests. In *Yearbook of the Department of Agriculture, 1923*. Washington DC: Department of Agriculture.

Greenwood, R. J. 1981. Foods of prairie raccoons during the waterfowl nesting season. *J. Wildl. Manage.* 45:754–60.

———. 1982. Nocturnal activity and foraging of prairie raccoons (*Procyon lotor*) in North Dakota. *Am. Mid. Nat.* 107:238–43.

———. 1986. Influence of striped skunk removal on upland duck nest success in North Dakota. *Wildl. Soc. Bull.* 14:6–11.

Greenwood, R. J., A. B. Sargeant, D. H. Johnson, L. M. Cowardin, and T. L. Shaffer. 1987. Mallard nest success and recruitment in prairie Canada. *Trans. N. Am. Wildl. Nat. Resour. Conf.* 52:298–309.

Griffin, C. R., T. S. Baskett, and R. D. Sparrowe. 1982. *Ecology of bald eagles wintering near a waterfowl concentration.* Spec. Sci. Rep.—Wildl. 247. Washington DC: U.S. Fish and Wildlife Service.

Griffith, P. W. 1976. Introduction to the problems: Shelterbelts on the Great Plains. *Proc. Great Plains Agric. Council* (Denver) 78:3–7.

Guither, H. D., H. S. Baumes and W. H. Meyers. 1994. Farm prices, income, stability, and distribution. In *Food, agriculture, and rural policy into the twenty-first century*, ed. M. C. Hallberg, R. G. F. Spitze, and D. E. Ray. Boulder CO: Westview Press.

Guttenberg, A. Z. 1976. The land utilization movement of the 1920s. *Agric. Hist.* 50:477–90.

Hart, J. F. 1972. The Middle West. *Ann. Assoc. Am. Geo.* 62:258–82.

Hays, R. L., and A. H. Farmer. 1990. Effects of the CRP on wildlife habitat: Emergency haying in the Midwest and pine plantings in the Southeast. *Trans. N. Am. Wildl. Nat. Resour. Conf.* 55:30–39.

Heimlich, R. E., and O. E. Kula. 1991. Economics of livestock and crop production on post-CRP lands. ed. L. A. Joyce, J. E. Mitchell, and M. D. Skold. In *The Conservation Reserve—yesterday, today and tomorrow.* Symposium Proceedings, 14 January 1991. Gen. Tech. Rep. RM-203. Fort Collins CO: U.S. Forest Service.

Henry, A. 1897. *The manuscript journals of Alexander Henry, 1799–1814.* vol. 1. Ed. E. Coues. New York: Francis P. Harper.

Hergenrader, G. L. 1962. The incidence of nest parasitism by the brown-headed cowbird (Molothrus ater) on roadside nesting birds in Nebraska. *Auk* 79:85–88.

Herkert, J. R. 1993. The influence of two centuries of habitat change on grassland bird populations in Illinois. *Meadowlark* 2(1): 4–8.

———. 1994a. Breeding bird communities of midwestern prairie fragments: The effects of prescribed burning and habitat-area. *Nat. Areas J.* 14(2): 128–35.

———. 1994b. The influence of habitat fragmentation on midwestern grassland bird communities. *Ecol. Appl.* 4(3): 461–71.

Hester, F. E. 1991. The U.S. National Park Service experience with exotic species. *Nat. Areas J.* 11(3):127–28.

Hewes, L., and P. E. Frandson. 1951. Occupying the wet prairie: The role of artificial drainage in Story County, Iowa. *Ann. Assoc. Am. Geog.* 42:24–50.

Higgins, K. F. 1977. Duck nesting in intensively farmed areas of North Dakota. *J. Wildl. Manage.* 41:232–42.

Higgins, K. F., T. W. Arnold, and R. M. Barta. 1984. Breeding bird community colonization of sown stands of native grasses in North Dakota. *Prairie Nat.* 16:177–82.

Higgins, K. F., and R. O. Woodward. 1986. Comparison of wetland drainage during and after protection by 20-year easements. *Prairie Nat.* 18:229–33.

Hill, R. A. 1976. Host-parasite relationships of the brown-headed cowbird in a prairie habitat of west-central Kansas. *Wilson Bull.* 88:555–65.

Hines, T. D., and R. M. Case. 1991. Diet, home range, movements, and activity periods of swift fox in Nebraska. *Prairie Nat.* 23:131–38.

Hjertaas, D. G. 1993. The burrowing owl recovery program. In *Proceedings of the third prairie conservation and endangered species workshop*, ed. G. L. Holroyd, H. L. Dickson, M. Regnier, and H. C. Smith. Natural History Occasional Paper 19. Edmonton: Provincial Museum of Alberta.

Howe, H. F. 1994. Managing species diversity in tallgrass prairie: Assumptions and implications. *Cons. Biol.* 8:691–704.

Hurt, R. D. 1986. Federal land reclamation in the Dust Bowl. *Great Plains Quart.* 6:94–106.

———. 1994. *American agriculture: A brief history*. Ames: Iowa State Univ. Press.

Huszar, P. C., and J. E. Young. 1984. Why the great Colorado plowout? *J. Soil and Water Cons.* 39:232–34.

Illinois Department of Energy and Natural Resources and Nature of Illinois Foundation. 1994. *The changing Illinois environment: Critical trends*. N.p.

Inouye, R. S., N. J. Huntly, D. Tilman, J. R. Tester, M. Stillwell, and K. C. Zinnel. 1987. Old-field succession on a Minnesota sand plain. *Ecology* 68:12–26.

James, S. W. 1991. Soil, nitrogen, phosphorus, and organic matter processing by earthworms in tallgrass prairie. *Ecology* 72:2101–09.

Johnson, D. H., and A. B. Sargeant. 1977. *Impact of red fox predation on the sex ratio of prairie mallards*. Res. Rep. 6. Fort Collins CO: U.S. Fish and Wildlife Service.

Johnson, D. H., A. B. Sargeant, and R. J. Greenwood. 1989. Importance of individual species of predators on nesting success of ducks in the Canadian Prairie Pothole Region. *Can. J. Zool.* 67:291–97.

Johnson, D. H., and T. L. Shaffer. 1987. Are mallards declining in North America? *Wildl. Soc. Bull.* 15:340–45.

Johnson, R. G., and S. A. Temple. 1990. Nest predation and brood parasitism of tallgrass prairie birds. *J. Wildl. Manage.* 54:106–11.

Joyce, J., and J. P. Morgan. 1989. Manitoba's tall-grass prairie conservation project. In *Proceedings of the eleventh North American prairie conference*, ed. T. B. Bragg and J. Stubbendieck. Lincoln: Univ. of Nebraska.

Judd, E. T. 1917. *List of North Dakota birds found in the Big Coulee, Turtle Mountains and Devils Lake region*. N.p.

Kantrud, H. A. 1981. Grazing intensity effects on the breeding avifauna of North Dakota native grasslands. *Can. Field Nat.* 95:404–17.

———. 1993. Duck nest success on Conservation Reserve Program land in the prairie pothole region. *J. Soil Water Cons.* 48:238–42.

Kantrud, H. A., and K. F. Higgins. 1992. Nest and nest site characteristics of some ground-nesting, non-passerine birds of northern grasslands. *Prairie Nat.* 24:67–84.

Kantrud, H. A., and R. L. Kologiski. 1982. *Effects of soils and grazing on breeding birds of uncultivated upland grasslands of the northern Great Plains.* Res. Rep. 15. Washington DC: U.S. Fish and Wildlife Service.

———. 1983. Avian associations of the northern Great Plains grasslands. *J. Biogeog.* 10:331–50.

Kellert, S. R. 1980. American attitudes toward and knowledge of animals: An update. *Int. J. Stud. Anim. Prob.* 1(2): 87–119.

———. 1985. Social and perceptual factors in endangered species management. *J. Wildl. Manage.* 49 (2):528–36.

———. 1993. Values and perceptions of invertebrates. *Cons. Biol.* 7:845–55.

Kimmel, R. O. 1988. Potential impacts of ring-necked pheasants on other game birds. In *Pheasants: Symptoms of wildlife problems on agricultural lands*, ed. D. L. Hallett, W. R. Edwards, and G. V. Burger. Bloomington IN: North Central Section, Wildlife Society.

Kirby, R. E., J. K. Ringelman, D. R. Anderson, and R. S. Sojda. 1992. Grazing on National Wildlife Refuges: Do the needs outweigh the problems? *Trans. N. Am. Wildl. Nat. Resour. Conf.* 57:611–26.

Kirsch, L. M., H. F. Duebbert, and A. D. Kruse. 1978. Grazing and haying effects on habitats of upland nesting birds. *Trans. N. Am. Wildl. Nat. Resour. Conf.* 43:486–97.

Kirsch, L. M., and K. F. Higgins. 1976. Upland sandpiper nesting and management in North Dakota. *Wildl. Soc. Bull.* 4:16–20.

Klett, A. T., H. F. Duebbert, and G. L. Heismeyer. 1984. Use of seeded native grasses as nesting cover by ducks. *Wildl. Soc. Bull.* 12:134–38.

Klett, A. T., T. L. Shaffer, and D. H. Johnson. 1988. Duck nest success in the Prairie Pothole Region. *J. Wildl. Manage.* 52:431–40.

Knopf, F. L. 1986. Changing landscapes and the cosmopolitan of the eastern Colorado avifauna. *Wildl. Soc. Bull.* 14:132–42.

———. 1988. Conservation of steppe birds in North America. ICBP Tech. Pub. 7:27–41.

————. 1992. Faunal mixing, faunal integrity, and the biopolitical template for diversity conservation. *Trans. N. Am. Wildl. Nat. Resour. Conf.* 57:330–42.

————. 1994. Avian assemblages on altered grasslands. *Studies Avian Biol.*, no. 15:247–57.

Knopf, F. L., R. R. Johnson, T. Rich, F. B. Samson, and R. C. Szaro. 1988. Conservation of riparian ecosystems in the United States. *Wilson Bull.* 100:272–84.

Knopf, F. L., and F. B. Samson. 1996. Conserving the biotic integrity of the Great Plains. In *Conservation of the Great Plains ecosystems,* ed. S. R. Johnson and A. Bouzaher. Boston: Kluwer Academic Publishers.

Knowles, C. J. 1986. Some relationships of black-tailed prairie dogs to livestock grazing. *Great Basin Nat.* 46:198–203.

Knowles, C. J., and P. R. Knowles. 1984. Additional records of mountain plovers using prairie dog towns in Montana. *Prairie Nat.* 16:183–86.

Kraenzel, C. F. 1955. *The Great Plains in transition.* Norman: Univ. of Oklahoma Press.

Krapu, G. L., K. J. Reinecke, and C. R. Frith. 1982. Sandhill cranes and the Platte River. *Trans. N. Am. Wildl. Nat. Resour. Conf.* 47:542–52.

Kromm, D. E., and S. E. White. 1992. Groundwater problems. In *Groundwater exploitation in the High Plains*, ed. D. E. Kromm and S. E. White. Lawrence: Univ. Press of Kansas.

Landres, P. B. 1992. Temporal scale perspectives in managing biological diversity. *Trans. N. Am. Wildl. Nat. Resour. Conf.* 57:292–307.

Lang, R. E., F. J. Popper, and D. E. Popper. 1994. *Progress of the nation: The settlement history of the enduring American frontier.* New Brunswick NJ: Urban Studies Dept., Rutgers Univ.

Langner, L. L. 1989. Land-use changes and hunter participation: The case of the Conservation Reserve Program. *Trans. N. Am. Wildl. Nat. Resour. Conf.* 54:382–89.

Laycock, W. A. 1988. History of grassland plowing and grass planting on the Great Plains. In *Impacts of the Conservation Reserve Program in the Great Plains*, ed. J. E. Mitchell. Symposium proceedings, 16–18 September 1987. Gen. Tech. Rep. RM-158. Fort Collins CO: U.S. Forest Service.

————. 1991. The Conservation Reserve Program—How did we get where we are and where do we go from here? In *The Conservation Reserve—yesterday, today and tomorrow*, ed. L. A. Joyce, J. E. Mitchell, and M. D. Skold.

Symposium proceedings, 14 January. Gen. Tech. Rep. RM-203. Fort Collins CO: U.S. Forest Service.

League of Conservation Voters. 1994. *The scorecard: February 1994, 103rd Congress, first session.* Washington DC: League of Conservation Voters.

Leopold, A. 1933. *Game management.* New York: Charles Scribners' Sons.

———. 1966. *A Sand County almanac.* New York: Sierra Club/Ballantine Books.

Lewis, M. E. 1989. National grasslands in the dust bowl. *Geog. Rev.* 79:161–71.

Licht, D. S. 1994. The Great Plains: America's best chance for ecosystem restoration. Parts 1 and 2. *Wild Earth* 4 (2): 45–53; 4 (3): 31–36.

Licht, D. S., and S. H. Fritts. 1994. Gray wolf (*Canis lupus*) occurrences in the Dakotas. *Am. Mid. Nat.* 132:74–81.

Licht, D. S., and K. D. Sanchez. 1993. Association of black-tailed prairie dog colonies with cattle point attractants in the northern Great Plains. *Great Basin Nat.* 53:385–89.

Lingle, G. R. 1992. History and economic impact of crane-watching in central Nebraska. In *Proceedings of the North American crane workshop no.6,* ed. D. W. Stahlecker. Grand Island NE: North American Crane Working Group.

Litvaitis, J. A., and J. H. Shaw. 1980. Coyote movements, habitat use, and food habits in southwestern Oklahoma. *J. Wildl. Manage.* 44:62–68.

Lokemoen, J. T. 1984. Examining economic efficiency of management practices that enhance waterfowl production. *Trans. N. Am. Wildl. Nat. Resour. Conf.* 49:584–607.

Lokemoen, J. T., and H. F. Duebbert. 1976. Ferruginous hawk nesting ecology and raptor populations in northern South Dakota. *Condor* 78:464–70.

Luckey, R. R., E. D. Gutentag, F. J. Heimes, and J. B. Weeks. 1988. *Effects of future ground-water pumpage on the High Plains aquifer in parts of Colorado, Kansas, Nebraska, New Mexico, Oklahoma, South Dakota, Texas, and Wyoming.* Professional Paper 1400-E. Washington DC: U.S. Geological Survey.

Luttschwager, K. A. 1991. Effects of two haying provisions on duck nesting in Conservation Reserve Program (CRP) fields in South Dakota. M.S. thesis, South Dakota State Univ., Brookings.

Lysne, L. A. 1991. Small mammal demographics in North Dakota conservation reserve program plantings. M.S. thesis. Univ. of North Dakota, Grand Forks.

Mader, H. J. 1984. Animal habitat isolation by roads and agricultural fields. *Biol. Cons.* 29:81–96.

Manning, R. 1995. *Grassland: The history, biology, politics, and promise of the American prairie.* New York: Penguin Books.

Mather, E. C. 1972. The American Great Plains. *Ann. Assoc. Am. Geog.* 62:237–57.

Matthews, A. 1992. *Where the buffalo roam.* New York: Grove Press.

Mead, J. R. 1986. *Hunting and trading on the Great Plains, 1859–1875.* Norman: Univ. of Oklahoma Press.

Meagher, M. M. 1978. Bison. In *Big game of North America: Ecology and management,* ed. J. L. Schmidt and D. L. Gilbert. Harrisburg PA: Wildlife Management Institute, Stackpole Books.

Mech, L. D. 1970. *The wolf: The ecology and behavior of an endangered species.* Garden City NY: Natural History Press.

Mech, L. D., S. H. Fritts, G. L. Radde, and W. J. Paul. 1988. Wolf distribution and road density in Minnesota. *Wildl. Soc. Bull.* 16:85–87.

Mengel, R. M. 1970. The North American central plains as an isolating agent in bird speciation. In *Pleistocene and Recent environments of the central Great Plains,* ed. W. Dort and J. K. Jones. Lawrence: Univ. of Kansas Press.

Miller, B., G. Ceballos, and R. Reading. 1994. The prairie dog and biotic diversity. *Cons. Biol.* 8:677–81.

Milner, C. A., II. 1994. Introduction and chronology. In *The Oxford history of the American West,* ed. C. A. Milner, C. A. O'Connor, and M. A. Sandweiss. Oxford: Oxford Univ. Press.

Missouri Department of Conservation. 1992. *The biodiversity of Missouri: Definition, status, and recommendations for its conservation.* Jefferson City MO: Biodiversity Task Force, Missouri Department of Conservation.

Mlot, C. 1990. Restoring the prairie. *BioScience* 40:804–9.

Mooers, G. 1987. Plowout on the Great Plains: Causes, consequences and prospects for change. *West. Wildl.* 13(3): 26–31.

Morgan, D. 1979. *Merchants of grain.* New York: Viking Press.

Mortensen, T. L., F. L. Leistritz, J. A. Leitch, R. C. Coon, and B. L. Ekstrom. 1989. Landowner characteristics and the economic impact of the Conservation Reserve Program in North Dakota. *J. Soil Water Cons.* 44:494–97.

Murphy, R. K. 1993. History, nesting biology, and predation ecology of raptors in the Missouri Coteau of northwestern North Dakota. Ph.d. diss., Montana State Univ., Bozeman.

National Park Service. 1991. *The national parks: Index 1991*. Washington DC: U.S. Department of Interior.

National Wildlife Federation. 1993. *1993 conservation directory*. Washington DC: National Wildlife Federation.

Nelson, H. K., and H. F. Duebbert. 1974. New concepts regarding the production of waterfowl and other gamebirds in areas of diversified agriculture. *Proc. Intl. Congr. Game Biol.* 11:385–94.

Nielsen, L. A., and S. L. McMullin. 1992. The fisheries and wildlife agency in 2020. In *2020 vision: Meeting the fish and wildlife conservation challenges of the 21st century*, ed. Tony J. Peterle. West Lafayette IN: North Central Section, Wildlife Society.

Niesar, S. L. 1994. Vertebrate richness of waterfowl production areas in the Prairie Pothole Region of Minnesota. M.S. thesis, South Dakota State Univ., Brookings.

Norall, Frank. 1988. *Bourgmont, explorer of the Missouri, 1698–1725*. Lincoln: University of Nebraska Press.

Norland, J. E., and C. B. Marlow. 1984. Use of wooded draws by free-roaming bison. In *Wooded draws, characteristics and values for the northern Great Plains*, ed. D. L. Noble and R. P. Winokur. Symposium proceedings, 12–13 June. Rapid City: South Dakota School of Mines and Technology.

Norman, R. F., and R. J. Robertson. 1975. Nest-searching behavior in the brown-headed cowbird. *Auk* 92:610–11.

Noss, R. F. 1994. Wilderness—now more than ever. *Wild Earth* 4(4): 60–63.

Noss, R. F., and A. Y. Cooperrider. 1994. *Saving nature's legacy*. Washington DC: Island Press.

Noss, R. F., E. T. LaRoe III, and J. M. Scott. 1995. *Endangered ecosystems of the United States: A preliminary assessment of loss and degradation*. Washington DC: U.S. Dept. of Interior, National Biological Service.

Nowak, R. M. 1979. *North American Quaternary Canis*. Lawrence: Museum of Natural History, Univ. of Kansas.

———. 1995. Another look at wolf taxonomy. In *Ecology and conservation of wolves in a changing world*, ed. L. N. Carbyn, S. H. Fritts, and D. R. Seip. Proceedings, Second North American Wolf Symposium. Occasional Paper 35. Alberta: Canadian Circumpolar Institute.

Odum, E. P. 1994. Conservation of biodiversity. In *Biological diversity: Problems and challenges*, ed. S. K. Majumdar, F. J. Brenner, J. E. Lovich, J. F. Schalles, and E. W. Miller. Easton PA: Pennsylvania Academy of Science.

Olson, T. E., and F. L. Knopf. 1986. Agency subsidization of a rapidly spreading exotic. *Wildl. Soc. Bull.* 14:492–93.

Omernik, J. M. 1987. Ecoregions of the conterminous United States. *Ann. Assoc. Am. Geog.* 77:118–25.

Orwig, T. T. 1992. Loess Hills prairies as butterfly survivia: Opportunities and challenges. In *Proceedings of the twelfth North American prairie conference*, ed. D. D. Smith and C. A. Jacobs. Cedar Falls: Univ. of Northern Iowa.

Osborn, B., and P. F. Allen. 1949. Vegetation of an abandoned prairie dog town in tall grass prairie. *Ecology* 30:322–32.

Osborn, C. T., F. Llacuna, and M. Linsenbigler. 1990. *The Conservation Reserve Program: Enrollment statistics for signup periods 1–9 and fiscal year 1989*. Statistical Bulletin 811. Washington DC: Economic Research Service, U.S. Department of Agriculture.

Paquet, P. C. 1991. Winter spatial relationships of wolves and coyotes in Riding Mountain National Park, Manitoba. *J. Mammal.* 72:397–401.

Paton, P. W. C. 1994. The effect of edge on avian nest success: How strong is the evidence? *Cons. Biol.* 8:17–26.

Pedan, D. G., G. M. Van Dyne, R. W. Rice, and R. M. Hansen. 1974. The trophic ecology of *Bison bison* L. on shortgrass plains. *J. Appl. Ecol.* 11:489–98.

Peterjohn, B. G., and J. R. Sauer. 1993. *Temporal and geographic patterns in population trends of brown-headed cowbirds*. North American research workshop on the ecology and management of cowbirds, 4–5 November. Austin TX.

Popper, D. E., and F. J. Popper. 1987a. *The fate of the Plains*. New Brunswick NJ: Rutgers Univ.

———. 1987b. The Great Plains: From dust to dust. *Planning* 53(6): 12–18.

———. 1994a. Great Plains: Checkered past, hopeful future. *Forum for Appl. Res. Pub. Pol., winter,* 89–100.

———. 1994b. The buffalo commons: A bioregional vision of the Great Plains. *Landscape Arch.*, 84(4): 144.

Porneluzi, P., J. C. Bednarz, L. J. Goodrich, N. Zawada, and J. Hoover. 1993. Reproductive performance of territorial ovenbirds occupying forest fragments and a contiguous forest in Pennsylvania. *Cons. Biol.* 7:618–22.

Potter, C., P. Burnham, A. Edwards, R. Gasson, and B. Green. 1991. *The di-*

version of land: Conservation in a period of farming contraction. London: Routledge.

Powell, J. W. 1879. *Lands of the Arid Region of the United States*. Washington DC: Government Printing Office.

———. 1970. *Selected prose of John Wesley Powell*. Ed. G. Crossette. Boston: D. R. Godine.

Ray, D. E., and R. Frederick. 1994. The economic setting for U.S. food and agriculture. In *Food, agriculture, and rural policy into the twenty-first century*, ed. M. Hallberg, R. G. F. Spitze, and D. E. Ray. Boulder CO: Westview Press.

Reading, R. P., S. R. Beissinger, J. J. Brensten, and T. W. Clark. 1989. Attributes of black-tailed prairie dog colonies in northcentral Montana, with management recommendations for the conservation of biodiversity. In *The prairie dog ecosystem: Managing for biological diversity*, ed. T. W. Clark. Wildlife Technical Bulletin 2. Billings: Montana Bureau of Land Management.

Rising, J. D. 1983. The Great Plains Hybrid Zones. Curr. Ornithol. 1:131–57.

Risser, P. G. 1988. Diversity in and among grasslands. In *Biodiversity*, ed. E. O. Wilson. Washington DC: National Academy Press.

Risser, P. G., E. C. Birney, H. D. Blocker, S. W. May, W. J. Parton, and J. A. Wiens. 1981. *The true prairie ecosystem*. Stroudsburg PA: Hutchinson Ross.

Robbins, C. S., D. Bystrak, and P. H. Geissler. 1986. *The breeding bird survey: Its first fifteen years, 1965–1979. Res. Pub.* 157. Washington DC: U.S. Fish and Wildlife Service.

Robins, J. D. 1971. Movements of Franklin's ground squirrel into northeastern Minnesota. *J. Minn. Acad. Sci.* 37:30–31.

Robinson, S. K. 1988. Reappraisal of the costs and benefits of habitat heterogeneity for nongame wildlife. *Trans. N. Am. Wildl. Nat. Resour. Conf.* 53:145–55.

Rockel, M. L., and M. J. Kealy. 1991. The value of nonconsumptive wildlife recreation in the United States. *Land Econ.* 67(4): 422–34.

Rohlf, D. J. 1991. Six biological reasons why the Endangered Species Act doesn't work—and what to do about it. *Cons. Biol.* 5:273–82.

Rolfe, E. S. 1896. Nesting of the ferruginous rough-leg. *Osprey* 1:8–10.

Royer, R. A., and G. M. Marrone. 1992. *Conservation status of the Dakota skipper* (Hesperia dacotae) *in North and South Dakota*. Denver CO: U.S. Department of Interior, Fish and Wildlife Service.

Ruelle, R. 1993. Contaminant evaluation of interior least tern and piping plover eggs from the Missouri River in South Dakota. In *Proceedings, the Missouri River and its tributaries: Piping plover and least tern symposium/workshop*, ed. K. F. Higgins and M. R. Brashier. Brookings: South Dakota State Univ.

Ryan, M. R. 1986. Nongame management in grassland agricultural ecosystems. In *Management of nongame wildlife in the Midwest: A developing art*, ed. J. B. Hale, L. B. Best, and R. L. Clawson. Chelsea MI: Bookcrafters.

Ryan, M. R., R. B. Renken, and J. J. Dinsmore. 1984. Marbled godwit habitat selection in the northern prairie region. *J. Wildl. Manage.* 48:1206–18.

Samson, F. B. 1980. Island biogeography and the conservation of nongame birds. *Trans. N. Am. Wildl. Nat. Resour. Conf.* 45:245–51.

Samson, F. B., and F. L. Knopf. 1982. In search of a diversity ethic for wildlife management. *Trans. N. Am. Wildl. Nat. Resour. Conf.* 47:421–31.

———. 1994. Prairie conservation in North America. *BioScience* 44:418–21.

Sargeant, A. B. 1981. Road casualties of prairie nesting ducks. *Wildl. Soc. Bull.* 9:65–69.

———. 1982. A case history of dynamic resource—the red fox. In *Midwest furbearer management*, ed. G. C. Sanderson. Wichita: North-central Section of the Central Mountains and Plains Section and Kansas Chapter, Wildlife Society.

Sargeant, A. B., and S. H. Allen. 1989. Observed interactions between coyotes and red foxes. *J. Mammal.* 70:631–33.

Sargeant, A. B., S. H. Allen, and R. T. Eberhardt. 1984. Red fox predation on breeding ducks in mid-continent North America. *Wildl. Monogr.* 89:1–41.

Sargeant, A. B., S. H. Allen, and J. P. Fleskes. 1986. Commercial sunflowers: Food for red foxes in North Dakota. *Prairie Nat.* 18:91–94.

Sargeant, A. B., S. H. Allen, and J. O. Hastings. 1987. Spatial relations between sympatric coyotes and red foxes in North Dakota. *J. Wildl. Manage.* 51:285–93.

Sargeant, A. B., R. J. Greenwood, M. A. Sovada, and T. L. Shaffer. 1993. *Distribution and abundance of predators that affect duck production—Prairie Pothole Region*. Res. Pub. 194. Washington DC: U.S. Fish and Wildlife Service.

Saunders, D. A., R. J. Hobbs, and C. R. Margules. 1991. Biological consequences of ecosystem fragmentation: A review. *Cons. Biol.* 5:1–15.

Schaible, G. D. 1989. *Irrigated acreage in the Conservation Reserve Program.*

Agriculture Economic Report 610. Washington DC: Economic Research Service, U.S. Department of Agriculture.

Schalles, J. F. 1994. The Platte River: A conflict between a managed water resource and regional biodiversity. In *Biological diversity: Problems and challenges*, ed. S. K. Majumdar, E. J. Brenner, J. E. Lovich, J. F. Schalles, and E. W. Miller. Easton PA: Pennsylvania Academy of Science.

Schlicht, D., and M. Saunders. 1994. Completion of status surveys for the Dakota skipper (*Hesperia dacotae*) and the poweshiek skipper (*Oarisma poweshiek*) in Minnesota (with additional data on the regal fritillary [*Speyeria idalia*]). Report to U.S. Fish and Wildlife Service by Minnesota Department of Natural Resources, Natural Heritage and Nongame Research Program. St. Paul MN: n.p.

Schmutz, J. K. 1984. Ferruginous and Swainson's hawk abundance and distribution in relation to land use in southeastern Alberta. *J. Wildl. Manage.* 48:1180–87.

Schmutz, J. R. 1993. Grassland requirements by ferruginous hawks. In *Proceedings of the third prairie conservation and endangered species workshop*, ed. G. L. Holroyd, H. L. Dickson, M. Regnier, and H. C. Smith. Natural History Occasional Paper 19. Edmonton: Provincial Museum of Alberta.

Schorger, A. W. 1955. *The passenger pigeon*. Madison: Univ. of Wisconsin Press.

Schwartz, O. A., and P. D. Whitson. 1986. A 12-year study of vegetation and mammal succession on a reconstructed tallgrass prairie in Iowa. *Am. Mid. Nat.* 117:240–49.

Scott, M. J., Jr., and R. A. Seigel. 1992. The management of amphibian and reptile populations: Species priorities and methodological and theoretical constraints. In *Wildlife 2001: Populations*, ed. D. R. McCullough and R. H. Barrett. London: Elsevier Applied Science.

Seton, E. T. 1929. *Lives of game animals*. Vol. 4, pt. 1. Garden City NY: Doubleday, Doran.

Shafer, C. L. 1990. *Nature reserves: Island theory and conservation practice*. Washington DC: Smithsonian Institution Press.

Shaffer, M. L. 1981. Minimum population sizes for species conservation. *BioScience* 31:131–34.

Sharps, J. C., and D. W. Uresk. 1990. Ecological review of black-tailed prairie dogs and associated species in western South Dakota. *Great Basin Nat.* 50:339–45.

Shoemaker, R. 1989. *The Conservation Reserve Program and its effect on land values*. Agriculture Information Bulletin 554. Washington DC: Economic Research Service, U.S. Department of Agriculture.

Sims, P. L., and J. S. Singh. 1971. Herbage dynamics and net primary production in certain ungrazed and grazed grasslands in North America. In *Preliminary analysis of structure and function in grasslands*, ed N. R. French. Range Science Department Science Series 10, Fort Collins: Colorado State Univ.

Smith, D. D. 1992. Tallgrass prairie settlement: Prelude to demise of the tallgrass ecosystem. In *Proceedings of the twelfth North American prairie conference*, ed. D. D. Smith and C. A. Jacobs. Cedar Falls: Univ. of Northern Iowa.

Soule, M. E. 1980. Thresholds for survival: Maintaining fitness and evolutionary potential. In *Conservation biology: An evolutionary-ecological perspective*, ed. M. E. Soule and B. A. Wilcox. Sunderland MA: Sinauer.

Soule, M. E., and D. Simberloff. 1986. What do genetics and ecology tell us about the design of nature reserves? *Biol. Cons.* 35:19–40.

Spencer, G. 1989. *Projections of the population of the United States by age, sex, and race: 1988 to 2080*. Current population reports, ser. P-25, no. 1018. Washington DC: Bureau of Census.

Squires, J. R., S. H. Anderson, and R. Oakleaf. 1993. Home range size and habitat-use patterns of nesting prairie falcons near oil developments in northeastern Wyoming. *J. Field Ornithol.* 64(1): 1–10.

Steinauer, E. M., and T. B. Bragg. 1987. Ponderosa pine (*Pinus ponderosa*) invasion of Nebraska Sandhills prairie. *Am. Midl. Nat.* 118:358–65.

Stevens, T. H., J. Echeverria, R. J. Glass, T. Hager, and T. A. More. 1991. Measuring the existence value of wildlife: What do CVM estimates really show? *Land Econ.* 67(4): 390–400.

Stromberg, M. R., and M. S. Boyce. 1986. Systematics and conservation of the swift fox, *Vulpes velox*, in North America. *Biol. Cons.* 35:97–110.

Stromberg, M. R., R. L. Rayburn, and T. W. Clark. 1983. Black-footed ferret prey requirements: An energy balance estimate. *J. Wildl. Manage.* 47:67–73.

Sugden, L. G., and G. W. Beyersbergen. 1986. Effect of density and concealment on American crow predation of simulated duck nests. *J. Wildl. Manage.* 50:9–14.

Sullivan, B. D., and J. J. Dinsmore. 1990. Factors affecting egg predation by American crows. *J. Wildl. Manage.* 54:433–37.

Swihart, R. K., and N. A. Slade. 1984. Road crossing in *Sigmodon hispidus* and *Microtus ochrogaster*. *J. Mammal.* 65:357–60.

Terres, J. K. 1982. *The Audubon Society encyclopedia of North American birds*. New York: Alfred A. Knopf.

Thwaites, R. G. 1905. *Early western travels, 1748–1846*. Vols.14–21. Cleveland: Arthur H. Clark.

Tilman, D. 1987. Secondary succession and the pattern of plant dominance along experimental nitrogen gradients. *Ecol. Monogr.* 57:189–214.

Times Mirror Magazines Conservation Council. 1992. Can they be saved? Pop. Sci. 241(1): 8–10.

Turner, F. J. 1901. The Middle West. *Int. Month., December,* 794–820.

Twedt, C. M., and C. W. Wolfe. 1978. Botanical pioneers of the Nebraska Sandhills. In *Fifth Midwest prairie conference proceedings*, ed. D. C. Glenn-Lewin and R. Q. Landers Jr. 22–24 August 1976. Ames: Iowa State Univ.

Ulrich, R. S. 1983. Aesthetic and affective response to natural environment. In *Behavior and the natural environment*, ed. I. Altman and J. F. Wohlwill. New York: Plenum Press.

Uno, G. E. 1987. Buffalo wallows: Ephemeral pools in the Great Plains. *Am. J. Bot.* 74(5): 663.

Uresk, D. W., and J. C. Sharps. 1986. Denning habitat and diet of the swift fox in western South Dakota. *Great Basin Nat.* 46:249–53.

U.S. Bureau of Census. 1955. *Statistical abstract of the United States: 1955.* Washington DC.

———. 1992. *USA counties*. Washington DC CD-ROM.

———. 1993. *Statistical abstract of the United States: 1993*. Washington DC.

———. 1994. *USA counties*. Washington DC CD-ROM.

———. 1995. *1992 Census of agriculture*.

———. 1950. *Agricultural statistics, 1950*. Washington DC: U.S. Government Printing Office.

———. 1964. *Agricultural statistics, 1964*. Washington DC: U.S. Government Printing Office.

———. 1978. *Agricultural statistics, 1978*. Washington DC: U.S. Government Printing Office

———. 1992. *Agricultural statistics, 1992*. Washington DC: U.S. Government Printing Office.

———. 1993. *Agricultural statistics 1993*. Washington DC: U.S. Government Printing Office.

U.S. Fish and Wildlife Service. 1981. *The Platte River ecology study*. Spec. Res. Rep. Jamestown MD: U.S. Fish and Wildlife Service.

———. 1988a. *Black-footed ferret recovery plan*. Denver CO: U.S. Fish and Wildlife Service.

———. 1988b. Lespedeza leptostachya *recovery plan*. Twin Cities MN: U.S. Fish and Wildlife Service.

———. 1989. Trifolium stoloniferum *recovery plan*. Twin Cities MN: U.S. Fish and Wildlife Service.

———. 1990. *Have you seen an Eskimo curlew?* Grand Island NE: U.S. Fish and Wildlife Service.

———. 1991a. *American burying beetle* (Nicrophorus americanus) *recovery plan*. Newton Corner MA: U.S. Fish and Wildlife Service.

———. 1991b. Endangered and threatened wildlife and plants: Animal candidate review for listing as endangered or threatened species. *Fed. Reg.* 56 (225): 58804–36.

———. 1991c. *Neosho madtom recovery plan*. Denver CO: U.S. Fish and Wildlife Service.

———. 1992. *Blowout penstemon* (Penstemon haydenii) *recovery plan*. Denver: U.S. Fish and Wildlife Service.

———. 1993a. *1991 national survey of fishing, hunting and wildlife-associated recreation*. Washington DC: U.S. Government Printing Office.

———. 1993b. *Pallid sturgeon* (Scaphirhynchus albus) *recovery plan*. Bismarck ND: U.S. Fish and Wildlife Service.

———. 1993c. Plant taxa for listing as endangered or threatened species: Notice of review. *Federal Register* 58 (188): 51144–90.

———. 1994. Platanthera praeclara *(western prairie fringed orchid) recovery plan*. Technical/agency draft. Fort Snelling MN: U.S. Fish and Wildlife Service.

U.S. Fish and Wildlife Service and Environment Canada. 1986. *North American waterfowl management plan*. Washington DC: U.S. Fish and Wildlife Service.

U.S. Forest Service. 1989a. *An analysis of the land base situation in the United States, 1989–2040*. Gen. Tech. Rep. RM-181. Fort Collins CO: U.S. Forest Service.

————. 1989b. *An analysis of the minerals situation in the United States, 1989–2040.* Gen. Tech. Rep. RM-179. Fort Collins CO: U.S. Forest Service.

————. 1989c. *An analysis of the wildlife and fish situation in the United States, 1989–2040.* Gen. Tech. Rep. RM-178. Fort Collins CO: U.S. Forest Service.

————. 1989d. *The evolving use and management of the nation's forests, grasslands, croplands, and related resources.* Gen. Tech. Rep. RM-175. Fort Collins CO: U.S. Forest Service.

————. 1990. *An analysis of the outdoor recreation and wilderness situation in the United States, 1989–2040.* Gen. Tech. Rep. RM-189. Fort Collins CO: U.S. Forest Service.

————. 1992. *Draft environmental impact statement: Mountain plover management strategy.* Fort Collins CO: U.S. Forest Service.

————. 1994. *Land areas of the National Forest System: As of September 1993.* FS-383. Washington DC: U.S. Forest Service.

U.S. Accounting Office. 1993. *Conservation Reserve Program: Cost-effectiveness is uncertain.* GAO/RCED-93-132. Washington DC.

————. 1994. *National Wildlife Refuge System: Contributions being made to endangered species recovery.* GAO/RCED-95-7. Washington DC.

U.S. National Park Service. n.d. *Endangered species in the national parks.* Washington DC.

U.S. Office of Technology Assessment. 1987. *Technologies to maintain biological diversity.* Washington DC: Congress of the United States, Office of Technology Assessment.

————. 1992. *A new technological era for American agriculture.* Washington DC: Congress of the United States, Office of Technology Assessment.

————. 1993. *Harmful non-indigenous species in the United States.* Washington DC: Congress of the United States, Office of Technology Assessment.

Vance, D. R., and R. L. Westemeier. 1979. Interactions of pheasants and prairie chickens in Illinois. *Wildl. Soc. Bull.* 7:221–25.

Volkert, W. K. 1992. Response of grassland birds to a large-scale prairie planting project. *Pass. Pigeon* 54 (3): 191–96.

Waggoner, P. E. 1994. *How much land can ten billion people spare for nature?* Task Force Rep. 121. Ames IA: Council for Agricultural Science and Technology.

Wakeley, J. S. 1978. Factors affecting the use of hunting sites by ferruginous hawks. *Condor* 80:316–26.

Wallach, B. 1985. The return of the prairie. *Landscape* 28(3):1–5.

Weaver, J. E. 1943. Resurvey of grasses, forbs, and underground plant parts at the end of the great drought. *Ecol. Monogr.* 13:63–117.

Webb, W. P. 1931. *The Great Plains*. New York: Grosset and Dunlap.

Wedin, D. A., and D. Tilman. 1992. Nitrogen cycling, plant competition, and the stability of tallgrass prairie. In *Proceedings of the twelfth North American prairie conference*, ed. D. D. Smith and C. A. Jacobs. Cedar Falls: Univ. of Northern Iowa.

Wells, S. M., R. M. Pyle, and N. M. Collins. 1983. The *IUCN invertebrate Red Data Book*. Gland, Switzerland: IUCN.

Wendtland, K. J., and J. L. Dodd. 1992. The fire history of Scotts Bluff National Monument. In *Proceedings of the twelfth North American prairie conference*, ed. D. D. Smith and C. A. Jacobs. Cedar Falls: Univ. of Northern Iowa.

Westemeier, R. L. 1988. An evaluation of methods for controlling pheasants on Illinois prairie-chicken sanctuaries. In *Pheasants: Symptoms of wildlife problems on agricultural lands*, ed. D. L. Hallett, W. R. Edwards, and G. V. Burger. Bloomington IN: North Central Section, Wildlife Society.

Wetrogan, S. I. 1988. *Projections of the population of the states, by age, sex, and race: 1988 to 2010*. Current Population Reports, ser. P-25, no. 1017. Washington DC: Bureau of Census

White, F. C., J. A. Langley, and M. A. Edelman. 1994. Agricultural supply control. In *Food, agriculture, and rural policy into the twenty-first century*, ed. M. C. Hallberg, R. G. F. Spitze, and D. E. Ray. Boulder CO: Westview Press.

Whitman, W. 1982. *Complete poetry and collected prose*. Literary Classics of the United States. New York: Viking Press.

Wiedner, D., and P. Kerlinger. 1990. Economics of birding: A national survey of active birders. *Am. Birds* 4(2): 209–13.

Wiens, J. A. 1973. Pattern and process in grassland bird communities. *Ecol. Monogr.* 43:237–70.

Wiens, J. A., and M. I. Dyer. 1975. Rangeland avifaunas: Their composition, energetics, and role in the ecosystem. In *Proceedings of symposium: Management of forest and range habitats for nongame birds*, ed. D. R. Smith. Gen. Tech. Rep. WO-1. Washington DC: U.S. Forest Service.

Wild Earth. 1992. National overview: Roadless areas map. *Wild Earth*, special issue.

Wildlife Society. 1991. *Restoration of wolves in North America*. Tech. Review 91–1. Bethesda MD: Wildlife Society.

Williams, J. E., and R. R. Miller. 1990. Conservation status of the North American fish fauna in fresh water. *J. Fish Biol.* 37:79–85.

Wilson, E. O. 1992. *The diversity of life*. Cambridge: Harvard Univ. Press.

Wilson, S. D., and J. W. Belcher. 1989. Plant and bird communities of native prairie and introduced Eurasian vegetation in Manitoba, Canada. *Cons. Biol.* 3:39–44.

Wooten, H. H. 1965. *The land utilization program, 1934 to 1964: Origin, development and present status*. Agric. Econ. Rep. 85. Washington DC: U.S. Department of Agriculture, Economic Research Service.

World Almanac. 1994. *The world almanac and book of facts, 1994*. New York: Funk and Wagnalls.

World Resources Institute. 1994. *Environmental almanac*. New York: Houghton Mifflin.

World Wildlife Fund Canada. n.d. *Prairie conservation action plan: 1989–1994*. Toronto: World Wildlife Fund Canada.

Wuerthner, G. 1994. Subdivisions versus agriculture. *Cons. Biol.* 8:905–8.

Young, C. E., and C. T. Osborn. 1990. *The Conservation Reserve Program: An economic assessment*. Agric. Econ. Rep. 626. Washington DC: U.S. Department of Agriculture, Economic Research Service.

Zimmerman, J. L. 1990. *Cheyenne Bottoms: Wetland in jeopardy*. Lawrence: Univ. Press of Kansas.

———. 1992. Density-independent factors affecting the avian diversity of the tallgrass prairie community. *Wilson Bull.* 104:85–94.

Index